Mexican Painting in Our Time

OROZCO. *Hidalgo y Costilla*. FRESCO. CENTER WALL OF STAIRCASE, GOVERNMENT PALACE, GUADALAJARA

BERNARD S. MYERS

Mexican Painting

in Our Time

NEW YORK · OXFORD UNIVERSITY PRESS | 1956

Printed in Germany at J.J. Augustin, Glückstadt

For

THE EIGHTEENTH ANNIVERSARY
OF OUR FIRST TRIP TO MEXICO

Foreword

Modern Mexican painting, like that of any other culture, springs from a combination of individual and environmental circumstances. In Mexico, however, the development of art since the Revolution of 1910 has been overwhelmingly affected by the political and social milieu, which provides a general background for most of the painters, however powerful their individual personalities. With very few exceptions, they are Revolutionary painters.

Periodic changes since 1910 have cut across the personal development of masters such as Orozco, Siqueiros, and Rivera, in spite of their obviously separate styles. Thus in the years 1920–24, immediately after the end of the Revolution, Mexican painting is quite different in character and accomplishments than during the subsequent increasingly reactionary era dominated by President Calles. With the advent of Cárdenas as president in 1934, there comes an upsurge of reforming enthusiasm and public sponsorship of art, interrupted by World War II. After a war period of internationalism, postwar Mexican art expresses a renewed national consciousness.

Although the leading Mexican painters seemed to go their respective ways after the dissolution in 1925 of their early association, the Syndicate, other organizations arose sporadically to keep artists together, while federal and state patronage of art continues as a basic influential factor down to the present day. Through such groups as the League of Revolutionary Writers and Artists (L.E.A.R.) or the new Frente Nacional de Artes Plásticas, the traditions of the early Syndicate days have been perpetuated. In the same way, official sponsorship of art extends beyond the initial period of 1922–4 to the federal school mural commissions and state projects (e.g. Orozco's in Guadalajara) of the 'thirties and the national projects of the 'forties and 'fifties. While in the United States federal aid to art falls by the wayside, in Mexico it becomes established practice for schools, hospitals, and other types of public buildings to receive mural and in some cases sculptural treatment. The architecture itself advances along lines of modern design, abandoning the conventional form of government buildings.

Mexican painting, however, because of the circumstances surrounding its origin and its almost constant didactic function, has been mainly representational in character rather than abstract. This art was influential in the United States during the social-conscious 'thirties, but the figurative expressionism of Orozco, the dynamic realism of Siqueiros, and the decorative narratives of Rivera now have little appeal for advanced artists in other countries. This rejection by itself hardly invalidates the contribution of modern Mexican art, which expresses the needs of its particular culture with undeniable directness. Moreover, the body of material turned out by such painters as Orozco and Siqueiros presents a quality of accomplishment that many contemporary nations would find difficult to match. Further, in its development of new painting techniques and procedures, the Mexican school is bringing art up to date in a new way, utilizing the products of technological progress.

Second only in importance to its mural painters are Mexico's graphic artists, stemming from the native tradition of the nineteenth century. Although they have evolved their own forms and techniques, they show a close relationship to the mural tradition (especially to Orozco). Either as individuals or as members of print groups, particularly the Workshop of Popular Graphic Art, they offer a continuous series of works from the early part of the century to the present day.

Easel painting in Mexico has had a less fortunate history than either mural or graphic work. Overwhelmed by the fame of the muralists (who received government help because of the 'useful' nature of their art), discouraged by the lack until quite recently of private middle-class patronage, easel painting remained a pale reflection of mural and graphic art or an isolated Magic-Realist or Surrealist phenomenon. Rapid industrialization during and after World War II has created middle-class patrons and collectors as well as new art dealers to perform the middle-man function. Easel painting in this period has entered a more promising phase, and is emerging from the subordinate position it held for so long. This becomes increasingly clear not only through the sensuous abstractions of Tamayo and the dynamic pyroxilin paintings of Siqueiros but also through the work of a number of younger men. It is in their work that the hope for future Mexican painting may lie.

New York   B. S. M.
1956

Acknowledgments

The author wishes to express his gratitude to the many friends and acquaintances, both in Mexico and in the United States, who have given him help, advice, and encouragement.

In Mexico City, Sra. Inés Amor of the Galería de Arte Mexicano; the distinguished collector Sr. Dr. Alvar Carrillo Gil; Professor Justino Fernández; and Sr. Fernando Gamboa, former Chief of the Departamento de Artes Plásticas made available the resources of their particular institutions and their own profound knowledge of the Mexican scene. Among artists who have given generously of their time, advice, and photographic help, special thanks go to Sr. y Sra. David Alfaro Siqueiros, Sr. José Chávez Morado, Sr. y Sra. Jorge González Camarena, Sr. y Sra. Ricardo Martínez, Sr. Leopoldo Méndez, Sr. y Sra. Juan O'Gorman, Sr. Manuel Rodríguez Lozano, Sr. Rufino Tamayo—and particularly to Sr. y Sra. José L. Gutiérrez for their kind aid in a variety of ways.

For special photographic assistance the author wishes to thank Sr. Francisco Caracalla of the Galería de Arte Moderno, Sr. Alberto Misrachi, Jr., of the Central de Publicaciones, Sr. Daniel Núñez Rochet of the United States Information Service, Srta. Gabriela Orozco Marín of the Galería Artes Plásticas, Sr. Walter Reuter, Sr. Victor M. Reyes, Chief of the Departamento de Artes Plásticas, Mr. John Roberts (now of San Francisco), Sr. José Verde of the Departamento de Artes Plásticas, and Sr. Guillermo Zamora.

In this country Mr. Henry Clifford of the Philadelphia Museum of Art, Dr. MacKinley Helm of Santa Barbara, California, Professor Loren Mozley of the University of Texas Department of Art, and many friends in the Museum of Modern Art and the Metropolitan Museum in New York have all been very helpful.

The greatest thanks are to the author's wife, who has lived through this Mexican experience with him from the beginning and with whose constant encouragement and direct help this book was brought into being. Her feeling for Mexico and its people, her knowledge of the background, have been as valuable for this study as her many months of devoted editing of the manuscript and her aid in preparing it for the press.

Table of Contents

List of Illustrations

Mexican Painting in Our Time

Après le pain
l'éducation
est le premier besoin
du peuple.

DANTON
(Convention Nationale, Discours du 13 Août 1793)

Background for a New Art

The mountain highway leading into Mexico, with hairpin curves and violent contrasts of upward and downward movement along beautiful but dangerous precipices, symbolizes the modern history of that country. The revolt in 1810 against three centuries of Spanish rule was the beginning of a long tortuous road leading to the Revolution of 1910, which produced, as its chief cultural manifestation, modern Mexican painting.

Even at that point of climax, however, the struggle for liberation of the peasant, against a deeply entrenched hacienda system and clergy, had merely reached a new level. This problem was to remain among the most important in Mexican politics for a long time. It persists in its current form as part of the still unfulfilled Mexican Revolution, whose visible symbol and conscience is the Mexican painting and graphic work of our time. This art constantly refers to the revolutionary and reforming heroes of the past. It invokes their memory in reminder of the nation's struggles, and consciously suggests through repetition of their stories that the Revolution is far from over.

The revolt initiated in 1810 by the patriot priests Hidalgo y Costilla and Morelos not only led to the break with Spain but set forth the social and political aims for which Mexico has been fighting ever since. More than a century later, there had not yet been achieved all the ideals expounded by Morelos in 1813: no special privilege for army or church, a living wage for all, racial equality, division of the large estates into small parcels for the poor peasants, and better distribution of the nation's wealth.

Although independence in 1821 meant only the substitution of local for foreign oppressors, the future course of the land was clearly marked along a circuitous path toward reform. The short-lived imperial career of the opportunist Iturbide was followed by a few stormy years under a liberal constitution, 1824–32, and then by the quarter-century long on-and-off dictatorship of the flamboyant Santa Anna. During this time Mexico lost Texas and found itself at war with the United States in 1845–8. These conflicts revealed dramatically the ineffectualness and corruption of the politicos and army officers of that day. The liberal constitution of 1824 had been replaced in 1836 by a far more conservative document, which permitted those individuals to make the republic their private possession. The Scottish born and American bred wife of the first Spanish ambassador to Mexico during this period recounted her continual astonishment at the disparity between the magnificent displays of the wealthy clergy and rich families and the tremendous number of beggars and suffering poor in the streets.

The long course of Santa Anna's intermittent control ended in 1855. Mexico returned once more to the road of liberal accomplishment under the leadership of Miguel Lerdo de Tejada and the great Indian Benito Juárez, author of the constitution of 1857 and hero of the Reform. A new attack was made on the problems of church domination and special privileges of the clergy and military. More than anything else, the new constitution was intended to break up the great estates of the church for the advantage of the general public. At the height of the violent civil strife which ensued, Juárez as president continued to carry out his program. He and his cabinet framed the Reform measures which confiscated properties of the church, disbanded monastic orders and church schools, made marriage a civil rather than a religious arrangement, abolished all titles of nobility, and stipulated freedom of worship for all faiths as well as freedom of the press and the right of free assembly.

By 1861 the Juárez forces had defeated the reactionaries, but a large unrepaid French loan to the leader of the opponents of the Reform gave France a pretext for the disastrous intervention of 1861–7. Supported by French troops, the Austrian Archduke Maximilian and his wife Carlotta ascended the throne of Mexico as representatives of Napoleon III. When, in the period immediately following the United States Civil War, the French were forced to withdraw by United States pressure, by Mexican arms, and by exigencies in Europe, Maximilian was dethroned and executed. Juárez now tried to bring order out of the chaotic conditions. Improvement of the situation of the Indian masses—still landless, poverty-stricken, and uneducated—seemed to him the primary job. Hampered by the disaffection of the poor ex-soldiers, the greed of a horde of petty politicians, and the difficulty of working democratically in a country by no means accustomed to democracy, Juárez often used a firm and even autocratic hand.

Porfirio Díaz, military hero of the war against the French, who had fought unsuccessfully against Juárez's election to a fourth term, also opposed the re-election of Juárez's successor, Sebastián Lerdo. On a platform of 'effective suffrage and no re-election,' Díaz was able to gather a good deal of liberal support, dislodge Lerdo, obtain recognition by the congress, and set himself up as defender of the democratic process and the constitution. The Reform of Juárez, however, had tried to establish both a democratic form of government and a general economic development, while Díaz inevitably drifted in the direction of a dictatorship whose purpose was to achieve the latter aim, however much the former had to be sacrificed. For thirty-four years he remained in control of a

Mexico which in the period since Iturbide (from 1822 to 1876) had had forty presidents, two emperors, a number of temporary governments, innumerable revolts, exilings, summary executions, and political switches. His career presents the constant paradox of a zealous liberal who comes to power and finds it easier or more advantageous to become a conservative.

In his terrific drive for power and his equally strong need for peace, Díaz welcomed all adherents, offering opportunities for enrichment to his supporters and ruthlessly crushing those who opposed him. The Reform movement of the immediate past no longer functioned, and the lower classes figured very little in his plans. To encourage economic development, he offered liberal concessions to foreign investors, in the course of which Mexico's natural resources were given away. The profits from these usually untaxed enterprises went abroad to Europe and the United States, minimizing the advantages to Mexico of the original investment and stirring up a powerful nationalistic feeling that reinforced the existing antiforeign attitudes. Since no consistent plan was followed in this process of industrialization, it enriched the investors more than it aided the economy of the nation.

Under Díaz, enslavement of the peasant population rose to far greater heights than ever before, and possession of land became concentrated in the hands of a small number of Mexican and foreign companies. Not only was land given away as a form of political bribery, but peasants were forced off their little plots into the debt-peonage of the hacienda system. It is estimated that by the end of the agonizingly long era of Díaz about 95 per cent of the rural population owned no land. Similarly the ecclesiastical measures of the Reform were ignored as Díaz entered into a working arrangement with the church. He passed on its major appointments and permitted re-establishment of monastic institutions and accumulation of property. Naturally the grateful clergy preached obedience to his dictatorship.

Opposition to his regime was virtually impossible, as he bought or suppressed newspapers, controlled the police, played off one official against another, and nominated the members of congress and the judiciary. The rural areas were controlled by reducing the Indian population to peonage and establishing an efficiently brutal corps of *rurales*—the mounted police, often former bandits, whose treatment of the peasants was so vividly demonstrated in Eisenstein's famous film, *Thunder over Mexico*. In one scene of this motion picture, these agents of Díaz take a group of rebellious farmers and bury them up to their necks so that the gallant *rurales* could play a ghoulish form of polo with their heads. This may be an extreme instance, but it effectively dramatizes that side of the regime.

Most significant for the development of Mexico was the growth of a powerful *mestizo* (part Indian) class of state and local politicians, which took its place beside the older creole (native white) group of landowners. Although capital kept pouring in from abroad, this huge political apparatus maintained by Díaz necessitated large high-interest loans that were to plague the country at a later date.

During the later years of the dictatorship, from the 1890's on, a new generation of so-called *científicos* (scientific ones) became increasingly influential in the government. These materialists believed strongly in progress through science rather than through the liberalism of the Juárez period. Distorting the ideas of Darwin on survival of the fittest, they advocated the domination of whites not only over Indians but over *mestizos*, who at that moment played a major part in the administration. *Científico* lawyers, economists, and intellectuals brought Mexico even closer to Europe in the cultural sphere than it had been before, while Anglo-Saxon economic dominance grew greater than ever. Although they undoubtedly improved the efficiency of the administration, the *científicos* took for themselves (and by legal means) large portions of the nation's wealth.

Whatever superficial prosperity Mexico may have shown in the era of Porfirio Díaz, however many new mansions, broad avenues, railroads, telegraph lines, and flourishing business enterprises may have appeared, the fact remains that the bulk of Mexican people—the Indians—were in a state of medieval misery. On the haciendas, brutal managers kept this enormous portion of the population in virtual serfdom. Forced to buy their necessities at the hacienda store at arbitrary prices, the peasants remained in constant debt-peonage, lived on a bare subsistence diet, suffered from disease, and were harried by the rapid increase of prices. Here was one potential and immediate source of revolt.

As for industrial workers in the service of foreign-dominated and foreign-owned companies, their condition was equally miserable, and just as in the case of the peasants there was no recourse to higher authority for fair treatment. The foreigner, according to Díaz, was always right. In spite of brutal repression, unions were formed and strikes, though unsuccessful, organized. In such instances Mexican soldiers were forced to shoot down their countrymen to keep inviolate the privileges of foreign mine and mill owners. The infiltration of anarcho-syndicalist and socialist ideas by way of the United States and Spain and other parts of Europe provided another important background factor in the rising discontent with the status quo.

Díaz, whose position during this long period had been almost impregnable, since he had both his own and foreign support, went so far in giving privileges to United States and European businessmen that he finally realized he had given them, especially the 'North Americans,' too much power. Trying to play one foreign group against another in his usual way, he found that the 'North Americans' withdrew their support and encouraged his political enemies. The question of the succession to the aging dictator, a pressing one for some time, arose again, while the financial crisis of 1907, combined with a disastrous harvest and starvation, increased the prevailing restlessness. A new Democratic party appeared, demanding improvements, while post-*científico* intellectuals worked along the same lines.

Francisco Madero had become famous in 1908 for the forthrightness of his book, *The Presidential Succession in 1910.* The diminutive, mild-mannered idealist now rose as spearhead of the new movement. This son of a wealthy family organized his own newspaper and a group of anti-re-election clubs, whose convention nominated him as their presidential candidate. From a jail cell, Madero, for whom 30,000 supporters had previously demonstrated, learned that he had been counted out by the government's tally officials with less than two hundred votes for the entire nation. On his release, he fled to the United States, from where he announced publicly that the elections had been dishonest, appointed himself provisional president, and called for a general revolt.

By 1911 Díaz had been forced to resign, but Madero, elected late the same year, was too much the pacifist and idealist for that bloody and brutal time. He refused to put the dangerous ones out of the way and hoped to reform Mexico by his own pious example. The disappointed masses were once more stirred to revolt. The peasant leader Emiliano Zapata called for return of the lands that had been stolen from the villages. As the revolution spread, conservatives of the old Díaz group, aided by the treacherous General Huerta and encouraged by United States ambassador Henry Lane Wilson, forced the resignation of Madero and his vice-president Pino Suárez. These two were promptly murdered by Huerta, who then became president, supported by the landowners, old Díaz officials, and the church.

But the torrent unleashed by the gentle Madero could not be stopped. In the north a movement to avenge him began under Venustiano Carranza, who, with the help of Obregón, de la Huerta, and Calles, formed the Constitutionalist army to oust the vicious Huerta. Pancho Villa, who had fought on the side of Madero, now returned from the United States to gather a rapidly growing Army of the North, whose counterpart in the south was the forces of Emiliano Zapata. The existence of these three groups soon forced Huerta (now deprived of United States support by President Woodrow Wilson's refusal to recognize him) to flee.

For some time the three victorious armies jockeyed for mastery of Mexico. Villa marched on the capital abandoned by the government troops of Carranza, but Zapata and his army of peasants forestalled him. The two came to some sort of working agreement, and both armies occupied Mexico City—the Zapatistas with simple peasant decorum, the Villistas running amuck in every kind of excess, inflamed by the example of their flamboyant leader.

Carranza, who had retired to Vera Cruz, now promulgated a series of reform decrees, allocating land to the peasants. Obregón, endeavoring to recruit the aid of the working men for Carranza, wooed the socialist Casa del Obrero Mundial (House of the Worker of the World) and made friends with Luis Morones, the future labor leader. To these people he promised the help of the government in labor disputes and unionization problems, thus setting the stage for the later government-labor co-operation, first under Obregón and then under Calles. Ultimately Villa was driven back to the United States border, while Zapata retired to Morelos, where he held out for three years. Although the United States recognized the Carranza government in October 1915, the depredations of Villa across the border brought the entry of United States troops into Mexico in 1916. This act was much resented by the Mexicans. After a strong protest from Carranza, the 'North Americans' withdrew in February 1917.

The constitution of 1917, especially in Articles 27 and 123, marks a turning point in the story of the Mexican Revolution. Under Article 27, concessions for private exploitation of Mexico's natural (particularly subsoil) resources were still permitted, but it was clearly stipulated that these resources belonged to the nation, which retained the right of expropriation, with compensation to the private owners. Further, the *ejidos*, community-owned farm lands that had been taken from the villages, were now returned to them. Article 123, equally famous in the history of Mexican economic reform, was labor's Magna Charta. It guaranteed the right to form unions and to strike, the right to a minimum wage and an eight-hour day, and the abolition of child labor and peonage. In Mexico City there is a street called Artículo 123.

Despite the dishonesty with which these two articles (and those reaffirming the Juárez position on the church) were administered in the time of Carranza, despite the plundering and corruption by the new revolutionary leaders, this coming to grips with the economic problems of Mexico changed the entire complexion of the Revolution. Under Carranza also, the agrarian leader Zapata was treacherously murdered in 1919, but in the heroic example of his life Zapata has remained a legend, the hero of innumerable folk songs and a favorite theme for painters such as Rivera and Orozco.

When the time came for another election, Carranza tried to put in his own candidate, but Obregón had the support of the newly formed craft union, C. R. O. M. (Regional Workers Confederation of Mexico), led by Luis Morones. Obregón was elected and took office in 1920. Thus after ten years of civil war and many occupations of the capital by rival armies, with attendant bloodlettings, Mexico was once more at peace, and able to take another step along the route of economic and social progress.

A Culture in Revolution | **II**

Spontaneously and without plan, the variety of pressures against Díaz had broken through and swept the land, growing into the Revolution that continues today on another plane. It remains the vision to which both left and right still refer—for some a genuine ideal, for others a gaudy cloak in which to dress opportunist political or artistic aims.

In its beginning the Revolution had no formal program, nor was there any one reason for so many different types of humanity to be swept up in its fury. Peasants left the haciendas on their own, feeling themselves released from peonage, or wishing to take advantage of the opportunities for looting. Sometimes they followed a member of the owner's family going off to war; sometimes they were already in hiding from Díaz press gangs and drifted toward the scene of revolt. An important source of recruits was those who, like Zapata, had been stripped of their farms by the big district landowners.

From these individuals bands were formed, then troops, and finally armies. Everyone felt there was something for him in the Revolution, something to make up for the things lacking in the life of a worker or a peasant, a professional or an intellectual. The small armies were usually led by minor landowners (traditional enemies of the *hacendados*, or estate owners, their friends the land sharks, money lenders, and others such as the local judges, mayors, and priests). In these armies there were often young students, lawyers, and the like, who wrote the speeches and kept the records, and poets who sang their own songs to guitars. Artists were also involved; some played important roles as officers or propagandists, e.g. Orozco as a cartoonist and Siqueiros as a young officer inspiring his men. The pacifist Goitia became a recording artist to a Villa group, while other noncombatant painters opposed the conservative art authorities and the Academy.

Apart from such expressions of feeling as the lusty Villa anthem *La Cucaracha* (The Cockroach), the haunting marching song of Zapata's barefoot peasants, *Quatro Milpas* (Four Fields), or an occasional wordy manifesto, the troops did their fighting with no definite purpose. They carried on local actions for the most part, against nearby estates and towns, took tribute from all, and added to their numbers and resources. They had in common an undying hatred for past tyranny, a rather vague dream of a better life somewhere in the future, loyalty toward their leader, and a love of the adventurous and occasionally profitable life they were leading. Writers and artists, many of whom had felt intellectually oppressed, forced to admire the foreign and to scorn the native and the ordinary, were able to share these feelings and become absorbed into the Revolution.

The identification of intellectuals with this dynamic spirit emerges in the greatest book of the Revolution, *Los de Abajo* (Those from Below), written by a participant, Dr. Mariano Azuela. 'You ask me why I am still a rebel?' says one of his characters. 'Well, the revolution is like a hurricane; if you're in it, you're not a man . . . you're a leaf, a dead leaf, blown by the wind.' Azuela makes us aware less of social idealism than of man's inevitable suffering and cruelty, his mystical need for belonging to the vast Revolution, feelings shared by Orozco, which made him the ideal illustrator for this book. The author says further: '. . . Villa? Obregón? Carranza? What's the difference? I love the revolution like a volcano in eruption; I love the volcano because it is a volcano, the revolution because it's the revolution! What do I care about the stones left above or below after the cataclysm? What are they to me?'[1]

Dr. Azuela himself exemplifies the involvement of professionals, intellectuals—indeed all Mexicans—in the suffering of that period. This involvement has given a specifically national and Revolutionary character to Mexican literature, art, and politics. Even today artists are criticized if they did nothing for the cause, and politicians are attacked for some dubious action at that time. Most artists of both the first and second generations of the modern Mexican movement were part of the Revolution; their paintings and prints deal with that material, in a way that leaves no doubt of their direct experiences.

As the Revolution grew, Díaz's federal army melted away, many going over to guerrilla generals, some forming their own revolutionary units with the help of local rebel leaders. This new element helped to turn the earlier guerrilla warfare into a more regularized type of fighting.

The constitution of 1917 illustrates the lack of agreement among the generals about what they expected from the Revolution. They did know, however, what they hated: foreign domination, church power, large estates, special privilege, and concentration of wealth. The dynamic and effective side of Mexican art, as seen in Orozco and Siqueiros, often expresses the same attitudes.

As the army that was the Revolution became the government, the generals had to reward as many followers as possible and yet give evidence of revolutionary zeal. Of the projects suggested by revolutionary intellectuals, art and education seem to have been selected as activities

[1] Mariano Azuela, *The Under Dogs*, trans. by E. Munguía, Jr., introd. by Carleton Beals, illus. by J. C. Orozco, Brentano's, N. Y., 1929, pp. 101, 207.

involving the least possible danger to the generals or expense to the new regime. Within a few years, however, art rose to a point where it began to show up the hollow promises of the politicians and had to be held in check.

Most Mexican intellectuals of the early post-Revolution 'twenties, unlike their European and United States counterparts, rejected the pessimism of Dada, New Objectivity, and Magic Realism. They gave instead an exalted and fervent response to the promise of the future, charting a route that still remains to be traversed. The beginning of the modern Mexican art movement, like the Revolution itself, seems to have been without program; its strong political character was a later development. A common dislike of the academic, the European, the inferior, and the artificially sentimental brought the artists together to find a means of expression understandable to the people. The mural became the apparent answer and, since they knew little about murals, this also had to be developed.

The new movement was in a sense a rehabilitation. After centuries-long dependence on the art of Spain, the break with the mother country and the later split between church and state in 1857 had torn up the roots of Mexican art without replanting them elsewhere. Under Maximilian, Mexico City had been remodeled in the French style. Homes, clothes, jewels—everything followed Paris. The trend was accentuated by increasing wealth among the upper classes and the practice of sending young people to France for their education. During the confused period between the revolt against Maximilian and the accession of Díaz in 1876, art was distinctly secondary. In the Díaz era of 'peace and prosperity,' buildings of all kinds were erected: theaters, jails, post offices, city halls, and so on, all in a second-rate French academic style. French academic painting of the most blatant sentimentalism was taught at the official Academy, where copying from casts, sketching from Greek vases, and copying from Murillo were standard procedures. The National Theater building, begun in 1900 and finished later as the Palacio de Bellas Artes, shows vividly the shallow eclecticism of that period.

Some painters at the beginning of the twentieth century reflect an awareness of Impressionism, either the Zuloaga-Sorolla version brought in from Spain or the more genuine form produced by Joaquín Clausell (1866–1935) and Alfredo Ramos Martínez (1881–1946). The first decade of our century also offers the first evidences of Mexicanism in the work of painters such as Saturnino Herrán (1887–1918), who was one of the first to use regional themes, although sentimentally. These paintings portray idealized Indians in a naturalistic studio light, and mark a transition between the European-influenced Mexican art of the late nineteenth century (Zuloaga and Sorolla) and the more realistic product of the next epoch.

More important, this period felt the initial effect of one of the real fermenting influences of the Mexican movement, the celebrated Dr. Atl. Born Gerardo Murillo (c. 1875), he began to paint under an old-fashioned portraitist. In 1896 he left Mexico to study philosophy and law in Rome, and wandered through Italy, Spain, and France. In Paris the future Mexican Revolutionary organized a protest demonstration against the censoring of Jacob Epstein's tomb for Oscar Wilde.

In 1904 Dr. Atl returned to Mexico to take a leading part in the early stirrings of the art movement, preaching mural painting for the first time and the Mexicanization of culture. (He had dropped his family name—the hated academic symbol Murillo—for the Nahuatl Indian *atl*, i.e. water.) He organized expeditions, subsidized artists, led strikes, defended neo-Impressionism, and wrote criticism, other prose, and poetry; he did articles on volcanology as well as work in botany, mining, and astrology. At this point the fiery Dr. Atl was an anarcho-syndicalist whose aesthetic point of view paralleled the political and social attitudes of the Casa del Obrero Mundial, which he himself had recently organized.

During these last years of the Díaz dictatorship, preparations were being made for the centenary celebration of the 1810 revolt from Spain. In his usual grandiose fashion, Díaz hoped to make this the climax of his career—and in a way it was. To make sure that the celebration of Mexican independence was not turned over to foreign artists, the nationalist-minded Dr. Atl created in 1910 Mexico's first artists' organization, the Centro Artístico. Although the Centro was given a commission to decorate the Anfiteatro Bolívar in the National Preparatory School (later painted by Rivera), the outbreak of the Revolution that very year changed everything.

Dr. Atl left Mexico again to study volcanology in Naples. In Lausanne he talked politics with Lenin and, together with a young socialist newspaper man named Benito Mussolini, put out an anticlerical paper in Switzerland.

The beginning of political revolution in Mexico was paralleled by revolt among the art students at the National Academy of San Carlos in 1911, against the academic methods of the past. From this essentially anti-Díaz gesture there developed, early in 1913, a number of open-air schools under Alfredo Ramos Martínez, the enthusiastic Impressionist recently returned from Europe. That same year, during the brief incumbency of the usurper Huerta and as a sop to the insurgent forces, Ramos Martínez was made director of the Academy.

The students of the open-air school studied this painter's version of Impressionism in their Barbizon-like retreat in the suburbs of Mexico City, deriving benefit from direct contact with nature but aesthetically, through no fault of their own, somewhat behind the times. Many of these youngsters plotted against Huerta and joined the revolutionary forces attempting to unseat him. As for the open-air school, which was later moved to Coyoacán, in spite of its rather mild artistic progressivism at that moment, it had the effect of imparting to Mexican painting the highly keyed color quality that is retained to this day.

The 1913 coup of Huerta brought Dr. Atl back to Mexico City, where he joined the Carranza forces, taking an active part in the revolutionary excitement of the time. In addition to organizing the 'red battalions' of workers, he brought together a group of young writers and intellectuals. One night early in 1914 he convinced a band of workers who had about decided to join the oncoming Villa forces to switch to Carranza, and the entire crowd fled on the last freight leaving for Orizaba, carrying away a load of precious printing equipment. There, in a complex of abandoned church buildings, Atl enlisted the aid of his writers and artists (among the latter the young Orozco) to produce an illustrated newspaper, posters, and other propaganda material.

The nativism or Mexicanism implied in the paintings of Herrán and the preachments of Atl received a powerful impetus during this early revolutionary period from the work of Francisco Goitia, one of the most important precursors of the modern development. Born in Zacatecas in 1884, Goitia came to the Federal District as a boy. He studied at the Academy of Fine Arts and made his living as a pressman for etchings. On a government scholarship he went to Europe in 1904, spending most of his time in Italy and Spain.

In 1912 the pacifist Goitia returned to Mexico, where, as a recording artist, he followed the corps of General Angeles under Villa in the north until 1917, when Carranza finally won out. In the course of those years Goitia began to produce his increasingly naturalistic scenes of Mexican life. Such pictures as the 1916 *Dance of the Revolution* and the *Viejo del Muladar* (fig. 1) of the same date mark the point at which the great tragedy of the Mexican people finally begins to emerge in art. His later paintings are better known, especially the *Tata Jesucristo* (fig. 2), but are not nearly so significant historically, coming after the Preparatory School murals of Orozco. Goitia's earlier art is an important step away from folklorism, from the picturesque nativism of Herrán and his contemporaries toward the new, more socially conscious point of view that was to be developed through the 'twenties by others.

Goitia's growing awareness of the Mexican heritage is typical of those artists who, like Orozco and Siqueiros, had direct contact with the realities of the Revolution. Their broadened knowledge and sympathy with the people were expressed in a constantly expanding aura of nationalistic form and fervor. Even painters and writers who were not in Mexico for the actual fighting realized—perhaps because of the spreading vogue for primitivism—that they had an Indian tradition.

Among the many intellectuals drawn home because of the political emergency was the anthropologist Manuel Gamio. To Gamio must be given the credit for reducing to scientific terms one of the great spiritual components of the Revolution, its awareness of the grandeur of its own

1

GOITIA. *El Viejo del Muladar* (*The Old Man of the Dump Heap*). OIL.
MUSEO NACIONAL DE ARTES PLÁSTICAS, MEXICO CITY.

tradition. Instead of trying to educate the Indian and integrate him into the development of modern technological society, Gamio called for the re-education of the so-called literate ones, who would, in the process of absorbing this tradition, help to 'weld a fatherland.'

Gamio set up a National Department of Anthropology, choosing the important region of San Juan Teotihuacán near the capital for special investigation. Into this area he sent missionaries to study the country and its people. Partly as a result of their work, specific political and economic changes were made there, as well as important archaeological and sociological studies. To climax these investigations, Gamio called in an artist to crystallize and pictorialize the material, a procedure that often recurs in the later development of the 'Mexican renaissance,' when exciting new ideas, especially in the field of education, are carried out or sparked by artists. The artist chosen for Teotihuacán was Francisco Goitia, who worked there from 1918 to 1925, seeking 'the sorrows of the race.' He also continued to produce his native types, his personal expression of the way of life of the Mexican people, especially their misery.

In 1925 Goitia went to Oaxaca to study native customs, still painting in his own manner the beggars, cripples, oppressed, and poor—some in light, almost remote colors, others in the powerful expressionist tones of his famous *Tata Jesucristo* (1926–7). A mystic spirit, Goitia is often overcome by his own feelings, but he is a characteristic product of his time, is typically Mexican, and is one of the earliest honest painters of native life. For this last reason especially, Goitia has been an important progenitor and influence in the modern Mexican school.

Disagreeing with the mural development and with the political direction of Mexican art during the 'thirties, Goitia withdrew to Xochimilco on a permanent government scholarship designed to give him time to paint. There he has taught school for many years, his art turning toward sunny landscapes as he retired from the movement. The early directness and honesty of Goitia's painting are emphasized by his words concerning the *Tata Jesucristo*:

I tried my models sitting this way and that, but no, I didn't feel it exactly right. At last I investigated everything I could about them. I then made them come and sit for me on the Day of the Dead, when of their own accord they would be dwelling on sorrow, and little by little I uncovered their sorrow and the revolution and their dead. And they writhed, and one turned her foot up in the pain. Then I knew I had it! Those hands and feet gave their grief the genuine form. I would never have thought of it myself, but of course that is the way grief is, and so I was satisfied at last. They weep tears of our race, pain and tears our own and different from others. All the sorrow of Mexico is there.[2]

The nativism of other intellectuals during the Revolutionary period— and even later—was somewhat more self-conscious. A genuine expression of Mexicanism, however, appeared in the work of José Guadalupe Posada (1851–1913), a pure emanation of the humor and imaginativeness of the people. Posada also reflected the dissatisfaction with the political situation at the end of the Díaz era. His work began in the 'seventies with a series of political lithographs, related technically to the delicate French caricature style of the 'sixties. Coming to Mexico City in 1887 to work for the conservative publishing house of Vanegas Arroyo, Posada devoted a good deal of energy to illustrating for various papers in opposition to Díaz, anticipating the caricaturists of the Revolution period. The great importance of Posada for artists such as Rivera and Orozco has long been recognized; these two and many others of the first modern generation have freely acknowledged their indebtedness. The same is true of artists of the second and even the third generations, especially in the graphic field.

---

[2] Anita Brenner, *Idols behind Altars*, Payson & Clarke Ltd., N.Y., 1929, p. 297.

2

GOITIA. *Tata Jesucristo*. OIL.

As early as the 1890's, Posada maintained an open shop fronting on the street and occupying the former carriage entrance of a house on the Calle Santa Inez. Here everyone could see him at work, including students on their way to and from the Academy of San Carlos. According to Jean Charlot,[3] Orozco recalled that at the age of ten he saw Posada at work on his metal plates, turning out the sensational *corridos*, or throw-away sheets, for which he is famous. A little farther along the street, the boy would stop before the shop of Antonio Vanegas Arroyo the publisher,

[3] Jean Charlot, *Art Making from Mexico to China*, Sheed & Ward, N.Y., 1950.

16

where the ladies of the family were occupied in hand-coloring Posada's sheets for public sale. This was done with stencils and gaudy colors. The historical and contemporary themes of these broadsheets, in Posada's bold line and blatant colors, made an ineradicable impression on young Orozco. They were a violent contrast to the academic routine of his school, with its anatomy charts and plaster casts, its occasional landscape exercise for relaxation. Rivera also has recorded his early reactions to the work of Posada and the Vanegas Arroyo workshop.

After the early lithograph style, Posada used a second technique in a coarser manner designed for the penny pamphlets that Arroyo got out as a kind of poor man's bible for the nearly illiterate. Since in those days this meant a high percentage of the population, the impact of Posada's prints had to be immediate and forceful—either horrible or ludicrous or both. Arroyo also put out a *Gaceta Callejera*, a 'newspaper of the streets' with handcut pictures, very much like the late nineteenth-century illustrated papers in the United States. Exciting extras of the journal were issued with scenes of street demonstrations, fights, murders, religious phenomena, and so on. The demand for this material was so great that Posada often used stock compositions which could be slightly changed and freshly labeled for the occasion.

Among the most exciting art forms produced by Posada in this period were the *calaveras*, or skeleton pictures, cut in wood or type-metal with a burin to form a white line on a black background. A preoccupation with death is part of the Mexican tradition, as seen in the moralistic engravings of the colonial period or in the celebration of the Day of the Dead, with the skeleton-shaped candies, toys, and foods. The skeleton print itself emerged for the first time in the 'seventies in the work of one of Posada's immediate predecessors, Santiago Hernández.[4] Taken up by Posada, this new form was applied to every kind of social and political problem, achieving tremendous acceptance among the Mexican people. It was used for historical themes such as the French Intervention, in the *calavera* of that name, and even more for contemporary problems, as in the *Calavera Federal* (fig. 3), a portrayal of one of the scourges of the early Revolutionary period, the federal soldier. Perhaps the most famous of Posada's *calaveras*, done shortly before the print-maker's death in 1913, is the devastating and horrible *Calavera Huertista* (fig. 4), which created a sensation throughout Mexico. It shows the vicious Huerta as a loathsome tarantula with a skeleton head, devouring the skeletons of his victims.

Here at an early stage was a political prophet and a pioneer social realist. Within a relatively short time many of his prophetic scenes came to life as the Revolution broke out afresh. One can almost say that the ideal of a 'people's art,' so ardently sought after by the artists of the

[4] Fernando Gamboa, 'Calaveras,' *México en el Arte*, Nov. 1948, no. 5.

3

POSADA. *Calavera Federal.*
WOOD ENGRAVING.
INSTITUTO NACIONAL DE
BELLAS ARTES, MEXICO CITY.

Revolution, was already a fact in the art of Posada. Orozco is quoted as having remarked, as the mural movement began and he himself had not yet been involved: 'Why paint for the people? The people make their own art.'[5]

The people of Mexico do have a popular art tradition of great strength, extending from pottery and other crafts to the beautiful papier-mâché figures of the Day of Judases, the striking *pulquería* or saloon murals, and the graphic works of men like Posada. What the Revolution produced was a series of so-called fine arts, drawing strength from the popular arts and the events of the time: mural and easel painting, sculpture, and graphics. It remains an open question, however, to what extent these forms may be referred to as 'people's art,' however broad their aims. Surely some of the political harangues of Rivera's murals or the philosophical symbols of Orozco must baffle many of their intended audience. Moreover, the locale of most of the early murals, inside the National Preparatory School, the Ministry of Education, and so forth, did not bring these works before a very large number of the people. Only in the graphic-arts area has the popular tradition of Posada continued to flourish, and here only when practiced by specifically political groups such as the Taller de Gráfica Popular (Workshop of Popular Graphic Art). The Taller con-

---

[5] Charlot, op. cit.

tinues to produce *corridos* and *calaveras* in the spirit and with the technique of Posada, from whom they proudly trace their lineage.

Posada's techniques, as we have seen, included the early lithograph and wood and metal cuts. To these should be added the relief etching, made by drawing on a zinc plate with acid-resistant inks, then allowing the rest of the plate to be bitten by an acid bath that dissolves some of the non-inked metal, leaving the inked and protected lines to stand out in relief. This was a freer and more casual method than that of the engraved *calaveras*, the latter necessarily being more primitive and naïve in feeling; but in either technique the accent was upon the real and the everyday. Although the prints of Posada did not have the status of art when they were done, their effect on at least two major figures in the Mexican movement (Rivera and Orozco) seems quite clear.

During 1914–15 Orozco did caricatures for *La Vanguardia*, the Carranzist paper put out in Orizaba under the leadership of Dr. Atl. Other artists in Orizaba who stored up visual memories for their future roles in the movement were Siqueiros, José Guadalupe Zuno, Ramón Alva de la Canal, and Francisco Cahero. Late in 1916, Orozco (already known for his drawings of women) showed a number of his schoolgirls and

4

POSADA. *Calavera Huertista.*
WOOD ENGRAVING.
INSTITUTO NACIONAL DE
BELLAS ARTES, MEXICO CITY.

prostitutes, some of the newspaper caricatures, and sketches for an oil painting. Although poorly received, this show was another step in the realistic graphic Posada tradition. Orozco's caricature comments on the extremist behavior of the Carranza forces after their 1915 return to the capital made him unpopular with those in power, and this may have been a contributing cause of his leaving Mexico for the United States in 1917.

The nativism developing in Goitia and Posada moved another step forward in 1918 with the presentation of a Mexican ballet starring the famous Anna Pavlova. With specifically Mexican music composed for the occasion and equally nativist costumes and scenery designed by Adolfo Best-Maugard, this work ran for a month in the capital, raising enormously the prestige of Indian-derived material. (In 1921, Best-Maugard was to organize an elaborate fair in Mexico City's Chapultepec Park, featuring native dances and music.)

The success of the Pavlova ballet and the general use of native ideas helped to turn the theater in this direction. Like the prints of Posada, new dramatic efforts included salty references to contemporary political and social types, expressed with the same morbid humor found in Mexican painting. Like the soon-to-be-created modern Mexican school of painting, the theater developed a number of important stereotypes, such as the heroic peasant, the evil ranch owner, the dishonest politician, and the dissolute soldier, which may well have had a direct bearing on parallel forms in the plastic arts.

In 1919 a movement to regenerate the popular arts was begun by Roberto Montenegro, a talented painter and illustrator, who was responsible for the magnificent collection of popular arts in the Museo Nacional de Artes Plásticas. Dr. Atl's contribution to this movement was significant; after 1920, he made a survey of the popular arts for all Mexico. Although the new evaluation of these forms can be looked upon as part of a resurgent nationalism, it is a genuine folk art, varying in each section of Mexico and showing a remarkable degree of vitality in its many aspects. The interest in it is important not only as a symptom of change from foreign to native values but also as a source of influence on contemporary Mexican artists, who have been affected by precolonial and colonial forms as well.

In 1919 also, a revolutionary government of artists was established in the state of Jalisco under José Guadalupe Zuno (who had been at Orizaba in 1914). This painter-governor organized a Congress of Soldier Artists with the help of Siqueiros, Amado de la Cueva, Xavier Guerrero, and Carlos Orozco Romero, to investigate the possible new directions for art and culture in general. As one of the results, Siqueiros, Orozco Romero, and others were sent to Europe for additional study.

With the inauguration of Obregón as president in December 1920, the military phase of the Revolution ended.

The Obregón Period

1920 to 1924

The cultural advances during Alvaro Obregón's administration were strong enough to mark a definite break with the past. The social and political character of this era, however, was not startlingly different from that of the period immediately preceding.

The governmental apparatus, still substantially what it had been under Díaz, gradually began to administer the reforms set forth in the new constitution. In addition to the usual inertia, reform was hampered by the appearance of a new ruling class, the Revolutionary victors, which sought its own advantage in the tradition of Mexican politics. The government was still run by one man with the doubtful aid of local chiefs and far-from-idealistic state governors. Many of these figures began to refer to themselves as socialists and warriors against Yankee imperialism, an overworked if genuine issue.

Obregón himself, not so much a revolutionary idealist as a realist, was more concerned with political peace and economic stability than with democracy and individual freedom. With the rights of the workers now more secure, his basic aim was to develop a native middle class and to fight the still medieval system of landowners and clergy—but without any radical change in ownership of the land. Although there was more freedom of the press and of congressional criticism, Obregón still remained the master playing one faction against another. An important source of his power was the Labor Party, his old friends; as a result, C.R.O.M. unions were favored over others that arose. At the same time a rival agrarian union led by the murdered Zapata's counselor, Soto y Gama, was encouraged to offset the power of labor and to appease the peasants who had still not received their lands back from the *hacendados*. Labor's gains in this period were far more tangible than those of the peasantry because government encouragement built up the Grupo Acción of Luis Morones. This semi-secret group that controlled the Labor Party was destined for a very dubious role in the Mexican labor movement.

The most positive achievements of the regime were in education and in art. With the unusually large sum of money made available for these purposes, José Vasconcelos, Obregón's new Minister of Education, organized and launched Mexico's educational system. One of the most paradoxical figures in Mexican history, he created the ministry and gave it the basic form it retains today. His ultra-sensitive, even neurotic personality is reflected in his four-volume autobiography.

During his pre-1920 exile in Los Angeles, Vasconcelos had given a good deal of thought to public education, absorbing and improving on the ideas of Lunacharsky, the Soviet Commissar of Education. Vasconcelos's plan called for branches of the ministry in various parts of the country with three main departments: Schools, Libraries, and Fine Arts. The last-named department included all teaching of music, drawing, and physical training in schools, universities, the Academy, the National Museum, and the conservatories of music. Vasconcelos, who was essentially a poet rather than a professional educator, thought in Platonic terms rather than in the everyday realistic terms necessary for that period of building and rebuilding. In some ways he showed an astonishing lack of practicality. Feeling that it was necessary not only to teach people to read but also to furnish worthy reading matter, he organized a publishing program to provide cheap editions of Plato, Cervantes, Dante, Euripides, and Homer. At a time when most people were not merely illiterate but also hungry, the first publication was a 'people's edition' of Plato.

The story is told of an inspection trip made by Obregón and his cabinet into the north. In the backwoods the party lost its way, and the president asked an Indian and his wife where they were or what town they were near. When it appeared these good folk, born and brought up in that place, had no idea of where it was and were not especially concerned about their ignorance, Obregón turned to his Minister of Education and said: 'José, make a note of this man so that you can send him a complete edition of the classics you've just edited.'[1]

Yet in rural education generally, if we compare Vasconcelos's accomplishments with the vacuum of the centuries preceding, this period marks a tremendous forward step. Both roving and resident teachers were sent out, and within two and a half years schools were established in some of the most undeveloped parts of the country. Vasconcelos thought not in terms of an Indian problem but of the problem of ignorance, an ignorance made worse by the indifference of others. Because they started from absolute zero (no reading or writing materials in most places) and because of the opposition of the clergy and the 'know-nothings,' the missionary teachers were faced by the most difficult task imaginable and often were even attacked and killed. They are among the real heroes of modern Mexican history. As late as the end of the 'thirties, the active antagonism of the reactionaries resulted in a series of teacher murders.

Although Vasconcelos's rural schools, like his art program, are an accepted feature of Mexican education today, he himself was ousted in the

---

[1] Verna Carleton Millán, *Mexico Reborn*, Houghton Mifflin Co., Boston, 1939, pp. 44–5.

change-over from the Obregón to the Calles regime in 1924. As a presidential candidate, he campaigned unsuccessfully against the latter dictatorship in 1929. At that point he was still the great hope of the liberals and anticlericals, but his disappointment at the turn of events in Mexico (he has since frequently spoken of the 'failure of the Revolution') subsequently drove him into the arms of Mexico's reactionary clergy and toward an almost hysterical mysticism.

Yet his contributions to the development of art in Mexico are just as important as those to education in general. In art, though the problem was primarily one of patronage and encouragement, there was also the question of a new approach. Previously, art students had received instruction in the traditional academic way: cast drawings, vase drawings, copies of Murillo, and so on; and after some years the best students were sent abroad for further study. After five or more years in Europe without official supervision, they would return home, become teachers themselves, and repeat this formula with their students. As painters they would do very few pictures, seldom more than one a year—the kind of merchandise that only the wealthy could buy. Since there were few of the latter, even fewer with a taste for art, and no dealers at all to sell pictures, there was no way for art to develop.

Vasconcelos turned to a more popular form of art education and a more popular form of art, i.e. the mural, which presumably everyone could enjoy without special education or a great deal of money. To advance popular art education, Vasconcelos organized a department of drawing and handicrafts as well as a number of open-air schools for the general public. These schools were staffed by young artists, later well known: Carlos Mérida, Manuel Rodríguez Lozano, Rufino Tamayo, Leopoldo Méndez, Antonio Ruiz, Julio Castellanos, Miguel Covarrubias, and others. From the open-air school at Coyoacán alone were produced such talents as Fernando Leal and Fermín Revueltas, who were among the leaders in the early mural movement.

Even before Vasconcelos became Minister of Education and while he was President of the University of Mexico, he had commissioned Roberto Montenegro and Xavier Guerrero to paint murals in the former convent of San Pedro y San Pablo. This took place in June 1920, before Obregón took office. In this old church that had been converted into an annex of the Preparatory School, the works that are considered the first in the Mexican mural movement were done. With his appointment to Obregón's cabinet in December, Vasconcelos was in a better position to make available the walls and funds for the 'people's art' movement that got under way the following year, and to encourage artists such as Rivera and Siqueiros to return from Europe.

In many ways 1921 was a turning point. In the only issue ever published of the periodical *Vida Americana*, David Alfaro Siqueiros in Barcelona proclaimed his now famous manifesto, which is often credited with crystallizing the mural movement in Mexico.[2] The theories first set forth in this magazine, and since repeated in many books and articles by the painter, stress the need for abandoning easel painting (which according to him had long outlived itself) in favor of the mural. Another important idea he advanced then and later was that the theme or subject of any painting was as important as the style of the picture—an attitude in direct conflict with abstract painting, which has always been a favorite target of his. Siqueiros felt that the picture should derive its 'emotion, design, construction, and color from the model,' which should not be chosen purely as a motif or, in his words, as an excuse 'to demonstrate artistic gymnastics.'

He felt, moreover, that the contemporary artist had to identify himself with the native tradition, through which he could regain (in terms of today's needs) the old simplicity, solid structure, and profound religious feeling. Toward these ends the older arts should be used merely as a point of departure, as a source of emotional and structural energy 'without falling into lamentable archaeological reconstruction.' What he wanted was 'to create a monumental and heroic art, a human and public art, with the direct and living example of our great masters and the extraordinary cultures of pre-Hispanic America.'

These ideas were applied by Siqueiros in his own painting from the time of his return to Mexico in 1922. Neither he nor Rivera was in Mexico while the stage was being set for the new movement, and Orozco, who was there, does not seem to have been especially active. But other artists and intellectuals were arriving from every quarter as the Revolution came to an end and reconstruction began.

Jean Charlot, the part-Mexican painter from Paris, had developed ideas somewhat similar to Siqueiros's, and had done a number of murals in French churches. After his military service he came to Mexico in 1921, drawn by sympathy with the anticapitalist ideas of such liberal Catholics as Jacques Maritain and hoping to find an outlet for these feelings in the new Mexico. In addition to this Christian-socialist attitude, he approached the new material with a fervor, a sensitive feeling for the culture of the country, and a technical flair that give him a high place among the pioneers of the movement.

Carlos Mérida, from Guatemala via Paris and New York, had his first show of Indian-inspired subjects in 1921. This was also the year of Best-Maugard's *A Night in Mexico* fair at Chapultepec Park. From Guadalajara came Amado de la Cueva and Xavier Guerrero, both soon to be active on mural projects, as were Charlot and Mérida. Another group returning from Europe included Carlos Orozco Romero, who was to help found a school of woodcut art in Guadalajara and later to be an outstanding easel painter. More important for the immediate history of the

---

[2] David Alfaro Siqueiros, *El Muralismo Mexicano*, Ediciones Mexicanas, S.A., Mexico, 1950.

Mexican movement were the 1922 return of Siqueiros and the 1921 arrival of Diego Rivera, which acted as a kind of catalyst. The other member of Mexico's 'big three,' José Clemente Orozco, had been in the United States from 1917 to 1919 and was just about to take his place in the movement.

During this Obregón period the subsequently martyred governor of Yucatán, Felipe Carrillo Puerto, invited Vasconcelos, Rivera, and Best-Maugard to make a survey of the social and cultural needs of his state. Carrillo Puerto, himself a Maya Indian, had been aware of the oppression of the people since the time when Yaquis had been whipped to work on Yucatán plantations and Mayas completely peonized. He had translated the new Mexican constitution into the Maya language, and had preached from it to the Indians as though from some sacred text. For this he had been jailed and tortured almost to death. Taking an active part in the Revolution, Carrillo Puerto eventually became governor of Yucatán and tried to improve the condition of the Indians, the position of women, and to create roads, schools, and other necessities. During the confusion attendant on the election of Obregón's successor in 1923, he was taken prisoner by the reactionary supporters of de la Huerta and killed.

The nativism symbolized by the career of Carrillo Puerto is paralleled on another plane by the already mentioned new system of art education, based on native art and founded by Best-Maugard. He showed how a few simple straight and curved lines were the basis of the rather elaborate Mexican ornament. This ornament, dominated by a basic spiral, he then proceeded to break down into seven fundamental elements. Since these things concerned everyday objects and their decoration, his pupils applied themselves with considerable understanding and enthusiasm. Partly because of this new system and partly because of the immediate pedagogic utility of art in all its forms, the enthusiasm for art became so great that other academic subjects were taught in terms of art expression.

As the new director of the Department of Fine Arts, Dr. Atl made a systematic study of the popular arts of Mexico, adding his name to those of Roberto Montenegro, Manuel Rodríguez Lozano (who was to make a specialty of folk sculpture), Jorge Enciso, and many others—some of whom absorbed the influences from this material into their own art. In his official capacity Atl also chose the first walls for the painters to work on. He himself did a rather hasty series of murals in San Pedro y San Pablo, which, like the early 1920 job by Montenegro and Guerrero, soon deteriorated very badly. The archindividualist in a group of individualists, Atl worked in a personal wax-crayon technique known as 'Atl color,' which, although effective in his innumerable easel landscapes of volcanoes, had no permanence when applied to walls (fig. 5).

Having done this much for the Revolution and the art movement, Dr. Atl chose to drop out of the picture. During the 'twenties and 'thirties he wandered all over the world, continuing his studies of volcanoes and prolific writings. (His claim to have lived for six months inside the crater of Popocatépetl is not so unlikely as it may seem.) During World War II, disillusioned as was Vasconcelos with the direction of the Revolution, this former associate of Mussolini turned to fascism, publishing books and articles in support of that point of view. In 1943, when the Paricutín volcano erupted, Dr. Atl immediately hastened there and, to the gratification of the poor farmer whose fields had been destroyed, bought him out. On this site Atl produced 130 drawings, 11 paintings, and an enormous book dealing with the volcano. This material is now in the possession of the National Institute of Fine Arts.

In July 1921 Rivera had arrived from Europe bringing a great revolutionary enthusiasm, however theoretical, an agile mind, and a concrete knowledge of painting, though not of fresco technique. No one in Mexico at that time knew very much about fresco. Those who came from

5

DR. ATL. *Landscape, 1933.* ATL COLOR.
INSTITUTO NACIONAL DE BELLAS ARTES, MEXICO CITY.

Europe originally (e.g. Charlot) or had been there studying (Rivera, Siqueiros, and so on) knew what frescoes looked like, but not how they should be done—with the possible exception of Charlot. The technique had to be rediscovered.

When Montenegro, for example, received the 1920 commission for San Pedro y San Pablo, he took along young Xavier Guerrero as technical assistant. Guerrero, an Aztec Indian from Coahuila, was the son of a master house painter, had actually handled brushes as a child, and had acquired some experience as an architectural draftsman. At fourteen he got a job in Guadalajara decorating the house of a rich farmer, and by sixteen was an experienced commercial muralist in the tradition of thousands of painted walls in Mexican homes and *pulquerías* (saloons that sell the native *pulque*). While painting a map mural in a hacienda, Guerrero had been surprised by a Revolutionary band and pressed into service.

Working with Montenegro, he let the latter do the main part of the rear wall in oils, while he painted the rest (flowers, birds, and zodiacal decorations in the cupola) in tempera on a white plaster ground. When, late in 1921, Rivera received the commission for the first mural in the National Preparatory School, he inherited Guerrero from Montenegro. This mural in the auditorium, the Anfiteatro Bolívar, was done in encaustic, a laborious and traditional wax technique, which Rivera had used in Spain. Here Guerrero was able to suggest various cheap and practicable materials. The work was done with the assistance of Mérida, Charlot, and Guerrero, who ground the colors, incised the outlines on the cement, transferred details from drawings to the walls, and primed the wall with hot rosin at exactly the moment of painting. A touch of the blowtorch to the wall with each brushstroke solidified or crystallized the paint. The mural was finished in March 1923. Rivera's style at this point suggests the mosaics of Ravenna, whose gold background and haloes reappear in his rather formidable and pompous *The Creation* (fig. 6). In the handling of the necessary gold leaf, Guerrero's practical experience was again invaluable.

In May 1922 Vicente Lombardo Toledano, then director of the National Preparatory School (the Preparatoria), commissioned a group of painters to decorate the walls of the school with murals: Jean Charlot, Ramón Alva de la Canal, Fermín Revueltas, Fernando Leal, and Francisco Cahero. This somewhat unplanned commission, whose only requirement was Mexican themes, resulted in a group of tentative and by no means Revolutionary works. Although nativist in theme, they show a consciousness of the Mexican past rather than present and a reliance on Renaissance decorative traditions and techniques. The subjects include Alva de la Canal's idealized *Planting of the Cross by the Spaniards*, Charlot's decorative and Uccello-like *Fall of Tenochtitlán*, Leal's picturesque *Feast of Chalma*, and Revueltas's stylized *Allegory of the Virgin of Guadalupe*.

Yet with these rather self-conscious works, Mexican painting had taken an important forward step. It had moved from easel-painting Mexicanism like that of Herrán to a publicly projected and monumentalized nativism that was to be converted into a Revolutionary form of expression. Rivera's contemporary *Creation* in the same building does not even have the merit of nativism to compensate for its pretentiousness. Only in his first panels in the Ministry of Education, begun in March 1923, does he come abreast of the Mexicanist point of view.

In the same way, technical procedures moved along hesitantly from the laborious encaustic methods of Rivera, Leal, Cahero, and Revueltas (as well as the initial Siqueiros murals somewhat later) to the wet-cement painting of Charlot and the fresco experiments of Alva de la Canal in the Preparatoria, of Guerrero in 1923 in the Ministry of Education, and of Montenegro in 1922 in San Pedro y San Pablo. The last-mentioned was Montenegro's second job in that building, the charming glorification of a Mexican workingman's holiday, *The Feast of the Holy Cross*. Here, masons and bricklayers are shown decorating the building on which they are working, with large ornate straw and floral crosses. As an occasion for depicting various native types (including a full-length portrait of Vasconcelos, which was later removed), this traditionally conceived work corresponds to the general level of the early paintings in the Preparatoria. Like most of those, it has a curiously inappropriate religious flavor.

Although the question of who did the first true fresco may seem academic to the non-Mexican, it remains a bone of contention among many painters who have survived that epoch. Charlot apparently finished the first mural in the Preparatoria, but he was not the first to begin work there. This credit, as well as that for the first use of the traditional fresco medium, would seem to belong to Alva de la Canal, who has continued to paint a series of such works down to the present day. Charlot, on the other hand, though not so prolific, has done a certain number of aesthetically important works and has written a considerable number of significant books and articles on the Mexican movement.

In September 1922 Siqueiros and de la Cueva arrived from Europe. The former began to paint at the Preparatoria on the staircase of the so-called Colegio Chico, first in encaustic and then in fresco. His first efforts, already dynamic in technique, show a Christ and an angel; only on the third try did he progress to a contemporary Revolutionary theme. Yet at this point he sparked the organization of the Syndicate of Technical Workers, Painters, and Sculptors. This trade union, created late in 1922, was introduced to the public through a ringing manifesto that carries the ideas and influence of Siqueiros. For the brief period of its existence, it became the focal point of mural activity in Mexico. Its later influence is equally important. The text of the manifesto has been translated as follows:

Social, Political and Aesthetic Declaration from the Syndicate of Technical Workers, Painters and Sculptors to the indigenous races humiliated through centuries; to the soldiers converted into hangmen by their chiefs; to the workers and peasants who are oppressed by the rich; and to the intellectuals who are not servile to the bourgeoisie:

We are with those who seek the overthrow of an old and inhuman system within which you, worker of the soil, produce riches for the overseer and politician, while you starve. Within which you, worker in the city, move the wheels of industries, weave the cloth, and create with your hands the modern comforts enjoyed by the parasites and prostitutes, while your own body is numb with cold. Within which you, Indian soldier, heroically abandon your land and give your life in the eternal hope of liberating your race from the degradations and misery of centuries.

Not only the noble labor but even the smallest manifestations of the material and spiritual vitality of our race spring from our native midst. Its admirable, exceptional and peculiar ability to create beauty—the art of the Mexican people—is the highest and greatest spiritual expression of the world-tradition which constitutes our most valued heritage. It is great because it surges from the people; it is collective, and our own aesthetic aim is to socialize artistic expression, to destroy bourgeois individualism.

We repudiate the so-called easel art and all such art which springs from ultra-intellectual circles, for it is essentially aristocratic.

We hail the monumental expression of art because such art is public property.

We proclaim that this being the moment of social transition from a decrepit to a new order, the makers of beauty must invest their greatest effort in the aim of materializing an art valuable to the people, and our supreme objective in art, which is today an expression for individual pleasure, is to create beauty for all, beauty that enlightens and stirs to struggle.[3]

In the organization of the Syndicate, Siqueiros had the key post of executive secretary, Rivera acted as a kind of foreign minister, Guerrero worked on organization problems, and Leal conducted the treasury. Orozco also became affiliated with the Syndicate but in an inactive capacity. In addition to his other duties, Guerrero assumed responsibility for the Syndicate's newspaper *El Machete* (The Scythe). Its slogan was printed on the first page near a woodcut illustration of a machete:

> The machete is used to reap cane
> To clear a path through the underbrush
> To kill snakes, end strife
> And humble the pride of the impious rich.

---

[3] Guillermo Rivas, in 'David Alfaro Siqueiros,' *Mexican Life*, Dec. 1935. A more literal translation is available in Anita Brenner's classic *Idols behind Altars*, Payson & Clarke, Ltd., N.Y., 1929.

This forthrightly leftist sheet was printed in red and black and was set up so that it could be used as a poster. It was pasted on walls at street corners and other strategic spots where its large-scale woodcuts could be seen by all, and was usually put up just before dawn by Guerrero and Siqueiros (who were also chiefly responsible for its art work). *El Machete* survived the Syndicate itself by many years, and continued to appear long after the group was dissolved in 1925.

The various painting jobs of the Syndicate were done on a contract basis determined by the size of the mural or murals involved. Both master painter and master mason worked an eight-hour day; each was paid an average of about eight pesos per diem (the peso then was worth about two cents). The first contract was signed toward the end of 1922, although most of the members were already at work on pre-Syndicate jobs, as we have indicated. In March of 1923 the new Ministry of Education building (the Secretaría) was turned over to Syndicate artists. Rivera was to do the first court; the second was to be a joint job for de la Cueva, Guerrero, and Charlot. March 1923 also marks the completion of the Rivera mural in the Preparatoria, the turgid *Creation*. To celebrate this event a party was organized, with Rivera, Vasconcelos, and Lombardo Toledano (then director of the Preparatoria) as the guests of honor. Assistants on this pioneer project, as listed on the humorous orange-colored invitation sheet, had been Xavier Guerrero, Carlos Mérida, Juan (sic) Charlot, Amado de la Cueva, and Luis Escobar. One of its most striking features was the great affection and respect felt for Rivera at that time.

As it actually turned out, the Ministry of Education building ultimately became Rivera's private preserve (again with the technical aid of Guerrero, who had gone to Teotihuacán to learn how the ancients had done fresco). When Rivera finished the ground floor of his own patio in 1924, the rest of the building was turned over to him. In the larger courtyard Charlot had completed three panels, among the best he ever produced, one of which was removed by Rivera to make way for his own composition. In this same courtyard, near the panel of Charlot, are two by Amado de la Cueva. With the exception of these few sections, the Montenegro office paintings, and the 1923 Mérida decorations in the Children's Library, the Ministry is a monument to the industry and shrewdness of Rivera. This situation was also due in part to the change of administration in 1924, which brought the artistic Revolution to a temporary halt.

In the Preparatoria, which Rivera had abandoned for the greener fields of the Ministry of Education, the others continued to work. These included Siqueiros, Revueltas, Alva de la Canal, Leal, Emilio Amero, and the newcomer José Clemente Orozco. The last-named was assigned three rows of corridor panels as well as the remaining space on the main stairway, where Charlot and Leal had painted their panels. Siqueiros chose to continue on the dark little stairway of the Colegio Chico, contributing his magnificent *Burial of a Worker*.

Orozco began his work with a number of religious and allegorical themes: the effective if traditional *Maternity*, the eccentric *Spring* with its enormous nude sweeping downward (later completely removed by the artist), and the *Christ Destroying His Own Cross* (subsequently removed by Orozco except for the head of the Christ). When Orozco had about completed these and the slightly later *The Rich Banquet while the Workers Quarrel*, a number of eager church ladies of the Damas Católicas, who proposed to hold a church party in the patio, demanded that he 'temporarily' remove what seemed to them caricatures of religion. The *Christ Destroying His Own Cross* and the nude Madonna and Child of the *Maternity*, perhaps objectionable on religious grounds, could not conveniently be removed, such being the nature of fresco. The good ladies therefore proceeded to action, nailing flags, branches, and garlands on the walls (thereby marring the paintings) and earning for themselves immortality in Orozco's later violent caricatures on the second floor.

These caricatures were done early in 1924, during the last hectic weeks of Orozco's assignment in the Preparatoria, just before the Obregón regime came to an end. Orozco and others were 'terminated' from the government payroll by the incoming Calles administration. The direct action of the women against Orozco's works was a symptom of the rising tide of reaction. The battle for and against the murals raged hot and heavy, with the Minister of Education under strong pressure from the conservatives for 'wasting the public's money.' Broadsides from embattled members of the Syndicate did not improve the climate. The climax was reached in June of that year as students of the Preparatoria (the children of conservatives) attacked the murals physically, scratching and scraping them and writing childishly obscene words wherever they could reach. Some of Orozco's caricature murals on the second floor were mutilated almost up to the necks of the figures, and his sympathetic St. Francis was badly damaged. Siqueiros's work, too, suffered from these attacks, the marks of which are still visible.

The young vandals, much praised by the reactionaries, 'could not be found' by the not too eager police. Only after a considerable number of foreign residents had petitioned the government, pointing out that art is 'an international property,' were any steps taken to protect the murals. But the work in the Preparatoria was definitely over, at least for the time being. As the new president and cabinet came in, Vasconcelos and his program were automatically out. The new Minister of Education is quoted by Miss Brenner as saying: 'The first thing I'll do is whitewash those horrible frescoes.'

Over at the Ministry of Education, where Rivera reigned, the situation was somewhat different. At the height of the trouble he had armed himself and his assistants with pistols, a flamboyant and characteristic gesture, in view of the fact that nothing had been painted there that could give offense. The group ideals of the Syndicate were apparently forgotten by Rivera, who refused to extend any help to his colleagues in difficulty less than a block away in the Preparatoria.

Of all the available painters, only two were retained by the new ministry: the elegant Roberto Montenegro, who continued his work in the church of San Pedro y San Pablo, and the indefatigable Rivera, whose work in the Education building was to go on until 1928. Orozco retired to his suburban studio; de la Cueva and Siqueiros went to Jalisco to work on a commission from the governor of that state, although Siqueiros found himself doing more and more union work. Guerrero became editor of the increasingly Communistic *El Machete*, in opposition to the government. Revueltas was occupied with commercial work for United States gasoline stations, and later shifted to teaching in one of the open-air schools; Charlot turned to easel painting. By 1925 the Syndicate was disbanded, but its contribution had already been made. The idea of an art coming from and going to the people was to remain as a permanent goal of the modern Mexican movement.

Diego Rivera

Through 1924

IV

Most observers of Mexican art have long realized that Rivera is not the entire movement and that a good deal of his fame is due to his ability to create issues and to a phenomenal sense of publicity. Nevertheless, though one may discount his endless self-promotion, flamboyance, and occasional opportunism, Rivera remains truly important as a historical figure. Reappearing in Mexico at the psychological moment, with the Revolution over and the culturo-political groundwork prepared, Rivera acted as a catalytic agent in the development of a new approach. His influence, for better or worse, has conditioned an entire school of Mexican painting through his various assistants and others who have felt the impact of his personality and the strong decorative simplicity of his work.

The large simple forms and bold color areas of Rivera have contributed in no small way to the widespread popularity of his murals and easel paintings. They stand in strong contrast to the Expressionist and less 'pleasant' forms of Orozco or the dynamic and overwhelming figures of Siqueiros. In this sense, Rivera's art is quite palatable and perhaps the closest thing to popular art that Mexico has produced in the field of painting. He has the further attraction, for the Mexican as for the foreigner, of an outstandingly didactic style which invites close examination, as to a machine or the page of a manuscript.

Whereas the forms themselves are self-explanatory, the content is generally far less so. For the Mexican peasant and worker, to whom his art is presumably consecrated, Rivera is not always understandable without additional help. For the perhaps more literate visitor who can afford guide books and-or guides, a visit to such murals as those in the National Palace or the Palace of Fine Arts opens a vista of titillating and 'interesting' political subjects such as Marxism, imperialism, the role of the proletariat, and so on—a distant and safe view of social problems. What must be kept in mind, in spite of the apparent simplicity of form and expository quality, is that this is not the work of a naïve individual. Rivera is a highly complex and sophisticated person, who, after all his experience of the school of Paris and the modern movement, deliberately set about creating the 'art for the people' demanded by the post-Revolutionary situation in Mexico.

33

Among the earliest artistic influences on the career of Diego Rivera, a number of things stand out. First are the commercial rather than artistic saloon decorations known as *pulquería* paintings, especially panoramic types such as *The Battle of Waterloo*. This childhood favorite of his might be said to prefigure some of his later large-scale many-figured works. As a boy Diego was also interested in the painted façades with large figures in the part of Mexico City where his family lived. In this same neighborhood also there was the shop of Vanegas Arroyo, where the engravings of Posada were hand-colored. From these three sources one may possibly deduce Rivera's later interest in panoramic art, decorative figures, and narrative and critical ideas.

Born in 1886 (at Guanajuato), Diego showed a flair for drawing as a child, and was entered in the Academy of San Carlos at the age of ten. From 1896 to 1907 he studied there under the classicist Santiago Rebull, the brilliant landscapist José María Velasco, José Salomé Pina, and Félix Parra, the first Mexican painter to use Maya and Aztec material. During this period also Rivera came to know the work of Posada. In 1907, thanks to a prize donated by the governor of Vera Cruz, the twenty-one-year-old Rivera went to Europe to continue his studies.

After contact with so-called Spanish realism and travel in Belgium, Holland, and England, he settled down in Paris in 1909. There he showed at the Independents and was influenced by Cézanne. Except for a few months in Mexico during 1910 (he witnessed the outbreak of the Revolution), Diego stayed in Europe until 1921, primarily in Paris. He participated in the Autumn Salon of 1911, came under the influence of neo-Impressionism, and showed a number of pictures in that technique at the Independents of 1912.

Perhaps Rivera's most important works from those years are the many Cubist pictures, begun in 1913, which may be compared very favorably with those of other masters in that style. But Cubism as such apparently did not satisfy him for long, and he absorbed influences from other French formalistic sources: Renoir, Gauguin, and once again Cézanne. With Siqueiros, who had come over in 1919 after a long series of Revolutionary experiences, Rivera discussed the need for transforming Mexican art into a national and popular movement. His travels in Italy during 1920–21 brought him into contact with the masters of the Renaissance and the Middle Ages (notably the fourteenth-century Sienese, the fifteenth-century Florentines, and the mosaicists of Ravenna) and with the new classicism of the postwar period. This modern Italian trend toward a more monumental and frozen conception of form (Frenchmen and Germans were also moving in that direction by 1920) is of great importance in the evolution of Rivera's style and that of some other Mexican painters. In 1921, on the invitation of Vasconcelos, Rivera returned to Mexico to fulfill his role in the new movement.

His first Mexican mural in the Anfiteatro Bolívar of the Preparatory

School, begun in 1922 and finished in March 1923,[1] was done in the slow and laborious encaustic technique. This is *The Creation*, with its half-religious, half-philosophical content, its sentimental expression and meaningless gestures. The figure of Christ in the niche (with evangelist symbols) grows out of a kind of Tree of Life, while on the arched surface around the niche allegorical figures of humanistic intent are symmetrically placed. On top the artist has indicated a star-studded mystic circle from which symbolic hands point to Tragedy, Science, Fortitude, and Temperance at the right, and Music, Comedy, and the Dance at the left (fig. 6). These two groups are arranged behind a nude male figure and a nude female figure respectively and are capped by a number of gold-haloed virtues on each side. One may compare this work in its general religious character with the early murals of Rivera's contemporaries, but there are neither the realistic nor the social implications of the others at that time and nothing to offend the conservatives.

Although it is believed that Rivera had intended to decorate the auditorium further with the history of thought, including Marx and Engels, *The Creation* must stand as his contribution at this juncture of the movement. It may be looked upon as a blend of contemporary European neo-Classical tendencies, with the drawing of the Renaissance and the gold backgrounds and haloes of Byzantine art. In color, it is lamentably weak; as pictorial expression, it is a low point in Rivera's career.

Only after Diego's trip to Yucatán and other parts of Mexico, where he saw native life and made many sketches, did his art turn toward the contemporary. The new Diego is seen in his extensive murals for the then newly built Ministry of Education, where he was to work from 1923 to 1928, with interruptions for the simultaneous job at Chapingo and his 1927 visit to the Soviet Union.

The Ministry, or Secretaría, is divided into two three-storied patios. The smaller one constitutes Rivera's so-called Court of Labor and the larger one (originally intended for Charlot, de la Cueva, and Guerrero) his Court of Festivals. With the exception of two panels each by Amado de la Cueva and Jean Charlot in the second patio, all of this area contains the work of Rivera and his assistants.

The decoration of the Secretaría began with Rivera (assisted by Guerrero) working in the smaller patio, while Charlot and de la Cueva began their painting in the larger. At the same time, Montenegro was assigned the main office on the third floor and Mérida the Children's Library, which he decorated with a pleasant fairy-tale series. When Rivera finished his court, he found that Charlot and de la Cueva had been able to complete only five panels between them. This factor, together with Rivera's claim that their work did not harmonize with his and the general reactionary trend in 1924, led to the assignment of the second patio also to Rivera.

---

[1] Jean Charlot, 'Renaissance Revisited,' *Magazine of Art*, vol. 39, no. 2, Feb. 1946.

6

RIVERA. *The Creation*, detail. ENCAUSTIC.
ANFITEATRO BOLÍVAR, NATIONAL PREPARATORY SCHOOL, MEXICO CITY.

What was later called the Court of Labor began with a group of rather tentative decorations inspired by the picturesque women of Tehuantepec. The two panels showing large-scale but flatly executed if exotic Tehuantepec women are not much improvement over *The Creation* either in composition or in mural technique. After a brief interval the colors began to deteriorate, and subsequent repairs have not helped too much. Presumably at this point Guerrero, in his capacity as technical advisor, went to the Teotihuacán archaeological site to compare his own experiments in so-called fresco with the methods used by the ancients. After a number of attempts he worked out a method that Rivera could use, but unfortunately Guerrero suggested the use of nopal juice as an agglutinating medium—apparently in the belief that this had been the method of the pre-Spanish Indians. Although this detail naturally appealed to the nativists of the moment, it did not make for good fresco. The juice of the nopal plant would not be absorbed into the body of the plaster and remained as a surface irritant. It prevented the evaporation of water from the wet plaster and caused innumerable tiny paint blisters to form, thus clouding the colors. This difficulty applies to all the murals in the Court of Labor.

The south wall of the patio shows the industries of southern Mexico: weaving, dyeing, cane growing, and sugar refining. On the north side the artist illustrates the northern industries: iron mining, ranching—and Revolution. The eastern wall is dedicated to the industries of central Mexico: silver mining, corn, wheat, and pottery.

With the transition from the purely picturesque *Women of Tehuantepec* to scenes of industry, Rivera finally enters the arena of social-minded art. There are not only pictures of people at work but clear references to pre-Revolutionary abuses as well as to post-Revolutionary hopes. They are not merely photographic representations, for a great many of the panels show the beneficial influence of post-Impressionist (especially Gauguin) space composition and form abstraction. As design, they are far superior to the *Creation* mural in the Preparatoria or the first experiments with the women of the south. In *The Weavers* the lines of the threads and the frames have been arranged into a pattern whose counterpoint is in the cylindrical bobbins of the foreground. The ensemble is unified by different tonalities of blue.

The subsepuent panels show an even clearer patterning. Human forms are reduced to linear silhouettes integrated into planear arrangements with one space area superposed on another in a manner that brings to mind the painting of Gauguin. Thus *The Dyers*, *The Sugar Refiners*, the *Descent into the Mine*, and so on, show stylized forms against simplified landscape or architectural elements. The enclosing space is controlled and limited in accordance with the Cézanne-Gauguin idea. None of these pictures is concerned with emotions, personalities, or even ideals, Revolutionary or otherwise. This aesthetic decorative conception of labor

7

RIVERA. *Iron Foundry.* FRESCO.
MINISTRY OF EDUCATION, MEXICO CITY.

is illustrated in the *Iron Foundry* of the north wall (fig. 7). Here the emphasis is on organization of geometrical solids, which are slightly distorted in form and position to accommodate them to the painter's design concept.

A significant departure is made in a group of panels that brings in a more dynamic and emotional point of view, as Rivera introduces a number of pre-Revolutionary abuses as well as political and idealistic themes. The well-known *Weighing of the Grain*, with its surly *hacendado* standing over a number of bent peons, is paralleled by the symbolically presented *Exit from the Mine* (fig. 8). Here the stylized and anonymous peasant, his arms raised as though for a crucifixion, is being searched by the equally anonymous foreman. The worker's head is fitted into the outline of the background mountains, one arm into the mountain at the left and the other aimed toward the tops of the posts at the right. His figure continues the pattern of the base of the panel, which is dominated by the triangular mine exit. At the same time his head forms part of an oval which includes

8

RIVERA. *Exit from the Mine*. FRESCO. MINISTRY OF EDUCATION, MEXICO CITY.

the landscape sweep at the right, the bent backs of the two men at his side, and the curve of the hole below. This simple but effective device ties together background and foreground in a post-Impressionist manner.

A more idealistic and post-Revolutionary series of themes includes the symbolic *Worker and Peasant* shown embracing in religious fashion (evoking the Italian fourteenth century) and the often reproduced *The New School* (fig. 9). The latter is a gentle and even touching tribute to the ideals of the educational campaign initiated shortly after the Revolution. The panel presents a group of people of all ages grouped about their teacher, who reads to them from a book as a mounted soldier keeps watch. In the middleground peasants toil in the fields; farther back a pair of figures building a house forms the apex of a semicircle which moves left and right from that point and again unifies background and foreground. The mounted soldier acts as a link between the oval in the foreground and this semicircle. The hills sweeping down to the left are balanced by lines moving to the right and into the foreground.

9

RIVERA. *The New School.* FRESCO.
MINISTRY OF EDUCATION, MEXICO CITY.

PHOTO CENTRAL DE PUBLICACIONES

Here also we may notice a henceforth typical Rivera figure, a diminutive small-nosed Mexican with globular head, round shoulders, and ovoid torso. This creation of Rivera is not based on the actual physical appearance of the average Mexican, but is again an aesthetic formula, here apparently derived from Duccio and his fourteenth-century contemporaries. One is reminded of the early Renaissance not only in this physical type, which becomes standard for Rivera, but in his massing of large groups of people, as in the *May Day* and *Distribution of the Land* (both in the next patio) or the later *Burial of a Proletarian Victim*.

In these and similar works the painter arranges his many figures in superposed rows rather than directly behind one another, so that after the foreground row of full-length forms, only heads appear as the eye moves backward through this arbitrarily controlled space. Crowds such as these (*May Day, Distribution of the Land, Burial of Proletarian Victim, Day of the Dead,* and so forth) suggest the groupings at either side of the Madonna in the Duccio *Majestas* in Siena—even to the shape of the faces—while the movement of the crowds on the back of that altarpiece offers an even closer parallel to Rivera's massed figures.

In the Court of Labor, working under the stimulus of the first flush of the reconstruction period and his own increasing concern with political matters, Rivera made a number of direct and forceful statements. Together with his later Chapingo murals, they constitute perhaps his finest work. Yet however successful these panels are as decorations and abstractions in the modern sense, they do not have the degree of monumentality already evident in the early works of Orozco and Siqueiros. In the second patio of the Secretaría, done at the beginning of the Calles period, this difference in orientation becomes even more evident. There Rivera moves on to a consistently coloristic and decorative scheme. He concentrates increasingly on large masses of figures disposed as much for their picturesque possibilities as for their social significance.

V | José Clemente Orozco
Through 1924

In spite of a charmingly written autobiography[1] and innumerable anecdotes and accounts by contemporaries, Orozco the man remains a shadowy figure when compared with either Siqueiros or Rivera. Yet even without the urbane personality advantages of those two painters or their cosmopolitan experience, Orozco emerges as the towering figure of the Mexican school. His art is based on a personally evolved form of Expressionism stemming from his deep sympathies for the miserable and oppressed. Neither self-conscious polemics nor programmatic political attitudes have ever affected his point of view. Orozco's work remains at all times the sensitive, even mystic reaction of an individual to the inequities and weaknesses of his environment.

If his painting is less readily understandable than that of Rivera, it is because of his profound belief that what the artist says is peculiar to the artist and not to the writer, politician, or propagandist. He has said of his own art: 'My one theme is HUMANITY; my one tendency is EMOTION TO A MAXIMUM; my means the REAL and INTEGRAL representation of bodies in themselves and in their interrelation.'[2] Without a specific political point of view, his art is in many ways the most penetrating expression of the suffering that characterized the Revolution and its aftermath.

Justino Fernández, the distinguished analyst of Orozco's work, has said: 'Above the Periclean tradition and above the materialistic environment of our times, Orozco's work rises as a gigantic protest against inertia of conscience and human degradation, against dishumanization and affirming a genuine human existence.'[3] Orozco appears not only as the outstanding painter of the modern Mexican school—and the finest essence of its spirit—but also, through his unique quality as an artist, as one of the leading figures of our century.

Orozco was born in Zapotlán, state of Jalisco, in 1883; his family moved to Mexico City in 1888. The young man at first intended to be an

---

[1] José Clemente Orozco, *Autobiografía*, Eds. Occidente, Mexico, 1945.

[2] Jean Charlot, *Art from the Mayans to Disney*, Sheed & Ward, N.Y., London, 1939.

[3] Justino Fernández, 'El pintor de nuestro tiempo,' *Anales del instituto de investigaciones estéticas*, no. 16, 1948.

agronomist; he spent four years studying agricultural engineering, and took his degree in 1899. A few years later he studied mathematics and architectural drawing at the Preparatoria (1904–8), and then took occasional art courses at the Academy of San Carlos from 1908 to 1914. There he acquired the solid academic drawing of his first 'classical' period. Other early influences on Orozco's art include the atmosphere of the big city, the work of Posada with its bold caricature quality and vivid color effects, and finally the events of the Revolution from 1910 on.

Orozco first exhibited in a 1910 Academy group show commemorating the 1810 revolt from Spain. Here he offered caricatures and other compositions.[4] These no longer extant works were probably similar in style to a series done in 1911–12 for *El Ahuizote* during the Madero administration. In spite of the anti-Madero character of this paper, Orozco (according to his own account) was not yet affected by the Revolution one way or another. As he himself has pointed out, he could just as well have done pro-Madero caricatures at this stage.

Orozco next appears in the tragic days following the assassination of Madero in 1913 and the ensuing brutal dictatorship of Huerta. According to the well-known interview with José Juan Tablada,[5] Orozco was then making sketches of women. In this account the painter is quoted by Tablada as saying that '... nowadays he paints exclusively women, limiting himself to college girls and prostitutes.' Although there is no hint of the bloody events of those days in the delicately tinted watercolors, there is nevertheless a clear enough criticism of mankind in general. It is not accidental that so little difference appears between the simpering and provocative schoolgirls and the rapacious and greedy or melancholy and bored types in the bordello pictures. The latter range from the mordant irony of the light-blue *Despoiling* (fig. 10) to more somber and even tragic scenes that symbolize the fatalistic misery of Mexico.

Here one already sees the genesis of Orozco's social caricatures, a mode based on the typical macabre humor of the Mexicans exemplified by Posada and emerging in Orozco's Preparatoria murals of 1923–4 and many later easel paintings and graphics. Throughout his career he returns to the prostitute theme, not in any cynical metropolitan sense but rather as a Dostoyevskian symbol of the corruption and weakness, the sadness and isolation of the individual. Thus the wretched figures lurking in doorways—black shadows of despair (as in the 1946 *Waiting Women*, owned by Dr. Carrillo Gil)—or the obscene creature on her back in the Bellas Artes mural of 1934, all are taken from everyday life and converted into symbols of reality in terms of Orozco's 'one theme ... HUMANITY.'

---

[4] Jean Charlot, 'Orozco's Stylistic Evolution,' *College Art Journal*, vol. IX, no. 2, 1949–50.

[5] José Juan Tablada, 'Un pintor de la mujer: José Clemente Orozco,' *El Mundo Ilustrado*, 9 Nov. 1913.

In 1914 Huerta fled, making way for the three-cornered scramble for the presidency between Carranza, Zapata, and Villa. Orozco, under the influence of his friend Dr. Atl, followed Carranza in the famous retreat from the capital to Orizaba. At Orizaba, Orozco's Revolutionary impressions were further enriched by scenes involving the summary execution of Zapatistas and the looting of churches. From this period come the drawings he did for *La Vanguardia*, a paper produced throughout 1915 to encourage the Carranza forces at a bad moment in their careers.

In these drawings the style is simpler and more effective than in those of 1911–12, with their cross-hatchings and soft washes. Now a thick twisting powerful line is applied sparingly but with great effect. The drawings are generally attacks on Huerta or on Villa's puppet president, Gonzales Garza, caricatures of conservative ladies and clerics, or somewhat obvious efforts to cheer up his own side with pictures of attractive and brave women who are shown helping their men, waiting for them to return, and so on.

10

 OROZCO. *The Despoiling*. WATERCOLOR. MEXICO CITY, COLL. DR. A. CARRILLO GIL.

The year 1915 saw Carranza winning his way back into the capital, a process that furnished new Revolutionary impressions for a disillusioned Orozco. He now witnessed, among other excesses, the sacking of one of Mexico's churches under the leadership of his political and artistic mentor, Dr. Atl.

Orozco's drawing technique during this entire Revolutionary period seems to have been based on the deliberately nonacademic practice of avoiding the standing model and preferring the model in motion, whose movements are stored up for future reference. In a May 1916 group exhibition the artist showed drawings of prostitutes and schoolgirls, political and anticlerical caricatures, and a number of strong symbolic drawings.[6] In September 1916 he had his first one-man show in Mexico City with the same feminine subjects and political cartoons (some apparently anti-Carranza now). He also exhibited two sketches for his 1915 oil painting, *San Juan de Ulua Evacuated by Spanish Troops in* 1822, his first government commission. Apparently the famous *Mexico in Revolution* wash drawings, which are generally dated between 1913 and 1917, did not yet exist, since they do not appear in this show. The unpleasant reception of this exhibition discouraged Orozco to such a degree that for the next few years he was relatively inactive, and for a while left Mexico.

From 1917 to 1919 he was in California working as a photo finisher and enlarger. According to the painter's autobiography, on leaving the country he was stopped at the border by United States customs officials who confiscated and destroyed a number of his watercolors. Orozco considered this an 'immoral' act and apparently never forgave the northern republic.[7] As late as 1922, he had not yet begun to paint specifically Revolutionary material. Tablada, in a January 1923 article in *International Studio* magazine, and the United States critic Walter Pach, writing in *México Moderno* in October 1922, both speak of the same feminine material and cartoons mentioned previously.[8]

In June 1923 Orozco began to work on the frescoes in the Preparatoria. Here, like his fellow painters, he went through a period of experimentation both with the medium and with the subjects to be employed, and also utilized a literary and semireligious type of theme in the name of Revolutionary painting. In Orozco's case there is the additional impact of Dr. Atl's influence toward the grandiose and allegorical. In the Annex of

[6] Charlot, op. cit. p. 151.

[7] Orozco, op. cit. p. 60. There appears to be some uncertainty about the date of this incident. Charlot and others give 1919 as the date; Charlot speaks of a 1919 trip to the United States in the article mentioned above. Orozco himself mentions meeting Siqueiros in New York that year (when the latter was leaving for Europe with his wife), although he gives the impression that he arrived there from San Francisco. Professor Fernández in his introduction to the catalogue of the Carrillo Gil collection gives 1917–18 as the United States dates.

[8] Charlot, op. cit.

the National Preparatory School (the former convent of San Pedro y San Pablo) Atl had done a series of large-scale nudes of men and women as well as a number of landscapes symbolizing the forces of nature: Rain, Wind, the Night, the Sun, and the Moon. The most impressive was the gigantesque *The Man Who Came from the Sea*, a heavy-muscled, beetle-browed giant advancing from the water, his powerful hands beginning to move forward as though about to grapple with the world. (Dr. Atl's murals no longer exist.)

Orozco's first fresco experiments in the Preparatoria seem to have been influenced by Atl's point of view, and even his 1925 mural in the House of Tiles (now Sanborn's) in Mexico City is affected by this gigantism. Of the original Orozco studies only two remain as they were painted. The poetic *Maternity* (fig. 11) shows a giant seated female nude holding a child and surrounded by flying nymphs that suggest Botticelli's *Birth of Venus*. At the opposite end of this ground-floor corridor is the caricature mural *The Rich Banquet while the Workers Quarrel*. The first work emphasizes the relationship between Orozco and the traditions of the early Renaissance, first Giotto and then Piero della Francesca. The second work represents the native element in his painting, the local graphic caricature quality that combines the sardonic and the tragic. The monumental and the graphic sides of his art are blended in many later and more successful efforts. During this early period, however, and through the second phase at the Preparatoria in 1926, the 'classical' quality predominates.

The somewhat fanciful classicism of the *Maternity*, like the powerful hands of *The Rich Banquet*, is to be attributed to Atl's influence, which also existed in other panels of this time that were changed or obliterated later. These included the *Spring* with its huge downward-plunging nude (removed entirely), the Masaccio-like *Christ Destroying His Cross* (removed except for the head of Christ, later incorporated into *The Strike*), and the so-called *Trinity* (one figure substituted, one changed, the third remaining). The Revolutionary material in this corridor dates from 1926, when Orozco received his second opportunity to paint in this building: *The Trench*, *Destruction of the Old Order*, *The Strike*, and the reconstituted *Trinity*.[9]

Of the panels done in 1923 and apparently still on the walls as late as 1925–6,[10] there is in general a self-conscious striving for effect in a medium by no means conquered at this point. The caricature nature of *The Rich Banquet* is far removed from good mural quality; the upside-down figure in *The Spring* is exaggerated in the Atl sense; the powerful nude woman

---

[9] Charlot, op. cit. p. 152.

[10] Rosendo Salazar, in his 'socialist' *México en Pensamiento y en Acción*, Avante, Mexico, 1926, reproduces these murals and the Atl works of the Annex, mentioned above. See also the monograph by Clementina Díaz y de Ovando on *El Colegio Máximo de San Pedro y San Pablo*, Universidad de México, 1951.

in the *Maternity* prefigures Orozco's effectiveness at a slightly later date, but the rest of the composition is confused.

As for the *Trinity*, its original 1923 form (reproduced in Salazar's 1926 book[11]) showed a 'Scientist' with T-squares and drawing paper and a knobby-handed Worker holding tools and raising his battered face toward the symbol of Revolution. The muscles in this work are as exaggerated as in other panels of the period. In spite of the somewhat literal

---

[11] Ibid.

11

OROZCO. *Maternity*. FRESCO. NATIONAL PREPARATORY SCHOOL, MEXICO CITY.

symbolism, this painting is apparently the first reference to the Revolution in Orozco's murals, though the element of symbolic suffering, the agony of war and plunder, does not appear for some time. Like *The Rich Banquet*, also done in 1923, this panel indicates a disillusioned attitude, and reflects the oncoming end of the brief period of Revolutionary bliss, when opportunism and factionalism would change the entire direction of the movement.

Although Orozco has been quoted as claiming the present version of the *Trinity* (fig. 12) for the period before his dismissal in August 1924, the mural as it exists now belongs stylistically and spiritually to the next period of Mexican art under Calles, when these tendencies toward disillusionment and reaction were clearly in view. But it preserves the basic composition of the original and offers evidence of Orozco's transition from a tentative and strained expression toward a more symbolic and monumental attitude. The *Trinity* in its final 1926 form is a more concentrated and stronger version of the 1923 panel. Preserving only the central symbol of Revolution with its own red banner blinding it, the painter has changed the worker at the right, showing him without hands—in effect, betrayed. For the rather static Scientist at the left he has substituted an anonymous suppliant peasant placed back-to-back with the mutilated worker. This peasant, whose block-like form and costume may be seen in other panels of the time, is apparently drawn after one of Orozco's chief models during this second Preparatoria phase, the painter's own master mason (cf. figs. 12, 32).

The result of these changes is a more monumental arrangement which raises the Revolution on a kind of pedestal formed by the two bodies. The painting is also a clarification of the original disillusionment into frank betrayal. This is the path Orozco was to follow toward the classical works of 1926.

In the meantime, there came the affair with the Damas Católicas and the student attack in June 1924, which resulted in the defacing of Orozco's work. As retaliation, in the last few weeks before the enforced stoppage of the Preparatoria paintings in August, Orozco executed a number of violent caricature murals on the floor directly above the first series. Among these, the *Justice and the Law* shows a bloody and drunken female figure, bandage down on one eye, waving her scales with one arm, the other about the shoulders of an ugly-looking politician. In the *Final Judgment*, a cross-eyed Father God is flanked by a group of overdressed bourgeois, the 'saved,' while on the other side is a group of miserable poor, the 'damned.' Above these creatures a leering old hag, Liberty, is supported on golden cords. Farther on, the artist shows a rich man stabbed in the back and then a heap of symbolic objects, the *Social and Political Junk Heap*, the latter including at this early date a Nazi swastika. The panel immediately to the right is perhaps the most effective scene of this second floor corridor—two skinny hands emerging from ragged sleeves and

12

OROZCO. *The Trinity (The Revolutionary Trinity)*, FRESCO. NATIONAL PREPARATORY SCHOOL, MEXICO CITY.

| 49

dropping coins into a locked church box, under which a fat ring-covered hand is placed to catch the coins as they come through. The final caricature, *Reactionary Forces*, shows fat and thin male and female snobbish figures walking with noses in the air and ignoring the tiny miserable creatures over whom they tread.

However successful these panels may be as cartoons, they have little other quality (with the exception of the church scene). They are a mocking flare-up of Orozco's temper at that moment, his terrible disappointment at the treatment accorded him. Even if Orozco's contribution during this period is somewhat inconclusive, the future social critic and mystic, the humanitarian artist is already present in more than embryo. Within two years he would return to the Preparatoria to paint his first great works.

David Alfaro Siqueiros

Through 1924

VI

If the politics of Rivera reflect an opportunistic radicalism and those of Orozco a fatalism and negativism, the social attitudes of Siqueiros bespeak the highly individualistic Mexican approach to all problems, political or otherwise. Although he has been associated for many years with orthodox Communism and has been the author of many newspaper articles, books, and speeches on 'art for the masses,' his work remains essentially a personal expression. Where Rivera presents the picture of a Revolution realized or, failing that, the ideals of the Revolution, and Orozco its betrayals and deceits, Siqueiros rushes forward with a constant exhortation to fight.

Unlike Rivera, whose disciples can still be counted by the score, or Orozco, who in spite of himself engendered a large number of followers, Siqueiros has no 'school.' The few who have attempted in recent years to follow in his wake have produced watery imitations of an art that depends primarily on the spectacular personality and fiery energy of its creator.

The career of Siqueiros used to be cited as a horrible example of what could happen when an artist became too involved in politics, but since the late 'thirties his reputation has constantly grown. Today he is the outstanding living muralist of Mexico, one of its few important easel painters, and also a significant world figure. At the 1950 Biennale in Venice he was awarded the second painting prize of 500,000 lire (the first prize went to Henri Matisse). Nor has this worldly success turned him from the political convictions which, whether one agrees with them or not, remain the basis of his existence and the driving force behind his art.

Born in Chihuahua in 1896, Siqueiros was baptized José David. He lost his mother in 1898, and together with his older sister Luz and younger brother Jesús went to live with his paternal grandparents at Irapuato. There until 1906 he was under the influence of a grandfather who had been a colonel in one of the guerrilla Indian bands of Benito Juárez.

In 1907 he came to Mexico City with his father, a profoundly religious, almost mystical person, who entered him in the parochial Colegio Franco-Inglés. The outbreak of the Revolution in 1910 awakened in him the first stirrings of discontent. Partly through the influence of his sister and partly in revolt against the monastic character of his home, he became a somewhat romantic adherent of the Madero movement.

He entered the Academy of San Carlos as a night student in 1911, while he was attending the Preparatoria. With a number of others, including Orozco, Siqueiros participated in the epoch-making student strike of that year, his first contact with politico-artistic problems. While attending the open-air school of Santa Anita—one of the fruits of the strike—under Ramos Martínez, he became involved in the student plots against the dictator Victoriano Huerta. With the encouragement of Dr. Atl, he joined the Constitutionalist army late in 1911 (at the age of fifteen) under the name of José D. Alfaro, and soon advanced to the rank of sub-lieutenant. In 1913 he was in the mob led by cadets of the Colegio Militar and workers from the Casa del Obrero Mundial which followed Madero from Chapultepec Castle to the National Palace to challenge the reactionary forces opposed to him. Here Siqueiros witnessed his first bloodshed.

In 1914 he joined the general staff of the Carranzist General Manuel M. Dieguez, Chief of the Western Division which was comprised mainly of students, and rose to the rank of Capitano Segundo while participating in various battles in the north and northwest of Mexico. During this same period Siqueiros was one of the Orizaba group under Dr. Atl. These activities in which students participated so strongly were the real source of Siqueiros's knowledge of and feeling for the Revolution—as was also the case with Orozco. From these experiences he claims that he learned Mexican geography, history, archaeology, and social problems. For Siqueiros the events of 1916–18 brought a new kind of interest in the Mexican people as well as an end to the aesthetics of the Díaz period.

In 1919, with the help of Venustiano Carranza, head of the Constitutionalist Army, Siqueiros was sent to Europe to develop as an artist, although his official post was at the Mexican Embassy in Paris as a military attaché. Here he made friends with Rivera, and exchanged ideas on modern painting as well as on the problems of the socially oriented artist. From Barcelona in 1921 he issued his famous Manifesto to the Artists of America in *Vida Americana*, which he had founded. The following year (1922) Siqueiros returned to Mexico to join his contemporaries in building the 'Mexican renaissance.'[1]

Arriving home in September 1922, Siqueiros took a leading role in the formation of the Syndicate, its relations with the government, and the contracts for various mural projects. He is generally believed to have drafted the resounding Manifesto of the Syndicate cited earlier. The following year he conceived and helped to found *El Machete* with Guerrero and Rivera, a paper at first designed to emphasize the social role of mural painting and black-and-white graphic work. As this periodical turned increasingly to the left and the government in the opposite direction,

---

[1] According to Orozco, *Autobiografia*, p. 82, Siqueiros was recalled from Rome by Vasconcelos.

serious differences soon developed. Siqueiros and his friends Amado de la Cueva, Xavier Guerrero, and Roberto Reyes Pérez all ultimately lost their painting jobs.

Although *El Machete* was hailed by certain elements as the best answer to the need for a people's newspaper, it was more important as a political device in the city than as education for the illiterate peasants, who earned an average of thirty centavos a day—the paper cost ten. After the general firing of Syndicate artists in 1924, Siqueiros worked with Guerrero and Leopoldo Méndez on this newspaper until it was temporarily suppressed that same year.

From late in 1922 to June 1924, when the work on the Preparatoria was first suspended, Siqueiros painted his staircase murals in the patio of the Colegio Chico: the *Burial of a Worker*, *The Elements* (*Spring*, *The Sun*, et cetera, experiments that were destroyed), *The Angel*, and the *Christ*. These represent a self-conscious return to native values (in the heads of the Christ and the workers carrying the coffin) from Aztec sculpture, the spirit of which Siqueiros absorbed to a remarkable degree (fig. 13).[2] If this treatment is compared with the mechanical way in which Rivera utilized precolonial art in his *Day of the Dead in the Country* or in the Ministry of Education staircase mural, with its photographic copy of the Aztec flower god, one can see the difference between expressive adaptation and 'archaeological reconstruction'.[3]

A second point about these early murals is Siqueiros's claim[4] that from the beginning, in contrast to the flat two-dimensional work of most of his colleagues, he treated the mural as an integral part of the building. Before anyone else, he painted a vault (*The Angel*) with a consciousness that the mural is, or should be, the painting of architectural space and not of simple flat walls in two dimensions. He made a deliberate choice at this moment of a vault to paint, while his colleagues chose flat spaces.

From the outset, there is not only this consciousness of spatially designed painting but also a kind of sculptural and powerful form that remain characteristic throughout his career. Even though Siqueiros presents a certain amount of religious content here—as do the others at this juncture—his Christ, like that of Orozco, is a dynamic and angry figure.

The famous *Burial of a Worker* (fig. 13) is generally considered a memorial to the martyred governor of Yucatán, Felipe Carrillo Puerto, although it takes the form of a symbolic representation of the solidarity of the workers.[5] This sense of unity is reinforced by the way in which the

[2] Cf. porphyry mask in George C. Vaillant, *Aztecs of Mexico*, Doubleday, Doran & Co., N.Y., 1941, plate 49; also in Laurence Schmeckebier, *Modern Mexican Art*, Univ. of Minnesota, Minneapolis, 1939, fig. 41.

[3] Luis Cardoza y Aragón, *La Nube y el Reloj*, Mexico, 1940, plate 11, Rivera.

[4] *70 Obras Recientes de David Alfaro Siqueiros*, Instituto Nacional de Bellas Artes, Mexico, 1947, Introd. by Angélica Arenal, p. 16.

[5] Paul Westheim, 'David Alfaro Siqueiros, análisis de la forma, '*Espacios*, no. 4, Jan. 1950.

two rear workers have their hands on each other's shoulders. The shoulder of the third figure shows a similar hand, though the fourth figure was never added. The architectonic heads are designed to envelop the intensely blue coffin in a rectangle, paralleling the impressive cubical mass of that object with its unobtrusive but meaningful hammer and sickle on top. The entire effect here, as in later works of Siqueiros, is a forward motion toward the spectator.

At this stage of the Mexican movement, Rivera was painting his *Creation* in the Bolívar Amphitheater and Orozco was struggling toward realization of form ideas that still lay in the future. This mural of Siqueiros, on the other hand, already shows a definite maturity of feeling and form. His quickly achieved crystallization, though arrested by the turn of events of the next few years, would ultimately resolve itself into the long succession of works beginning in the 'thirties and continuing to the present day.

13

SIQUEIROS. *Burial of a Worker*, UNFINISHED. FRESCO.
NATIONAL PREPARATORY SCHOOL, MEXICO CITY.

VII The Calles Period

1924 to 1934

The decade during which Mexico wore the face of Don Plutarco Elías Calles began with a brave promise of reform, and reached its climax in a serious setback to the Revolution. It included Calles's own presidency from 1924 to 1928 as well as the following six years during which he controlled a series of puppet presidents.

Originally a belated follower of Madero, Calles had acted for a while as lieutenant to Obregón in the northern campaign. Under Carranza he became Governor of Sonora, where his anticlerical activities aroused the antagonism of various foreign governments. He came into the presidency in 1924 as Obregón's candidate, nipping in the bud (with the aid of United States-supplied arms) an uprising by de la Huerta.

Calles began his administration with a definite interest in improving conditions, but, in the fashion of many of his predecessors, he showed an equally marked preference for dictatorial methods. In some ways there were advances; roads, dams, powerhouses, and schools were built. But at the same time, all opposition to the government was ruthlessly crushed. The educational program of Vasconcelos was carried forward and agrarian reform was also promoted in various ways, including the founding of agricultural banks. The bulk of the money, however, was lent to wealthy farm-owners who knew the right people. Although Don Plutarco liked to refer to himself as a socialist, he and his friends became very wealthy. If any one thing can be said to have marked his 'socialist' administration, it is the fact that Mexican capitalism made considerable progress under the leadership of Calles. Nevertheless, within a relatively short time he became more and more the dictator and less and less the reformer.

An outstanding symptom of this process was in the labor movement. The unions had to join the government-controlled C.R.O.M., led by Luis Morones, the new Secretary of Industry, whose Grupo Acción smashed all rival unions. So-called labor leaders grew rich, since they were now in a position to control strikes and to blackmail employers accordingly. Rural resentment against the labor program was viciously suppressed, and foreign 'agitators' were simply shipped over the border.

Calles's 'radicalism' emerged in his long-felt antagonism toward the clergy, which opposed him and allied itself with certain privileged groups.

In return, he applied the anticlerical clauses of the constitution. In 1926 church schools were closed, foreign clergy deported, and native priests forced to register with the police—measures that caused a three-year-long but unsuccessful church strike. Part of the church's resentment was manifested in stirring up the Cristeros (so-called 'followers of Christ'), whose slogan *Cristo Rey*! (Christ the King) was the last thing heard on earth by frightened schoolteachers whom they murdered or by citizens whose trains were dynamited.

During the early years of his power, Calles became involved in a dispute with the United States over enforcing the anti-alien sections of the famous Article 27. He insisted that owners of oil lands turn in their titles for fifty-year leases. This quarrel lasted well into 1927; shouts for intervention were raised by United States big business and church authorities. The wise appointment of Dwight W. Morrow as ambassador to Mexico eased the strain considerably. He made tactful gestures toward salving Mexican pride (previous emissaries had treated Mexicans as inferiors), and displayed an interest in education and agriculture. This was climaxed by his inviting Lindbergh and Will Rogers to visit Mexico and by his commissioning Diego Rivera to paint murals in the Palace of Cortez at Cuernavaca. These efforts had their result in the decision of the Mexican Supreme Court whereby foreigners with pre-1917 concessions still retained their rights.

For the presidency of 1928, Calles managed to secure the election of his former chief, Obregón, but the latter was assassinated within a few weeks by an independently acting religious fanatic who resented the persecution of the church. With the Calles-supported Portes Gil chosen as president in 1928, the ex-president became the power behind the chair for the next six years as the 'supreme chief.'

Under Portes Gil, gestures were again made in the direction of reform. Most interesting, however, was the organization of a new government party, the P.N.R. (National Revolutionary Party), whose function from then on was to consolidate the group in power and make it self-succeeding. Every government employee had to contribute to its support; all political groups were subordinated to it and independents of any kind eliminated.

When the P.N.R. put up Ortiz Rubio as their candidate to succeed Portes Gil, Vasconcelos was nominated by the opposition to run against him. In spite of a vigorous nationwide tour during which he openly denounced Calles and his local and foreign friends, Vasconcelos did not have the remotest chance of success against this well-organized machine. He left for the United States, claiming fraud, which there undoubtedly was. If his books and other writings indicate a strong belief that the Revolution has failed, one can hardly be surprised.

Under the new president, Calles ran Mexico from his elaborate house in Cuernavaca, which was located on a street popularly nicknamed the

'Street of the Forty Thieves.' There, surrounded by wealthy 'socialists,' he exercised control by telephone to the capital. Despite its left-wing utterances, the P.N.R. was nothing now but a grafting dictatorship which permitted foreign capital to have its way (thanks to blocks of stock handed out in the right quarters), helping them to avoid strikes and otherwise smoothing the way. By 1933, according to Verna Millán, the labor leader Morones had 1,543,376 pesos registered in his name in Mexico City alone.[1] Even if we allow for the possibility of exaggeration in this and similar figures, there was still a substantial sum of money involved. One has only to look at the photographs of the well-fed, well-dressed, diamond-studded Morones during this period to sense the depths to which the Revolutionary movement had fallen.[2]

Yet by the end of the Calles period there were certain clear indications of a change for the better. Under the last of the Calles men (1932–3), Abelardo Rodríguez, the banker and gambling-house operator, fascism appeared in Mexico with the organization of the Gold Shirts—backed by the Calles crowd. This group was presumably dedicated to war on Jews (a minute part of the Mexican population) and Communists, against whom they fought street battles. From this low point in modern Mexican history a reaction set in. In 1932 the anti-C.R.O.M. movement was crystallized in the formation of a General Confederation of Workers and Peasants (C.G.O.C.) under the former director of the Preparatoria, the scholarly Vicente Lombardo Toledano. The years 1933 and 1934 saw younger and more progressive elements coming into the P.N.R. itself, and agrarian reform was once more put into forward motion as banks were established to help the peasants and land distribution was re-organized.

The end of Abelardo Rodríguez's administration also saw the appointment of a liberal Minister of Education, Narciso Bassols, under whom the school system was reformed. Incompetents and obstructionists were thrown out, teacher wages were raised, and a new government program was instituted. It became fixed policy at this time and thereafter for all new schools in the Federal District to be decorated with mural paintings. This was a considerable change from the lack of government patronage, the actual hostility, that had forced Mexican painting into exile during this period, when the 'big three' (Rivera, Orozco, and Siqueiros) did most of their important work abroad. During the next administration they would resume their rightful places in the Mexican scene.

But the liberal policies of Bassols were not to go unchallenged. Clerical elements organized against him with accusations of teaching sex in the schools, attacking religion, and so forth, and ultimately forced his resignation. This brilliant man, who had translated John Strachey's *Theory and Practise of Socialism* into Spanish, considering it a necessary tool for

[1] Millán, op. cit. p. 86.
[2] Salazar, op. cit. p. 35.

58

'socialist Mexico,' was shifted to the Department of the Interior in 1934, and later became ambassador to France.

Yet it was clear that the Callistas would have to make concessions if they were to remain in power. In 1934 Calles agreed to a presidential candidate acceptable to the left wing: Lázaro Cárdenas, a man with a well-deserved reputation for honesty and reform. He was elected in July 1934 for a six-year term with a Calles-designated cabinet, which was to insure Calles's control. The next epoch, however, tells the story of Cárdenas's 'dropping the pilot' and initiating the most progressive administration in modern Mexico.

Some of the developments in the art movement during the Calles era have already been mentioned. The firing of Siqueiros, Orozco, and others in 1924 with the incoming Calles administration left only a handful of painters working in Mexico City. Siqueiros and his group fled to Guadalajara, where, after a brief painting interval, Siqueiros turned to labor organization. On his return to Mexico City in 1930, he was promptly imprisoned for about a year and then kept under police supervision in Taxco. He left soon afterward for a stay in the United States, Argentina, and Cuba, and came back in 1934.

Orozco, after a brief period of retirement in his suburban residence, received a private commission and one small government commission. After being permitted to finish his Preparatoria paintings (with the help of foreign citizens), he left Mexico from 1927 to 1934. Jean Charlot worked for the Carnegie archaeological expedition in Chichén-Itzá from 1926 to 1929, expressing his Mexicanism, as did many others, in easel pictures, e.g. the *Tortilla Maker* with its charming primitivism and highly keyed color. He then came to New York and made his headquarters in the United States until after World War II, when he went to teach at the University of Hawaii. Julio Castellanos was abroad from 1925 to 1928, as were others.

Rivera was able to accommodate himself to the change of political scenery. He completed his Ministry of Education murals, and executed his Chapingo decorations as well as those in the Ministry of Health, the Palace of Cortez at Cuernavaca, and the staircase of the National Palace in Mexico City. In 1930, however, even he left Mexico and stayed in the United States for the next four years.

The sum total of murals done in Mexico during the Calles period, then, comprises those of Rivera, the 1927 Ministry of Health mural by Fernando Leal (removed by Rivera to make room for his own work), the staircase in the former church of San Pedro y San Pablo by Roberto Montenegro, the enforced completion of the Orozco murals in the Preparatoria, and his two relatively unimportant works in the House of Tiles and the Agricultural School at Orizaba.

On a perhaps less significant aesthetic level are the various school murals done under the new Bassols policy in 1933–4. These include a fairly extensive list in the Federal District, such as the Escuela Emiliano Zapata murals by Pablo O'Higgins, the Escuela Gabriela Mistral murals by Julio Castellanos and Juan O'Gorman, and the outstanding example in the Escuela Melchor Ocampo by Julio Castellanos. The last is a charming allegory of Heaven and Hell, beautifully and dynamically organized within itself and with relation to the side panels, which show such children's games as the *Little Fish*, the *Game of the Horse*, and so on. Generally speaking, however, the school murals are rather pedestrian affairs when compared to the heights Mexican painting reached even during this period.

Curiously enough, it was in the United States (and elsewhere) that Mexican art came of age in the long series of brilliant works by Orozco and Rivera and the experimental but important murals of Siqeiros in California, Buenos Aires, and Cuba. In Mexico itself, the lack of government patronage during most of this time and the general reactionary climate bred a kind of escapist turning away from current social problems toward a new interest in European literature and art.

Easel painting got its start under the leadership of painters such as Rufino Tamayo, Manuel Rodríguez Lozano, Julio Castellanos, Carlos Orozco Romero, Augustín Lazo, and Carlos Mérida. The influences coming from Europe varied all the way from the neo-Classicism of France and Italy to the Magic Realism of Germany in the 'twenties and the abstract Expressionism of Paul Klee. With the advent of the Cárdenas administration in 1934, however, the easel painters were overshadowed by the mural development and a renewed interest in graphic work. The art movement was once more harnessed to the chariot of the Revolution.

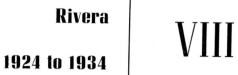
Rivera's work at the beginning of this era corresponds in spirit to the end of the Obregón period and the beginning of the Calles period. It represents a swing away from the simplicity and largeness of his Ministry Court of Labor murals toward a new kind of illustrative and picturesque quality, as in the Court of Festivals begun in 1924 and completed (together with the top floor of the earlier patio) in 1928. This second phase also indicates a change (for the time being) from a straightforward political attitude toward the compromise that had to be made in order to continue working in the Calles environment. This appears in the celebration of folklorism rather than of social problems. Where the latter are portrayed, they yield the stereotyped forms on the main floor of the Court of Festivals or the ineffective and superficial third-floor *corrido* illustrations.

Although Rivera had by this time mastered the true fresco technique, these walls show in the main a lack of color balance, not altogether compensated for by the increasing brightness and attractiveness of color schemes designed to act as unifying forces. The deficiency is overcome only in occasional panels on the third floor. During this phase one finds Rivera still steering a middle course between the coloristic and the monumental. The trend toward narration and didacticism takes on increasing importance.

The Court of Festivals is a typical instance of this mixture of tendencies, with the balance falling toward the coloristic and expository. On one wall is a series of crowd panels (bringing to mind the Sienese mass groupings), each around a doorway: *May Day*, *Distribution of the Land*, and *Market Day in the City*. Each shows a group of figures above the doorway, listening to speeches or watching the crowd. The optimistic *Distribution* shows an ideal situation reflecting the initial liberalism of the Calles administration, soon to be nullified. The *May Day*, identically arranged (although twice as long), is noteworthy for the portraits in the left-hand group, e.g. Máximo Pacheco and Paul (later Pablo) O'Higgins, two of Rivera's new staff of assistants, which now also included Ramón Alva Guadarrama, Emilio Amero, and others. The earlier generation of helpers had all gone off on their own, many to continue his point of view, others to develop something new.

14

CHARLOT. *Washerwomen*. FRESCO. MINISTRY OF EDUCATION, MEXICO CITY.

In *Market Day in the City*, the last crowd composition built around a doorway, Rivera turns frankly to the fiesta idea. We may mention here the four panels by Amado de la Cueva and Jean Charlot that flank the *Market Day*. These 1923 panels, which predate Rivera's taking over the patio, are the *Dance of the Santiagos* and the *Torito* by de la Cueva and the decoratively effective *Washerwomen* (fig. 14) and *Pack Carriers* by Charlot. The two by Charlot—and his *Dance of the Ribbons* later removed by Rivera—evidence great formal strength, and are as successful as anything of Rivera's in this court.

Other works by Rivera and his staff in this part of the Ministry include the symbolic *Yaqui Dance* (a carry-over from the simpler arrangements of the first patio), the *Sandunga Dance*, *Harvest Festival*, *Corn Festival*, *Burning of the Judases*, *Ribbon Dance* (a not very effective substitution for the Charlot mural), the flower *Festival of Santa Anita*, the *Day of the Dead in the City*, and the *Day of the Dead in the Country*. The majority of these consist of two-dimensional wall illuminations involving a considerable number of figures tastefully arranged in varicolored patterns—except for the deeply perspectivized *Festival of Santa Anita* with its far-reaching river and boats.

Typical of this phase is the *Day of the Dead in the City* (fig. 15), whose two-dimensional composition and packed crowds, featuring bourgeois *mestizo* city types, stand in strong contrast to the bare simplicity of the *Day of the Dead in the Country*. In the latter panel, as has been pointed out by others,[1] a didactic peasant honesty and frugality are offered in opposition to the sophisticated metropolitanism of the city scene. Nor is it accidental that the country types are all Indians, while those in the city are creoles and *mestizos*, including the painter himself in a wide-brimmed hat directly beneath the end of the skeleton platform. The city representation of one of the most attractive Mexican fiestas is far more successful than its counterpart in the country, which loses itself in static formalism, unconvincing piety, and undigested imitations of Aztec art.

These fiesta scenes show Rivera's constantly growing expository tendency as well as the turn from politically meaningful to purely picturesque thematology at a time when Orozco in the Preparatoria or at Orizaba was producing images that reflect a poignant awareness of the suffering of the Mexican people. The Court of Festivals offers a pleasant *May Day*, an optimistic *Distribution of the Land*, and a decorative *Day of the Judases*. The latter very charmingly shows a demonstration against the traditional betrayers, with effigies of the priest, politician, and soldier—straw men portrayed in a harmless stereotyped fashion.

In a series of grisaille decorations on the second and third floors of the front or smaller patio, the Court of Labor, Rivera enlarged on the scenes of labor first with conventional symbols of science and then with allegories

[1] Schmeckebier, op. cit. pp. 124–5.

15

RIVERA. *Day of the Dead in the City*. FRESCO. MINISTRY OF EDUCATION, MEXICO CITY.

on the arts, climaxed by the mawkish *Theater*. Under the heading of poetry are found the martyrs of Mexico, including the precolonial Cuauhtémoc and the contemporary Carrillo Puerto, Zapata, et cetera. Carrillo Puerto, dressed in a long shift and showing a pathetic little bullet hole, while the eyes turn upward in sheerest bathos, is the low point of this group. Simpler and more effective is the *Emiliano Zapata* (fig. 16), which shows the strength of Rivera's drawing, but reveals by contrast to the Zapatas of other artists a constant inability or unwillingness to rise above the level of gentle melancholy or lyric emotionality (compare Orozco, fig. 36).

16

RIVERA. *Emiliano Zapata*, detail.
FRESCO. MINISTRY OF
EDUCATION, MEXICO CITY.

17

RIVERA. FRESCO. WALL AND CEILING DECORATIONS. CHAPEL, CHAPINGO.

Before finishing the remainder of the murals in the Ministry, Rivera took on a simultaneous project in the newly founded Agricultural School at Chapingo. The chapel here is generally acknowledged as Diego's masterpiece. It was done during 1926–7, while the painter and his assistants were working on the second part of the murals described above. The Chapingo frescoes reach a high level of unified decorative planning, coloristic organization, and muted but expressive feelings (fig. 17). With an effective mixture of allegory and quasi-religious symbolism, Rivera portrays the different stages in man's social development through revolution, comparing these steps to the fertilization of the earth by mankind and making revolution as natural as the processes of nature itself. Toward this end, he has paired *Germination*, *Flowering*, and *Fruition* (a series of beautifully decorative brownish nudes simply disposed about small round windows, e.g. the central panel, fig. 18) with the corresponding revolutionary equivalents of *Agitation*, *Armed Struggle*, and *Reorganization* (in pink, blue, and gray).

66

The chapel is entered through a low vestibule, whose ceiling shows a tremendous red star on a blue background containing four yellowish hands, two open as though in greeting, the other two grasping a hammer and a sickle. On the side walls of this vestibule the high decorative quality of the series reveals itself from the start. The right-hand wall composition depicts the martyrs *Zapata and Montaño*. They are arranged mummylike beneath the earth in vivid orange-red with growing corn above against a green background and a splash of exciting color in the sunflower-rimmed window space. Here one thinks of the Egyptian Osiris legend and the symbolic fructification of the soil through his death. The opposite wall of the vestibule shows a group of peasants and workers spreading the seed of revolution by talking together in the gentle, almost lyrical fashion typical of these murals.

18

RIVERA. *Germination*. FRESCO. CHAPEL, CHAPINGO.

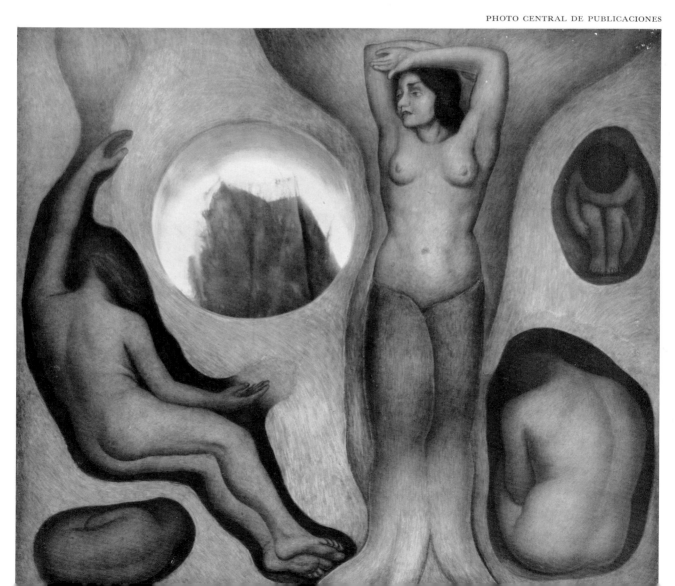

The chapel proper is a barrel-vaulted rectangular chamber, the most striking feature of which is the arched mural on the far wall. It features a huge buff-colored female nude (the *Liberated Earth*), eyes turned heavenward, one hand raised in the traditional gesture of blessing, the other holding a small budding plant which symbolizes her liberation. Against the blue and gray background are the gifts brought by this beneficent if somewhat overlarge figure: electric power, wind power, minerals, and so on. This rather top-heavy and crowded composition is not so effective as are other portions of the chapel.

Overhead, the simple rectangular arrangement of the lower panels changes to a more complex architectonic conception. A series of well-integrated geometric areas emphasizes the transverse arches of the vaults and the cornices, one area divided from another by vivid yellow lines. Thus the three vaults immediately inside the entrance show a polygonal-shaped central section from which triangles radiate; two symbolic Michelangelesque nudes are placed in each polygon and one in each triangle. The brown Indianized nudes against their blue decorative background (fig. 19) show far less organic function than in the original Renaissance source. Their use, however, and the linking elements employed give this chapel a unity and feeling of space that are seldom encountered in Rivera's work.

19

RIVERA. FRESCO. CEILING DECORATION. CHAPEL, CHAPINGO.

Significant subject matter is confined to the square wall panels or to the arched wall surfaces immediately above: e.g. the *Liberated Earth*, the wall over the vestibule entrance with its limpid *Virgin Soil*, and the adjacent *Earth Enslaved* over one of the wall panels. These allegories reveal both the strength and the weakness of Rivera's style. The *Virgin Soil* (fig. 20), the most poetic and in many ways most effective decorative moment in Rivera's painting, is a monumental single nude female figure, asleep with its hair flowing down over its eyes. Its right arm moves downward in the same direction, turns at right angles to parallel the base of the panel, and ends in the hand that offers symbolic protection to the little budding plant. Its left arm is subordinated to the flowing rhythm of the curved haunch that follows the rounded top of this wall section. Here, more than in the ceiling nudes, we feel that the lesson of Michelangelo has been absorbed. The superhuman figure emerges against a simple landscape background whose spaces, where they exist, are filled with the simplest additional elements.

In individual figures of this kind or in similar works with a limited number of forms, Rivera's outstanding ability as a draftsman comes to the fore with favorable results. Where, as in the *Earth Enslaved*, he begins to pile up the forms and involve them in an emotional complex, the chances of success are considerably less. (Similarly on the third floor of the Secretaría there is an unfortunate tendency to substitute caricature for

20

RIVERA. *Virgin Soil*. FRESCO. CHAPEL, CHAPINGO.

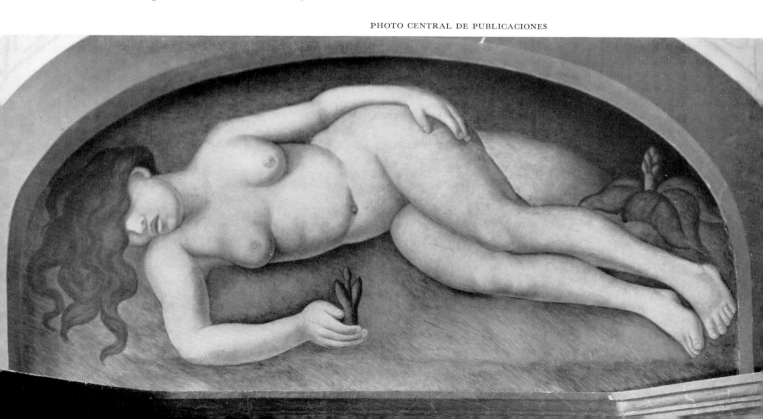

moral indignation and symbolic strength.) The beautifully drawn nude in this panel, with its back to the audience, has with it a fat 'moneybags,' a gross priest, and a bestial soldier with a gas-mask snout. The mixture of classical form and popular caricature does not come off well.

Where emotional content is kept on the lyrical level of the *Virgin Soil* or *Flowering*, with a few linear forms implying rather than expressing emotionality, it is most effective. Some panels, however, because of this muted quality are perhaps too withdrawn, considering the subject matter. Rivera's scenes of social revolution at this date (1926–7) are philosophical rather than activistic in character, compared with Orozco's 1926 panels of the Preparatoria. Rivera's *Agitation* is a quiet get-together, while the *Armed Struggle* shows a dead revolutionist over whose bodies three Marys or their Mexican equivalents mourn (one even has a halo furnished by the sombrero of a nearby man). The post-Revolutionary scene is a beatific conception in which the soldier, worker, and peasant perform the traditional, here Revolutionary, miracle of feeding the multitudes. By 1927 it was quite clear that the multitudes in Mexico were not going to be fed so soon.

In all these sections perhaps the most effective parts are the large symbolic hands, one over each scene. A magnificent open curved hand is meant to represent the tension that should emerge from *Agitation*; a clenched fist performs a similar function for the *Armed Struggle* pietà; and the open hand in the third, or *Reconstruction*, section is supposed to give the effect of benediction. The role of the monumentalized hand in the art of Diego Rivera is important; it emerges again with equal force in the murals at the Department of Health in Mexico City and those at the Detroit Institute of Arts some years later.

Rivera was already an international figure by 1927, when he finished the Chapingo murals, and received an invitation to visit the Soviet Union for the tenth anniversary of the Bolshevik revolution. There the question of an art for the people still remained to be solved after the liquidation of modern art a few years earlier. Rivera was the best-known figure of a movement that had achieved some sort of answer to this problem; he was given academic honors and invited to demonstrate his theories of socialist art. Just at this time, however, the great Stalin-Trotsky quarrel ended with the defeat of the Trotsky faction, with which Rivera apparently sympathized.

On his return to Mexico in August 1928, Rivera was warmly received by the Mexican Communist Party, with whom his relationship had been rather intermittent, but by 1929 he was expelled, presumably for his sympathies with Trotsky. Although reinstated for a short time, Rivera turned more and more to the world-embracing type of Communism preached by Trotsky's Fourth International. Trotsky, who was exiled from Russia in 1927, ultimately found refuge in Mexico in 1936, apparently through the intervention of Rivera.[2]

---

[2] At least according to Rivera himself, as quoted in Bertram D. Wolfe, *Diego Rivera*, Knopf, N.Y., 1939, p. 262.

21

RIVERA. FRESCO. STAIRCASE MURAL.
MINISTRY OF EDUCATION, MEXICO CITY.

The artistic result of Rivera's stay in the Soviet Union is to be found
in a series of forty-five spontaneous and well-composed watercolors
painted during the May Day celebration of 1928 (now in the collection
of the Museum of Modern Art, New York). Produced under the emotional stress of witnessing socialist history in the making and without the
opportunity to think and rethink the various problems, these papers are
among the most exciting things Rivera has done. One of the watercolors
with Red soldiers drawn up in a solid mass before a square building has
a geometric monumentality not found in Rivera's murals of the period. A
smaller mass rises directly over the inscription LENIN to complete a subtle
alternation of shallow and deep forms, horizontals and verticals, with
the mass of straight lines finally relieved by a whipping flag above.

| 71

Late in 1928 Rivera resumed his work at the Secretaría. He completed this huge job in 1929 with a number of frescoes in the elevator entrance, the effective staircase murals, and the panels on the third floor of the Court of Festivals. Those near the elevator are merely a reversion to the earlier Tehuantepec types in the Court of Labor. The staircase murals are far more interesting scenes depicting different parts of Mexico, from the lushly painted jungle areas of the south to the oppression of hacienda life in the center and the industrial life of the north. The Indian maidens in rich jungle foliage, some standing idol-wise (fig. 21) and frontalized, others with flutes, again evoke the decorative primitivism of Gauguin (and Henri Rousseau).

Toward the top of the staircase are the tyranny of the hacienda owner and the well-arranged *Burial of a Revolutionist* (fig. 22). In the *Burial* a semicircle of workers fits into the curve of the stairs in a sweeping compact

22

RIVERA. *Burial of a Revolutionist.* FRESCO.
MINISTRY OF EDUCATION, MEXICO CITY.

group, from which three white-clad figures bend forward, shoveling earth into the grave. At the side, three symbolic mourners, their backs to the spectator as in early Italian painting, are placed at the head of the stairs; a group of nude furies wheels disconsolately above this tragic scene in a manner that again suggests the fourteenth century. Here for the time being Rivera emerges from his decorative lyrical shell into a more dynamic sphere of action.

In the third-floor panels, however, the emotional quality dips again as he illustrates two *corridos* of the 1910–20 period, *The Proletarian Revolution* and *The Mexican Revolution*. Series of rectangular and arched panels are connected above by red ribbons bearing verses from the songs. Scenes such as *The Night of the Rich, Bourgeois Reformers, The Billionaires,* and so on, are shown. They are caricatures in the most conventional sense, suggesting newspaper cartoons far more than pictorial symbols.

This point of view is followed in many later murals which are evidence of Rivera's increasing political bent from the time of his return from Moscow. It would appear that in these paintings he is more concerned with a political message than with aesthetic quality. In many of the third-floor panels, Rivera tends to represent the Mexican Revolution not as a local phenomenon but as part of the world revolution. The bourgeoisie and millionaires whom he attacks, however, are primarily United States figures rather than the 'millionaire socialists' of Mexico who were busily plundering the land.

There are a number of other sections that abandon the most obvious associational elements to show a fine decorative and even lyrical quality. This may be seen in *The Rain* (fig. 23), which derives from the simple verses:

> Who does not feel happy
> When it begins to rain?
> It is a very obvious sign
> That we shall have food.[3]

In this unassuming panel, with its religious overtones of simple piety and thankfulness for blessings received, Rivera is manifestly more successful than in the somewhat pompous and smug speeches implied in the political works. Generally speaking, the third-floor area is more consistent coloristically than are other parts of the building. One long side shows a dominant red and greenish-yellow tonality; another wall is partly blue in one section and red in another.

Rivera's loudly proclaimed Communism and his anti-United States attitude did not prevent him from accepting a commission from the new ambassador Dwight Morrow in 1929, after the painter had finished his

---

[3] Translated in *Frescoes in the Ministry of Education by Diego Rivera* (Mexican Art Series no. 2), Frances Toor, 1937.

23

RIVERA. *The Rain*. FRESCO. MINISTRY OF EDUCATION, MEXICO CITY.

attacks on the United States in the Ministry of Education. By this time Diego was 'on the outs' with the Communist Party, and his acceptance of this assignment from the representative of the United States government was entirely in line with the general pacification of the period and its attempts at a rapprochement with northern capital.

Ambassador Morrow's commission was for the Palace of Cortez in the city of Cuernavaca, about forty miles from the capital and at that time the headquarters of the behind-the-scenes Calles dictatorship and the rich 'socialists.' Here, on the walls of an open balcony corridor on the second floor rear, facing the picturesque mountain valley, Rivera laid out a series of incidents from the history of Mexico culminating in the uprising of Zapata, one of the great heroes of this state of Morelos.

Beginning with the depiction of Aztec Mexico with its human sacrifice, the narrative moves along to the invasion by the Spaniards, the oppression of the Indians during the colonial period, and the fight for independence ending with Zapata. On the end wall we see an Indian sacrifice scene above the doorway; at either side, brilliantly dressed Indians sweep across to attack the armored Spaniards. The long wall at the left displays another battle between Indians and Spaniards, the armored and mounted enemy driving the Indians across the Cuernavaca canyon. This portion, with its native figures climbing across the rich canyon foliage and fallen trees, is one of the most effective sections in the entire building. Another part of the long wall deals with the taking of the city, its pillaging, and the violence done to the inhabitants.

The final sections of this wall treat the enslavement of the Indian (fig. 24). One scene shows the slave system on the sugar plantations of Morelos, with the mounted foreman and reclining owner; the other shows the building of this very Palace of Cortez under similar armed guards. The second end wall presents the building of churches with slave labor, the Inquisition, the conversion of the Indians, and finally the peasant revolution led by a handsome Zapata with a beautiful white horse. Two other walls offer an additional full-length portrait of Emiliano Zapata and a portrayal of Morelos, the great leader of the previous century (shown with the face of Rivera).

In the years 1929–30 Rivera also undertook to decorate the Council Room of the Ministry of Health in Mexico City, perhaps the lowest point in his creativity since *The Creation* mural. On the ceiling and walls of this room, a number of rather dismal allegorical nudes depict Purity and Continence, Life and Health, Knowledge and Fortitude. In contrast to these unfortunate and empty decorations are the powerful decorative hand holding sheaves of wheat and the symbolic blooming sunflower that represents growth. Without program notes or titles the nude figures are little more than generalized decorative forms against a blue background and on a greenish-yellow ground, capably drawn but empty of significance.

24

RIVERA. *Enslavement of the Indians*. FRESCO. PALACE OF CORTEZ, CUERNAVACA.

The National Palace staircase murals, begun in 1929 and completed in 1935 on Diego's return from the United States, may be compared with the contemporary murals at Cuernavaca. Both are primarily narrative and didactic in purpose. The Palace murals, in addition, refer to current problems, however ambiguously, and to the future, however gloriously. The enormous historical panorama projected by Rivera on this staircase has the merit of a better worked out decorative scheme and a more balanced and lasting color. It has retained its original quality, while the Cuernavaca murals have long since faded into an unbalanced jumble.

The portions of the staircase mural executed in 1929–30 include the right-hand wall and the large middle wall with its five arched sections and polygonal base, corresponding to the right-hand stairway and the wall of the landing. Although the scheme also included the left-hand staircase wall, this was not carried out until 1935. Like the Cuernavaca murals, the National Palace works relate the history of Mexico from precolonial times to the Revolution, but with comments on recent history as well.

The right wall, in contrast to the later prophetic Marxist left wall, portrays the mythical and precolonial past of Mexico. Its lower section is concerned with the customs (wars, ceremonies, industries) of the Indians and its upper section with their beliefs. Quetzalcoatl teaches the Indians, they quarrel, he leaves—in scenes that may be contrasted with those of Orozco at Dartmouth. This right side remains the most interesting part of the staircase murals. It is relatively simple in presentation, with a bright blue gentle sky, stunning orange sun, and orange-colored flames emerging from the ancient volcano.

The main wall, occupying the space on the first landing, tells the story of Mexico from the Conquest in the early sixteenth century up to the time when the mural was actually being painted. It is a continuous expanse interrupted by five arches in the upper section, and may be described in terms of those divisions, which set off the chief personalities and incidents of this long tale. The lower portion of the long landing wall deals with the colonial history of Mexico. Beginning at the right with the attack by the Spaniards and moving left, the various scenes show the enslavement of the Indian. A typical section from this lower third of the main wall (fig. 25) illustrates the wealth of material incorporated into every part of the vast historical panorama: the actual fighting, the slavery of the Indians, the cruelty of the Spaniards, and the protection extended the Indians by gentler elements among the clergy.

The upper portion of the wall (divided into five main parts) shows in the two outside arches later scenes of invasion and occupation, first by the French (at the left) and then by the United States (at the right). In the French-invasion area, the strongly outlined figures of Maximilian and his generals at the right and the soldiers at the left exist in a somewhat static relationship almost completely without emotional overtones.

Immediately adjacent to these outside panels are two inner arches with scenes of the struggles between progressive and reactionary forces in Mexican history. On one side (right) the problems of the Reform period are laid out; Juárez and his followers are opposed to General Miramón's party. Directly opposite, on the second arch from the left, is the Díaz era, with symbols of foreign capitalist invasion and the rising tide of dissatisfaction signified by Francisco Madero.

25

RIVERA. *Conquest of Mexico*, detail on staircase landing. FRESCO.
NATIONAL PALACE, MEXICO CITY.

In the center arch the resistance to reaction comes to a head. Here, directly above the struggling Indians and Spaniards of the colonial era, the Mexican eagle is placed as the symbol of a resurgent Mexico. In the upper portion of this panel the great leaders of Mexican independence from Spain—Hidalgo, Morelos, Allende, and so on—are placed below the leaders of the modern Revolution—Zapata, Carrillo Puerto, and others. At the left is the usurper Emperor Iturbide and a double portrait of Obregón and Calles, who appear to be backed up by a fat-faced individual who suggests the labor leader Morones, as well as by soldiers with United States campaign hats. These details may have contributed to Rivera's leaving Mexico for the United States, where he was to spend the next five years, returning later to complete the decoration of this staircase. Bold and large in effect, this mural shows clearly the painter's tremendous factual application and narrative facility.

In 1929 Rivera had been made director of the Academy of San Carlos, which he proceeded to reform in curriculum and staff. Juan O'Gorman, the architect-painter who has done so much for architecture in Mexico since the late 'twenties, was one of Rivera's appointees to the School of Architecture. It was in architecture that Rivera met his strongest opposition, because of commercial building interests. Although this struggle ended in the resignation of the daring director, it had the beneficial result of bringing into the open the question of the new architecture versus the old academic forms that still strangled Mexican design.

Rivera had now been working on murals in Mexico since 1922. Between 1924, when he assumed charge of the Secretaría murals, and 1930, when he left for his first United States visit, he was by all odds the dominant and best-known figure in the movement. Except for a brief interlude in 1926 when Orozco was permitted to finish his murals in the Preparatory School, it was the name of Rivera that came before the public. The controversy over an inscription on the *Exit from the Mine* (see fig. 8), the trip to Moscow and subsequent enthusiasm for 'Comrade Diego' in *El Machete*, followed by his expulsion from the Communist Party, the Morrow project in Cuernavaca, the difficulties in the Academy—all served to augment his fame. By 1930 he was hailed in many quarters as the outstanding muralist in the world. Certainly he was the best publicized, if not the most outstanding. Even at this point one must reckon with the monumental 1926 works of Orozco in the Preparatory School, one of the finest mural groups in Mexico.

The circumstances of Diego's coming to San Francisco at the end of 1930 have been recorded by his biographer, Bertram D. Wolfe.[4] The artist had been invited four years previously by William Gerstle, president

---

[4] Wolfe, op. cit.

of the San Francisco Art Commission, to paint a mural in the California School of Fine Arts. A second job, offered by the architect of the San Francisco Stock Exchange in 1929, finally made Rivera decide to visit the United States. After a number of difficulties with the State Department, which was reluctant to issue a residence permit to the Communist painter, Rivera finally arrived in San Francisco late in 1930 amid an outcry from local newpapers and artists who opposed his engagement on both political and economic grounds. Once the Riveras (Diego and his painter-wife, Frida Kahlo) had arrived, however, the clamor was stilled. After his one-man show late that year at the California Palace of the Legion of Honor and other private gallery exhibitions in Los Angeles, San Francisco, Carmel, and San Diego—plus the impact of the Rivera personalities—Diego was a real celebrity.

The year 1931 brought a continual procession of triumphs: the staircase mural in the Luncheon Club of the San Francisco Stock Exchange, the mural in the California School of Fine Arts, a fresco in the home of Mrs. Sigmund Stern in Fresno, and four transportable panels for his one-man show at the Museum of Modern Art in New York. However triumphant this series of commissions, exhibitions, and accompanying social events, the California murals are a not particularly brilliant segment of Rivera's work. Among the parties, the uncritical hosannahs, and the complete lack of significant purpose, the three California works emerge as a social rather than an artistic success.

At one of these parties the painter met Helen Wills, internationally famous tennis player, whose face and form became the allegorical figure of California in the Stock Exchange mural. This gigantic and conventional allegory, embracing the various natural and industrial resources of the state of California, derives from well-established academic sources. Although Diego professed to be excited by the fabulous environment, his pictorial statement seems noncommittal and unexciting.

The second large-scale work of that year was the original contract by Mr. Gerstle for the California School of Fine Arts. Here is another hymn to the glory of modern industry, this time in terms of building construction, visualized in a gigantic mural thirty-five feet wide and forty-five feet high. Its chief element, a scaffolding, stretches across the entire composition from bottom to top. The central vertical section shows a series of figures doing a huge fresco of a worker, their backs to the audience, and featuring the ample posterior of Rivera himself on the second plank from the top. In the rectangle at the bottom of this center area are two architects consulting with Mr. Gerstle (in the middle). Immediately to the right is another rectangular section devoted to architecture and showing a white-smocked Frida at a drafting table. The upper left section shows a friend of Diego's Paris years, the sculptor Ralph Stackpole, who was instrumental in bringing the painter to San Francisco. In this scene are also a number of industrial symbols, while at the lower left a group of mechanics is at work. The idea of industry and building is continued at the upper right with a skyscraper in the process of construction.

The figure of the painted worker overwhelms the rest of the composition, while Diego's plump bottom confronts the spectator from the geometric center of the painting. Apparently the artist was not completely pleased with all he had encountered, and in some ways this mural was a criticism of the United States. This is indicated in an article he wrote for a San Francisco periodical in 1931, entitled 'Scaffoldings,' quoted in Mr. Wolfe's biography.[5] Here he attacks United States standards of aesthetic judgment, appeals for a more functional approach, and urges a joining of northern and southern artists to 'form the NEW AMERICAN CULTURE.'

Between the work on the Stock Exchange and the Art School murals, the Riveras had spent a short vacation period at the home of Mrs. Sigmund Stern. The dining-room fresco executed by Diego in this charming environment is often referred to as *Abundance and Health*. It consists of a row of almond trees in the background, a group of workers occupied with a tractor in the middleground, and a wall in the foreground. There is a large fruit-filled basket on top, with three small children looking over the wall and taking the fruit. Two of these are the grandchildren of Rivera's hostess, the third an imaginary companion of theirs.

After a very brief stay in Mexico, Rivera (who had still not completed the National Palace murals) was recalled to the United States. This time a dramatic and successful one-man show was held at the Museum of Modern Art in New York, beginning late in December 1931. For this show he prepared a series of movable frescoes that would give some idea of what he could do and had done in this medium. Four of them were reworked fragments from his earlier Mexican murals; three new ones were the result of observations made in the United States: *Electric Welding, Pneumatic Drilling*, and the usual 'joker,' this time a panel called *Frozen Assets*. Here he showed in three registers the vault of a bank, a group of corpselike figures in a flop house, and in the topmost section the skyscrapers of New York formed like tombstones. This reference to the growing crisis of the depression was not too well liked, but the exhibition as a whole was an enormous success, owing partly to the publicity accorded the painter's gesture.

While Rivera had been in San Francisco, discussions had been initiated between him and the authorities of the Detroit Institute of Arts, to whom he had expressed a keen desire to portray the United States industrial scene. The increasing preoccupation with industry and the machine had emerged from the artist's first real contact with a mechanized culture. This brought a realization of the problems of labor that he could not have had in a still primarily agricultural Mexico. But the Detroit commission,

---

[5] Wolfe, op. cit. pp. 330–32.

made possible by the generosity of Edsel Ford and executed in 1932–3, is no indictment of capitalist society. The *Portrait of Detroit* resulted from months of careful study of the various factories, shops, and laboratories of that great city. It is a monumental glorification of industry, summing up the technology of a manufacturing center.

Rivera's murals in the courtyard of the Detroit Institute trace the evolution of industry to its basic components: Lime, Coal, Iron, and Sand, which are symbolized through the four races that comprise our population: White, Black, Red, and Yellow. Two of the walls here depict automobile manufacture (fig. 26), Detroit's chief industry; the third wall shows steam, electric power, and aviation (fig. 27); the final, or opposite, wall is devoted to a number of agricultural symbols. The sculpturesque nudes above this opposite side, like those above the two automotive walls, are reminiscent of similar earlier efforts at Chapingo and the Ministry of Health. The nude figures in the walls devoted to automobile-making represent the red and black races (left-hand wall), the white and yellow races (right-hand wall). In addition, the already familiar Rivera clenched hands here emerge from the earth to furnish the power of iron and coal, lime and sand.

The walls themselves in their infinite detail have dynamic movement and power, although these same details make for a certain difficulty of

reading or scanning, even more than in the Cuernavaca or National Palace murals. To Rivera these works represent the climax of his career, but many critics prefer the simplicity and decorative efficacy, the poetic quality and brilliant drawing of the Chapingo murals. A storm was aroused in the pulpit and press of Detroit by Rivera's materialistic conception of that city and his representation of *Preventive Medicine* (fig. 28) in a small panel of the left-hand wall in an arrangement reminiscent of a Holy Family. At that time, and indeed for a few years later, it seemed as though Rivera's murals might be whitewashed over.

The 'battle of Rockefeller Center' that occurred the following year points up the ambiguous position of a Communist artist trying to work for a capitalist patron. Whereas in San Francisco and Detroit the problem had been glossed over by the artist himself, the situation was quite different in the more active political environment of New York, with socially conscious artists acting as Diego's assistants. Rivera claimed that the disputed portrait of Lenin, which ultimately led to destruction of the entire mural, had been included in a less obtrusive form in the sketches submitted to the architect. His patrons may not have noticed it. Nevertheless, in Rivera's attempt to put over such a clear anticapitalist statement as this mural, he was either naïve or impelled by a desire for political martyrdom. Whether, as Rivera claims, the prominent and clearly portrayed figure of the Soviet leader at the right side of the mural was

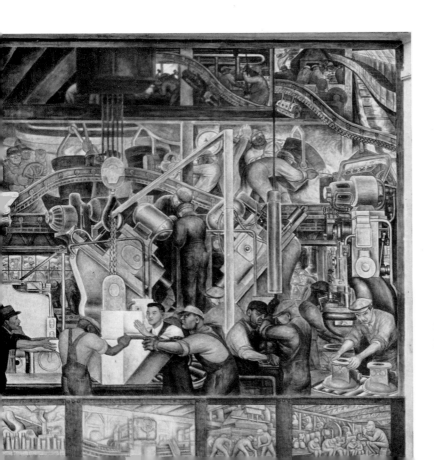

26

RIVERA. *Making of a Motor*, detail of left wall.
FRESCO. DETROIT INSTITUTE OF ARTS.

aesthetically indispensable to the conception as a whole is questionable in view of the lack of a comparable figure on the left side (see fig. 76 below).

Rivera was already reacting to the more liberal currents then apparent in Mexico, just as the 'battle of Rockefeller Center' itself must be regarded as part of the 1933 economic and political crisis in the United States. The painting was only covered up at the height of the battle in May 1933, and Diego was simply excluded from the building. But six months later the authorities of Rockefeller Center, feeling that the hubbub had subsided sufficiently, had the still-unfinished mural destroyed. The

27

RIVERA. *Steam, Electricity and Aviation*, west, or entrance, wall. FRESCO. DETROIT INSTITUTE OF ARTS.

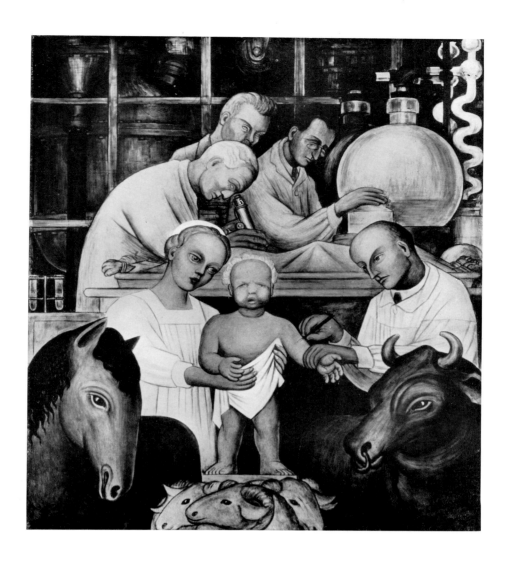

28

RIVERA. *Preventive Medicine*, detail of left wall. FRESCO.
DETROIT INSTITUTE OF ARTS.

ensuing clamor indicates, if nothing else, the awakening social conscience
of United States artists in the 'thirties, an awareness mirrored in their
turning toward a new social realism. Among the protesting artists was
José Clemente Orozco, then completing his Dartmouth College murals.
(The following year Rivera reconstructed the Rockefeller mural in the
Palace of Fine Arts in Mexico City—see Chapter XV.)

The dismissal left Rivera with a series of photographs of the mural and
a check in full payment for his services. After paying his expenses, he

applied the remainder to the production of a series of twenty-one removable fresco panels at the New Workers School in a rickety old building on West Fourteenth Street occupied by the Communist Party Opposition, the so-called Lovestonites. In this dingy environment, Diego painted his Marxist *Portrait of America*. Again, as in the Detroit murals, the painter had to familiarize himself with the subject matter by serious research. In this and other matters associated with these murals, he was aided by the school's director, Bertram D. Wolfe, his biographer and collaborator in their *Portrait of America*[6] and *Portrait of Mexico*.[7]

Perhaps the most conspicuous feature of these panels is the series of authentic portraits from United States and associated world history that were woven into the various scenes of the country's past and present. There can be little doubt of Rivera's phenomenal absorptive understanding of the material prepared for him by the staff of the New Workers School and his translation thereof into the stuff of his pictures. The general arrangement in these panels consists first of a group of slightly larger than life-size forms in the foreground, generally heroes or symbolic figures representative of a given period. In the middleground are masses of people in actions related to the large individuals; and the background depicts the country's landscape (fig. 29). The contrast and counterpoise of heroes and villains give these panels a dynamic quality seldom enjoyed by other Rivera works, although their mural quality is debatable.

While many objected to the Marxist interpretation of this nation's history, Siqueiros attacked Rivera for opportunism and inconsistency in depicting with photographic exactitude the villains who occurred in United States history up to the point at which the paintings were done, and then switching to symbols of N.R.A., the Blue Eagle, and so forth, instead of showing the specific individuals involved. This, according to Siqueiros, was an attempt to avoid offending people who might still give him commissions (a remote possibility after the Radio City incident).[8] These New Workers School murals were later removed to a new headquarters on West Thirty-Third Street in New York—the Independent Labor Institute—and then to the summer camp of the International Ladies Garment Workers Union at Forest Park, Pennsylvania (Unity House). The last Rivera works of this period are a pair of small panels dealing with the Russian revolution, done for the Trotskyist headquarters on University Place in New York, and featuring the leader of the Fourth International, Leon Trotsky.

---

[6] *Portrait of America*, Covici Friede, N.Y., 1934.

[7] *Portrait of Mexico*, Covici Friede, N.Y., 1937.

[8] Rivera's reply to Siqueiros's attacks on him is contained in the pamphlet, *Raíces políticas y motivos personales de la controversia Siqueiros-Rivera*, Imprenta Mundial, Mexico, 1935. Here Diego defends his 'Leninist Bolshevism' against the 'Stalinism' of his opponents, and also accuses them of envying his great reputation and the number of commissions he receives.

29

RIVERA. *Revolution and Reaction.* PORTABLE FRESCO. UNITY HOUSE, FOREST PARK, PA.

OMNI-CIENCIA

PINTADO POR
JOSE CLEMENTE OROZCO
POR ORDEN DE
GRAN ADMIRADO
FRANCISCO SERGIO ITURB
AÑO DE 192

30

OROZCO. *Omniscience*. FRESCO. HOUSE OF TILES (SANBORN'S), MEXICO CITY.

In 1924, a year of crisis for Orozco and many of his colleagues, the critic Salvador Novo said of the painter's work in the Preparatoria: '... repulsive pictures aiming to awake in the spectator, instead of aesthetic emotion, an anarchistic fury if he was penniless, or if wealthy, to make his knees buckle with fright.'[1] By August of that year, after the direct physical attack on the murals by students, Orozco was dismissed from the job and he returned to newspaper cartooning.

In 1925 Francisco Sergio Iturbe commissioned Orozco to paint a large mural over the staircase of the Casa de los Azulejos (House of Tiles), an impressive colonial building now occupied by Sanborn's Restaurant. This fresco may be considered the first climax of Orozco's 'classical' phase. The forms represent a philosophical statement rather than a revolutionary exhortation or horror scene; they deal with the nature of art. Below two pairs of powerful symbolic hands, like those used in the Preparatoria, Orozco has arranged a vertical composition called *Omniscience* (fig. 30), composed of yellow-brown and red-brown forms. In the center a magnificent smiling nude looks upward to receive the light of Inspiration. At the same time and with a decisive gesture she subdues Force and Intelligence, the male and female figures at either side of her, held in check by horizontally placed arms. Orozco, who at one time had said that 'Art is first of all GRACE. Where GRACE is not, there is no art. GRACE cannot be conjured up by so-called artistic recipes,' apparently means in this mural that Grace—or Inspiration—is a spiritual experience beyond Force and Intelligence.

The contrast with the mechanically combined figures of Rivera's *Creation* in the Anfiteatro Bolívar is very marked in this well-integrated horizontal-vertical arrangement. More important, Rivera used a group of conventional symbols inherited from Renaissance and Byzantine art, while Orozco evolved an altogether personal idea.

The year 1926 marks a serious change in Orozco's thematic approach, away from the generalized or religious subjects of the first Preparatoria murals (*Christ Destroying His Cross*, *Spring*, *Maternity*, and so on), the

---

[1] Jean Charlot, *Art Making from Mexico to China*, Sheed & Ward, N.Y., 1950, p. 129.

31

OROZCO. *Social Revolution*. FRESCO.
INDUSTRIAL SCHOOL, ORIZABA.

House of Tiles fresco, or the caricatures of the second-floor Preparatoria murals done in 1924. In the 1926 commission for the Industrial School at Orizaba (fig. 31) he turned to Revolutionary material in the impressive symbolic sense that would later characterize most of his work. This first tentative step toward portraying incidents of war, pillage, and rapine was taken against the background of Orozco's earlier experiences as an illustrator for *La Vanguardia*.

In the Orizaba work, men with rifles and spades are symmetrically and abstractly arranged over a doorway as builders of the post-Revolutionary period. In the side panels below, the Orozco of the forthcoming Preparatoria murals already emerges. Here are the first notes of Revolutionary tragedy in the huddled forms of the crying *soldaderas* at the left and the pathetically interlaced group at the right, with a woman wiping the face of a sweating and exhausted soldier.

Recalled to the Preparatoria shortly after completing the Orizaba murals, Orozco proceeded to remove most of the ground-floor material painted in 1923-4, leaving the *Maternity*, *The Rich Banquet*, and the head of the Christ from the scene of His destroying the Cross.[2] As for the rest, he found that their generalized Renaissance quality no longer met the increasingly powerful emotive needs of his art. He replaced them with the reworked *Revolutionary Trinity*, *The Strike*, the *Trench*, and the *Destruction of the Old Order*, in that order from left to right. At either end the two left-over murals remain, *The Rich Banquet* and the *Maternity* respectively.

Working against serious difficulties, such as low pay, constant student molestation, and the largest problem of all, that of perfecting his new style, Orozco painted on steadily, using his master mason as chief model. The latter's heavy moustache, slight paunch, and round shoulders appear in many compositions of this time, e.g. the left-hand figure in *The Strike* and presumably also the suppliant figure of the *Trinity* (see fig. 12).

The early *Maternity* panel, at the extreme right, had already shown some of the monumentality and restraint that characterize Orozco's style from this point on. Its colors are less fortunate, however, being hot and unpleasant. *The Destruction of the Old Order* (fig. 32), to the left of that panel, shows a pair of gray-white clothed men looking back at lavender and yellow-gray broken buildings—the symbols of the old order—seen against a dark-blue background. This is perhaps the high point of the first-floor patio. It offers a wonderful balance of inward and outward moving parts and a powerful assurance in the figures themselves, taking one last look backward as they move into the future.

The following panel, the *Trench*, betrays a rather strained symbolism involving a trio of dancelike figures clothed in the same colors as the foregoing but placed against a red background. *The Strike*, to the left, takes us back to the restrained monumentality of the *Destruction*. Again

---

[2] Jean Charlot, 'Orozco's Stylistic Evolution,' oc. cit. p. 152.

gray-white figures appear, now against a beautiful lavender building with a narrow red banner nailed across its doorway, the traditional strike symbol in Mexico. Here the head of Christ (left over from the previous composition in this space) hovers, as it were. over a solemn and hieratic scene of the people's misery. As for the *Revolutionary Trinity*, which we have already discussed (see fig. 12), it represents a reworking of what had been *Work, Science, and Revolution*, with its somewhat strained and awkward quality, into a more abstract symbol of man's suffering. The worker's hands have been cut off and the peasant begs for his life, while overhead the Revolution appears blinded by its own red flag. In this panel, as in

32

OROZCO. *Destruction of the Old Order*. FRESCO.
NATIONAL PREPARATORY SCHOOL, MEXICO CITY.

the final area containing *The Rich Banquet*, and so on, color combinations are more complicated and far less effective than in the *Trench*, the *Strike*, and the *Destruction*, which are related through the colors and forms of the men. These three panels, therefore, would seem to be a separate operation at a later date and related to the *Trinity* through the suppliant figure in the reworked version. Orozco may well have planned the first floor in its present form before his dismissal, but the homogeneity of these three panels and their relationship to the staircase and third-floor murals would argue a later date for the group. The ground-floor patio is also united by pairs of clasped and clenched hands on the dividing arches.

On the wall immediately adjacent to the ground-floor panels is the staircase leading to the upper floors. Here a group of figures at the bottom left drinks the waters of knowledge; at the right, series of gray builders employ the instruments of their trade. Ascending the staircase, we see on the vault directly overhead the magnificently powerful *Cortez and Malinche*, the conqueror and his Indian love, whose union symbolizes the joining of the Spanish and Indian cultures. These monumental and impressive nudes, he gray-yellow, she brown, are revealed against a background of lavender and brown. Their right hands are joined, while his left is placed across her body, restraining her from going to the aid of the stricken Indian at their feet.

Directly beneath this poetic symbol is the strong maguey decoration in its lavender-colored rectangle. Above, in the vault immediately over the top of the stairs, is the figure known as *Youth*. Here an exultant gray-white form soars through the air and flings its limbs to the corners of the panel. This figure sums up the hopefulness of that part of the building area, with its beneficent Franciscans comforting Indians, men imbibing knowledge, and others building the future. Among the most potent of these are *The Conqueror-Builder and the Indian Worker* and the *Ancient Warring Races* directly below. The latter symbolizes the constant struggles among the ancient inhabitants of Mexico, and shows a menacing, pyramidal, blanketed form looming over a prostrate figure. Out of this incessant warfare emerge the symbols of the round-headed Conqueror-Builder, who fashions modern Mexico with the aid of the Indian Worker. The dynamic restlessness of the former and the quiet strength of the seated Indian in the related group evoke the controlled power of Michelangelo.

The final statement in this building, and in many ways the most unified and effective of the murals, is the sequence of third-floor Revolutionary panels. Admirably set off by a group of flattened arches similar to those below, these scenes represent the logical climax of the earlier style. There is perhaps less dynamism and direct action than in some of the previous sections, but a sober strength and restrained emotional appeal are present instead. In accordance with the generally muted drama here, the accent is on rebuilding and not on revolt, on pity and not on anger. Although contemporary politics are not specifically referred to, one can point to the refurbished statement in the *Revolutionary Trinity* below, with its powerful accents of anguish, sorrow, and confusion, and to the *Return to the Battlefields* in this third-floor section, a symbolic indication that the struggle is not yet over.

On this wall, colors are still subdued, but they are far brighter than the browns on the stairs or the lower-floor colors, and more effectively unified by the use of a strong blue background throughout. The integration of the rectangular panels and the shallow arches is effected through a horizontal architectural background, in each painting, related to the panel itself, while the arched arrangement of the figures ties the foreground of each section to the curve of the arch. Through this means and the dominant deep-blue background that stretches from panel to panel, unity is achieved within the series and a relationship created between the paintings and the architecture. The figures, moreover, are consistently grayish, while the architectural backgrounds tend toward lavender.

The sense of subdued emotion, the rigidly controlled structure and balance of the compositions, the three-dimensional clarity of the individual forms, and the serene strength of the blue background and the gray figures before it are a summing up of Orozco's classical phase and the end of this particular direction in his painting. Although this wall is in many ways one of the most concentrated statements Orozco ever made, it must be differentiated from the works of the next phase, which become by turn more graphic and more Expressionistic.

These panels, as seen from across the patio, are a series of individual areas enframed by arches. Viewed at close range, they appear as a continuous composition, one scene flowing into the next. Thus at the left *The Wives of the Workers* shows a group of grayish figures before a yellow-gray building placed against the dark-blue background. Of these three women, the two at the right are turned toward the recesses of the building. The left-hand figure, a pregnant, sorrowing woman, is placed so that her glance and the horizontal of the plow carry the eye to the right toward the open grave of the next scene.

The Gravedigger is painted in dark gray and brown against a similar-colored hill of dirt, which carries us back to the left, as does the light-blue horizontal building, which is also part of the enclosure surrounding the three women. The sleeping digger lies half in and half out of the grave, his form paralleling the hill of dirt. The man and the hill make a simple dark triangle against the vivid light-blue horizontal architecture. The house reverses the perspective of the open grave. Both the pregnant woman and the gravedigger are shown with eyes closed.

The next few scenes show a more diverse handling of background in the various connected narratives. *The Mother's Benediction* turns the architecture at an angle to increase the sense of depth. At the right, a man on his knees faces away from the spectator and toward the seated

33

OROZCO. *The Mother's Farewell*. FRESCO. NATIONAL PREPARATORY SCHOOL, MEXICO CITY.

mother. She blesses him as he prepares to *Return to Labor*, the next panel to the right. The mother and son are placed against a lavender building, a more hopeful color than the dun background of *The Wives of the Workers*. The *Return to Labor* continues this happier lavender tonality; the architecture is similarly angled toward the spectator and recedes a considerable distance, implying that these people are going somewhere, toward an optimistic future. The figures themselves are more dynamic and varied than any so far. They move vigorously and decisively, as though they know what is to be done.

Here, as in many other panels, is the anonymous figure turned away from the spectator or in lost profile, a figure of symbolic meaning as well as a form in a composition. Once again, as in the pregnant woman of the first panel, we see the magnificent restraint and power of the Mexican woman, her capacity for service and suffering. Whether innate or developed by the circumstances of the Revolution, her heroic quality is a constant factor in Orozco's presentation.

The Mother's Farewell (fig. 33) takes place before a light-blue building

95

sharply angled toward the spectator, with its corner at the left. The panel shows two pairs of figures in broad curves set against the long wall that moves to the right. In the left-hand pair, the figure of a soldier bends forward in a smooth arc to kiss the hand of the abstract little gray form with its Aztec face—the theme of the panel. The mother's tight mouth and lined countenance, her unpupiled gray eyes shining out from the brown of her face, and the general simplified curves of the form make this one of the finest details in the entire wall. The bent soldier in the second group at the right is overlapped by the first soldier; the two backs, legs, and daggers join in a continuity of linear expression that carries us from one end of the panel to the other.

The sorrowful note of this scene is echoed in the *Peace* of the next section, where five figures in gray, white, and light brown form a semi-circle before brownish-gray architecture. Two women face the spectator: one holding a baby in her arms, the other supporting in her lap the head of a sleeping man whose form stretches horizontally across the group. The two women have their eyes closed in an uneasy sleep, while the other two people in the scene, a man and a woman, face away from the spectator, their arms about each other's shoulders, facing the generalized architecture in the background. These two may be looking toward the future, but they might also be looking at the large cloud in the upper right of the panel.

This is no final peace or moment of actual accomplishment, as is indicated in the final panel on this wall, the *Return to the Battlefields*, with its subdued but effective tones of gray and brownish gray. The implication of 'unfinished business' in this section, in which figures move off diagonally into an open and endless area, is quite different from the other panels, with their complete and tight statements.

During this period Orozco produced a number of ink and wash drawings, the famous *Mexico in Revolution* series. These have usually been attributed to the 1913–17 period to make them contemporary with the events depicted. But one can readily see by comparing any of them (fig. 34) with other material produced by Orozco during these years (cf. fig. 33), and even with the first mural paintings, that the Revolutionary drawings simply do not belong to that first period of Orozco's art. Stylistically, such drawings as the *En los Cerros* parallel the monumentality and closed form of the *Peace* or *The Mother's Farewell* in the Preparatoria murals. Others,[3] such as *The Flag (La Bandera)*, may be compared with the *Return to the Battlefields* and other similar compositions of this time. In a looser form, drawings such as *The Dead Comrade* (fig. 35) begin to approximate the Expressionistic intensity of many of his paintings, prints, and murals of the late 'twenties and early 'thirties, and in that sense they clearly fit into the pattern of Orozco's evolution as an artist. Among these

---

[3] Illustrated in Alma Reed, *José Clemente Orozco*, Delphic Studios, N.Y., 1932.

34

OROZCO. *In the Mountains* (*En los Cerros*). WASH DRAWING.
MEXICO CITY, COLL. DR. A. CARRILLO GIL.

works, we may mention the 1929 illustrations for Mariano Azuela's *The Under Dogs* (*Los de Abajo*), the 1928–9 lithographs and paintings in New York, and the Pomona College and Dartmouth College murals.

The conflict in style between the 'girls' of the pre-1917 era and these incisive and direct representations of suffering and despair is resolved by this redating of the drawings on stylistic grounds and through the external evidence gathered by the scholarly Jean Charlot,[4] who remembers that the drawings were done in the period of the 1926 murals and after. Moreover, he quotes from the contemporary diary of Anita Brenner, who lived in Mexico at the time and was in constant contact with Orozco. According to this diary, a number of the painter's friends—including Manuel Rodríguez Lozano and Miss Brenner herself—realized Orozco's

---

[4] Charlot, op. cit.

35

OROZCO. *The Dead Comrade*. WASH DRAWING.
MEXICO CITY, COLL. DR. A. CARRILLO GIL.

financial difficulties and invented a mythical United States purchaser
who wanted some illustrations for a book he was doing on the Revolution.
(Orozco's mural work was stopped for the second time in September 1926,
and Miss Brenner intervened on his behalf with the rector of the university.) The artist began to deliver the wash drawings toward the end of
September. According to the diary, he continued to turn them out until
August 1927, just before he left Mexico. In October 1928 they were first
shown as part of an exhibition at the Marie Sterner Gallery in New York.[5]
The next steps in his development now become very clear: *The Under
Dogs* drawings, the lithographs he did from 1926 on, the easel paintings
of the period, and finally the great murals from 1930 to 1934.

---

[5] Mrs. Reed, op. cit., lists them as 'Drawings and lithographs from sketches
made between 1913 and 1917.' The same position is maintained in her later
work, *Orozco*, Fondo de Cultura Económica, Mexico, D. F., 1955. English edition,
Oxford University Press, N.Y., 1956.

36

OROZCO. *Zapata*. OIL. MEXICO CITY, COLL. DR. A. CARRILLO GIL.

What had been impossible for Orozco to say openly in the third floor of the Preparatoria, he poured forth in these washes that could be shown only in New York City, far away from the Calles regime. They represent a reminder of the immediate past, of the sacrifices that had been made for the Revolution and the shift during the new generation, when Revolutionaries became politicians. Moreover, they emphasize the pessimistic interpretation of the Revolution that is characteristic of Orozco throughout. Their closest analogue is the desperate, mystical, and fatalistic prose of Azuela, and they are far removed from the bland optimism of Rivera in the Secretaría.

As a transition from the 'classical' character of the third-floor Preparatoria murals to the looser and more Expressionist quality of Orozco's next group of wall paintings, the drawings and easel pictures of this period, 1926–31, offer a strong body of material. Among the latter are some brilliantly designed, intense representations of the New York scene: subways, elevated railroads, street pictures, Coney Island, and so on, together with reminiscences of Revolutionary Mexico: soldiers, fallen columns, a family, a cemetery, reiterations of earlier subjects such as *Peace* and the *Barricade*, as well as the flamingly symbolic *Pancho Villa* and *Zapata* (fig. 36).

The last-named work shows how far Orozco had come within a few years from the carefully modeled, almost academically drawn figures of the 1923–6 period. Even had he not been in self-imposed exile during these years, one may imagine that his work would have taken on this somber quality, this sense of despair and futility; the economic collapse of 1929 no doubt augmented the feeling of misery and hopelessness. Very significant for the development of United States painting was this direct example of a social-conscious art on an extremely high level of symbolic and emotive quality, anticipating the perhaps less effective painters of the depression period here.

As early as 1928 such titles appear as *Eighth Avenue, The Subway, Fourteenth Street, The Elevated, Manhattan,* and so on.[6] The following year the melancholy aspect of local life appears in some of his works, while others, such as the beautifully abstract *Queensboro Bridge* (fig. 37), seem to have no ulterior social purpose. By 1930, however, he returns to Mexicanism once more, as in the brooding, haunting *Zapata,* visible symbol of Mexico's despair and his own. His new figurative Expressionist style is now formed, and will be applied to the murals of this period and the one following.

In 1930, after a few years in New York, Orozco finally received a commission to paint the far wall of the large student dining area known as Frary Hall in Pomona College near Los Angeles. In this huge pseudo-Gothic chamber, in a recess beyond a pointed arched opening, Orozco set forth his *Prometheus*—not without violent objections from local Cali-

---

[6] See Reed, op. cit.

37

fornians about the importation of a foreign artist. This was also the year
that Rivera was vigorously opposed in San Francisco.

Here Orozco presented the idea of Prometheus bringing the gift of fire
to mankind, apparently conforming to the idea of learning being con-
ferred on the sons and daughters of man. But the effect is of a tumultuous
Last Judgment combined with Moses Bringing the Tablets of the Law,
a frightening conception rather than a beneficent one (fig. 38). Mankind
here is terrified into a seething, milling mass by the awful spectacle. In
the center, the hero ascends from rich brown shadows in a series of
grayish browns to the lurid reds of the flames above. His Tintorettesque
body swings from left to right in a powerful diagonal that gives the impression of this titan supporting the heavens rather than drawing something out of them. Mankind recedes from the gigantic figure in helpless

waves and in varying degrees of terror, despair, smugness, and stiff-necked pride, depending on their respective reactions to the gift for which Prometheus has defied the gods.

This is Orozco's commentary on man's reception of social progress, as symbolized by Prometheus and his gift. Although the general arrangement suggests a Last Judgment, the effect is a flaming symbol of man in the mass. This is the first of many times that Orozco paints a dominant central figure about which seethe hordes of sketchily indicated, writhing, agonized human beings. The mural of the Palacio de Bellas Artes, the staircase fresco in the Palacio del Gobierno in Guadalajara, the *Departure of Quetzalcoatl* in Dartmouth are later instances of this symbolism.

Although the forms are still basically three-dimensional and figurative, there is considerable loosening (in the El Greco sense), especially in the masses of elongated, flamelike little figures that comprise the two sides of the composition. These two portions are compactly arranged, and cut

38

OROZCO. *Prometheus.* FRESCO. FRARY HALL, POMONA COLLEGE, CALIFORNIA.

across the right and left sides of the enclosing arch at a point considerably below the raised arms of the giant.

The twenty-five by thirty-five foot composition arranges itself into a kind of X shape as it sweeps across the wall. One line moves up from lower left through the main form of Prometheus and is continued by his right arm, which is paralleled by the upper part of the right-hand mass. The other line swings from the lower right across the body of the titan and up into his left arm, and is paralleled by the movement of the group at the left.

As is often the case, this mural suggests a variety of different influences —El Greco, Tintoretto (especially examples in the Accadèmia, Venice), and others—but it does not derive specifically from such sources. Orozco's mural remains in every case an extremely personal statement, no matter how much the non-Mexican art world has affected this painter. The calligraphic style of individual forms in the crowds belongs to the sphere of modern Expressionist painting, comparable in form and purpose to the art of the twentieth-century Germans, although again not relatable to any particular artist or group. It is doubtful to what extent Orozco was aware of the existence of the German material.

The side panels of the Pomona mural, not easily visible unless the spectator is close to the wall, are a poetic exposition of the relationship between *Chaos and the Monsters* and *Chaos and the Gods*. This kind of highly individual symbolism emerges in the later Hospicio at Guadalajara and the Hospital de Jesús in Mexico City.

Toward the end of 1930, Orozco returned to New York to begin work on a series of murals in another institution of learning, the New School for Social Research. Here he came forward with a more explicit, although far differently expressed, portrayal of the global social situation, the revolutionary movement in various parts of the world—Russia, India, and Mexico. This franker statement was made possible by the nature of the school for which the painter was working, for here a broad social and international point of view has always been fostered.

Thus the theme and execution of the murals in the third-floor refectory of the New School are the painter's own, with no restriction of any kind and with no serious fireworks resulting from the portrayal of Lenin, Stalin, British imperialism, or anything else. During 1930–31 Orozco worked out this international view in terms of a symmetrical and didactic presentation of such themes as the *Table of Brotherhood, Struggle in the Orient, Struggle in the Occident,*[7] *The Universal Family, Science, Labor, and Art,* and *The Strike.*

As with previous instances in which architecture and painting had to be integrated, he showed, if not the most subtle solution of these problems, at least a realization that the two had to be related. In the Preparatoria

[7] In 1953, however, the New School hung a yellow curtain over *Struggle in the Occident.*

103

the curved arches and rectangular panels are skillfully brought together, while in Pomona the figures are arranged with regard to the upward and side-curving motion of the pointed arch leading to the recess. Here at the New School, in the first modern building Orozco was given to decorate, the problem was considerably different; both the simplified shapes of the structure and the universal nature of the theme seemed to demand a new type of solution. Moreover, the walls did not have a frame, as the two previous jobs had had. This meant that the painter had to relate his long narrow panels to the building as a whole rather than to any part thereof. Since this building is a highly rational and functional structure, the painting had to be conceived along those lines, with individual forms reduced to parts of a machinelike structure, especially in the areas where mass action was portrayed. Orozco has said that he was influenced in the solution of this problem by the geometrical principles in the dynamic symmetry system of Jay Hambidge.[8]

In the reduction of humanity to a series of machined parts or their analogue, Orozco abandoned—actually he had to abandon—the flaming Expressionist technique of Pomona in favor of a static formulation, which many critics dislike, since it departs from the Orozco norm of violent emotionality. Yet, in spite of the relatively static character of some sections, the mural represents a courageous and open-minded solution of a problem the painter had never before encountered. We may contrast the integrated action of the two related east and west revolutionary panels with the individualistic treatment of the contrasting north and south sections, dealing with brotherhood and the family respectively. Inevitably those showing *Struggle in the Orient* and *Struggle in the Occident*,

---

[8] Orozco, *Autobiografía.*

39

 OROZCO. *Struggle in the Occident.* FRESCO.
THE NEW SCHOOL, NEW YORK.

symbolizing the rise of the oppressed masses, stress the reduction of the
individual to a cog in a political machine or movement. The other panels,
which stress the function of man as an individual and his right to racial
equality and a decent existence within the circle of his family, necessarily
treat the human being in the picture space more freely. Although the
figures in these two panels are still symbols—of race and of humanity in
general—they are not the flat, overlapping, mechanized forms of the
two revolutionary sections.

Struggle in the Occident (fig. 39) balances the revolutionary movement
in Russia at the right with the Mexican Revolution at the left. One
section shows an impressive portrait of Lenin over a group of anonymous
Soviet troops, with their winter caps pulled over their faces, while
immediately adjacent to them is a similarly arranged group of the various
races of the Soviet Union: Georgian (a portrait of Stalin), Negro,
Armenian, Indian, and so on, all marching forward toward their goal.
The left-hand portion features a somewhat spiritualized portrait of Felipe
Carrillo Puerto, the murdered governor of Yucatán. The simple pyramidal form is balanced by an actual pyramid, symbol of Carrillo Puerto's
belief in the Indians, who are shown as a simplified integrated entity
below him. They are arranged in a concave curve, with the pyramid
theme introduced again through the group of blue figures in the center,
which carries the eye back to the teacher figure above. Orozco stresses
the quiet dignity of this reformist scene as opposed to the regimented
forms of the Soviet section. For him the revolution is certainly more the
idea of reform; he criticizes the Russian version in his paintings time and
again, e.g. at the Hospicio in Guadalajara.

On the opposite wall *Struggle in the Orient* uses India as an example of the colonial nations oppressed by the West. Here again masses of people are pressed into a geometrical unity—enclosing the chained natives of the East—while above them a second smaller block includes the captive white-collar workers. These two entities are connected with a third geometric arrangement immediately to the right, showing a group of armed, gas-masked soldiers above a stylized colonial officer, all facing to the right and confronting a seated Gandhi. The latter is reduced to a right-angled triangle, and is seen against the outline of a tank that carries the eye back to the soldiers. Even more than on the west wall, there is a feeling here of diagonal and horizontal pistonlike movements which lend mechanized strength to the well-integrated composition. Color plays an unusually important part as it controls the backward and forward movements in space.

Between these two long horizontal panels is a third, far simpler, arrangement, the *Table of Brotherhood*, in which a glaring white table in reverse perspective moves up and down across the surface of the wall and unites the races of mankind around it. These figures are simplified into monumentalized block forms which have a crude simplicity and force. Among these compressed essences of the world's races the painter has placed in a special background niche the representatives of particularly oppressed groups: Mexican, Negro, and Jewish. This is the brotherhood of man that the revolutions will accomplish, in addition to the decent family life symbolized on the wall directly opposite.

By comparison with the brooding monumentality of the *Table of Brotherhood*, the *Universal Family* is a decorative and abstract conception utilizing the forms of pre-Cubist primitivism. Two workers come home to a waiting wife and mother; at the left in another group a beautifully painted woman is seen with two children. Between these two groups, a unifying gray-white table is shown (as on the wall opposite) uptilted in reverse perspective and garnished with a symbolic still life of food and books whose form suggests the Picasso-Braque Africanisms of around 1907. The panel outside the refectory, allegorizing *Science, Labor, and Art*, and the pseudo-symbolic worker's tools used to formulate the idea of *Strike* are the least successful portions of the work in this building.

Early in 1932 Orozco was called to Dartmouth College in Hanover, New Hampshire, to do a trial mural on a wall section about fifty feet in area over a doorway in the hall connecting the Baker Library and the Carpenter Art Building. For this square space he worked out a subject called *Release*, in which a hopeful, bright-eyed youth emerges from a wreckage heap of machine parts, broken cannons, and the like, dusting his hands briskly as he springs upward out of the mass.

On the basis of this satisfactory trial, Orozco was given the contract for the entire wall space in the reserve room of the Baker Library, an area of about 3000 square feet and a real challenge. The narrative and allegorical panels done here between 1932 and 1934 are in many ways the

40

OROZCO. FRESCO. WEST WING,
BAKER LIBRARY,
HANOVER, NEW HAMPSHIRE.

most exciting Orozco murals in the United States. Fourteen basic subjects have been conceived as a unit, with many themes arranged in a parallel and contrapuntal manner. They move in simple and dignified fashion from one panel to the next, along a flat wall with no architectural embellishments and with only an occasional door or ventilator to interrupt the flat even spaces.

The general theme of the Dartmouth murals is the history of America, seen as a blend of aboriginal and European elements and offering in juxtaposition the accomplishments of the precolonial past and those of the white man who followed. Part I of this epic (fig. 40) deals with the ancient culture of Mexico, along the short and long walls of the west wing. Part II, the contribution of the white man, runs along corresponding east-wing walls.

Surveying the whole, we find outlined in the first section the story of Quetzalcoatl, chief deity of the ancient precolonial peoples of Mexico, the great teacher and bringer of the arts, crafts, and civilization in general. He arrives in that precolonial world to confound the superstitions and barbarism of the old medicine men and offers a new, more civilized way of life. But since the people of Mexico soon relapse into their former habits as the influence of the witch doctors becomes strong again, Quetzalcoatl leaves in anger. Departing on a raft of serpents, he goes to the east, from which he had come originally, promising to return in five hundred years. From this ancient culture we look across to the east wing, where the contribution of the white man is set forth. The story is told of the arrival of Cortez and the Church, the age of the machine, the respective cultures of Anglo-American and Spanish America, the drying up of education, the Unknown Soldier, and, in the final scene, the return of Christ to destroy His own Cross.

Examining these works in detail, we see, on the short wall of the west wing, the first two scenes: *The Migration* and *Ancient Human Sacrifice*. The first indicates the connection between ancient America and the Orient, and shows the various types of aboriginal humanity. The general effect is one of gigantism and ruthlessness as the three groups of ten-foot-high nudes move in overlapping planes across the surface. The torrent of powerful humanity in a low-keyed brown-and-gray color scheme, with occasional touches of pink and blue, pours from one continent into the next.

The superstitions of ancient life are shown in the second scene through the human sacrifice made to the war god Huitzilopochtli. Masked priests surround the victim, who is arranged X-wise on the sacrificial block, and hold him spread-eagled as the officiating priest tears out his heart, with the ominous figure of the god dominating the background. In this *Ancient Human Sacrifice*, the forms themselves are still primarily brown, with white accents for the clothed figures in the foreground and spots of Pompeian red in the same area, green in the background, and masks colored red, green, purple, and black. Compositionally it is more tightly organized than the constantly moving *Migration* preceding it, closed where the other is open.

Moving on to the long west wall, we encounter over the doorway the brooding *Aztec Warriors*. These are the conquerors, the empire builders and militarists of ancient Mexico, whose counterparts, the European conquerors, one finds at the opposite end of this same wall and again over a door. Here the short, rectangular panel with its abbreviated figures shows the Indian warriors carrying flags of silver and feathers and dressed in traditional hoods in the shape of snakes, tigers, and eagles.

This long wall of the west wing is divided into three main sections: *The Coming of Quetzalcoatl*, the (pre-Columbian) *Golden Age*, and the *Departure of Quetzalcoatl*. It terminates in the short panel over the far door showing *The Prophecy*, which balances the short *Aztec Warriors* over the near door.

The first of the three main scenes is perhaps the least satisfactory in this wing. It features the horrified face of the great ruler and teacher Quetzalcoatl, a brilliant, white-robed, Orientalized figure with blazing blue eyes, who appears against a background of ancient gods arranged in a row across the rear of the panel. The forms of the older gods are taken from stone carvings and represent the deity of Greed, dressed in the purple-brown skins of his victims; olive-green Magic, with white feet of smoking mirrors; Rain and Storm (Tlaloc) with his green double-serpent masks; black Death with a skeletal mask; blue War with the feathered feet of stealth; and pink Fire. Quetzalcoatl appears over the pyramids of Teotihuacán, important site of his cult. All the god figures are in the upper half of the panel. Below we find two groups of brownish humans, their dull color in strong contrast to the tonalities above. The group at the left shows sleeping individuals who symbolize the past; on the right, a number of people converse in the shadow of a magnificently geometricized structure and represent the communion and co-operative activity of mankind. With this scene the general color key has been raised considerably higher than before, especially in the reds and blues of the gods, while the foreground shows a combination of rich browns combined with cool grays. The abstract house at the right is particularly effective with its modulated red-pinks.

The *Golden Age* (fig. 41) initiated by the coming of Quetzalcoatl consists of three main figures representing Industry, Art, and Science. The first of these, a powerful brown block form, is bent over some maize. Near him is a strongly stylized figure carving Aztec symbols on gray stone blocks, a form that parallels the shape and angularity of the stones themselves. Finally, behind the blocks of stone, a half-seen figure with its eyes closed thrusts an arm upward into the future to symbolize the science that will ultimately come (cf. the rising form in the abstract mural of the Normal School, 1947–8).

41

OROZCO. *The Golden Age.* FRESCO. WEST WING, BAKER LIBRARY.

The *Departure of Quetzalcoatl* (fig. 42) is motivated by the plotting of the priests and magicians to impose the old superstitions. Ancient practices such as human sacrifice are re-established and are followed by war, sickness, and the final end of the ancient civilization. From these events stems the high point in these murals, and one of the high points in Orozco's art—the ominous and prophetic departure of the god, a vivid, white, Michelangelesque figure against a dark sky, making his fateful and challenging gesture to the right, to the future. Balancing this violent rightward sweep of the god's right arm and the writhing movement of the serpents about him is the counterwave of frightened dark figures at the left—the priests, arranged in an ascending pyramid of raised arms and bent bodies (cf. the Pomona mural and the later Guadalajara example in the Palacio del Gobierno). The use of the pyramid, both architectural and human, has a symbolic and climactic purpose, underlined by the progression of color intensity from bottom to top in each case. The building goes from Pompeian red at the bottom to red-pink at the top, the human pyramid from gray-brown to flat white.

The awesome gesture of Quetzalcoatl, reminiscent of that of the creative God in the Sistine ceiling frescoes, keynotes the remainder of the representations in the library. It leads the eye first to *The Prophecy*, which

42

OROZCO. *Departure of Quetzalcoatl*. FRESCO. WEST WING, BAKER LIBRARY.

presumably fulfills Quetzalcoatl's promise to return with other white gods to set up a new civilization. Here, in a short mural over the doorway, is a symbol of European culture in general and of the conquest in particular. It shows armed soldiers and armored horses, the men carrying a stone Cross with reinforced pointed ends. This group appears against an arrangement of Romanesque and Doric columns and capitals that symbolize European civilization. This mural may be compared with the balancing small panel, *Aztec Warriors*, at the other end of this wall, symbolizing Aztec civilization.

The second section of the Dartmouth murals, in the east wing, deals with the general theme of the return of Quetzalcoatl, as symbolized by cultural manifestations since the time of Cortez. The diversity and complexity of this post-Columbian period bring a quicker tempo and a stepped-up color key, with a compositional change from masses of people to a stress on the individual leader, hero, or sufferer. This entire section carries a strong note of pessimism, ending on the sacrifices of World War I and the *Christ Destroying His Cross*, intended to show that this is not the civilization of man's hope, that the white god of peace has not yet returned.

This section begins with the rectangular *Cortez and the Cross*, an impressive black-clad, gray-visaged figure who, by a strange coincidence, arrived in Mexico at the exact time set by ancient legend for the return of Quetzalcoatl. Immediately behind Cortez is the great green Cross, held by a monk dressed in black. In the pinkish background are the burning ships. About the central figure are the wreckage of the older civilization and the bodies of the conquered, many of which are being fed into *The Machine* at the right.

This last is the arch-symbol of the New World for Orozco and one to which he will return many times, in the Palacio de Bellas Artes mural, in those of Guadalajara, and elsewhere. The machine, denoting the white man's contribution to America, is by no means a happy representation but a jagged broken symbol in black and white, relieved here and there by dark red spots. Not only is man fed into the maw of this splintery monster, but the general picture of the machine is one of powerful and conflicting mechanical forces that obliterate man. Although some of the forms are recognizable as smelters, turbines, and so on, the intent is symbolic and dehumanizing, introducing another age of confusion.

In Orozco's art, the machine is often something alive and malignant, not merely a series of streamlined forms. Thus, instead of turning mankind into robotlike figures, Orozco gives the machines themselves a specific emotional quality through their coloration, function, and distortion. He is not primarily concerned with the aesthetic possibilities of the machine, as are the post-Cubist painters, but rather with its moral and psychological connotations. Nor does he glorify it in the fashion of Diego Rivera's work at Detroit during this same period. To Rivera the machine is the potential savior of mankind that will bring the better life. The contrast between the glossy forms of Rivera's turbines on the entrance wall of the Detroit court and the menacing black forms of turbines here represents the contrast between two divergent methods of painting and thinking.

The next scenes, *Anglo-America* and *Hispano-America,* are on a perhaps less effective plane than the preceding ones to the degree that they contain clear elements of caricature. These two sections, like the following *Gods of the Modern World,* also offer direct criticism of the host nation and the host institution.

In *Anglo-America* a blank-faced, unpleasant-looking schoolteacher is surrounded by equally uninspiring youngsters. For Orozco, they reflect the supposed regimentation of American society, while the undistinguished forms in the town meeting at the left represent a kind of lifeless co-operation. The patch of yellow wheat at the lower left (comparable to a similar area in the *Golden Age*) is connected with the yellow in the upper right of the preceding composition and with the gold in the *Hispano-America* following.

The latter features the idealized bandit hero, a combination of the Zapata and Pancho Villa types that Orozco had done in easel paintings during 1930–31. Its intent is to contrast the dynamic revolutionary with the sheeplike schoolteacher. The brooding, brutal figure of the Mexican is surrounded by distorted leering millionaires and imperialist soldiers sprawling over tumbling heaps of gold. Fallen broken columns and a wrecked factory in red represent the havoc wreaked by these creatures.

The *Gods of the Modern World,* i.e. modern education, may be contrasted with the earlier panel in which Quetzalcoatl brought real knowledge. Here is Orozco's protest against traditional teaching, with the gowned collegiate figures seen as Posada-like *calaveras.* These forms surround a skeleton lying on heavy tomes, from whose womb stillborn knowledge issues with the aid of these academic midwives. The gowned gods of the modern world—Factual Knowledge, the Scientific and Materialistic Outlook, and so on—are seen against a world in flames (cf. the background color of Cortez's ships in flames). The yellow skeleton leads us to the next panel—from a denunciation of intellectual slavery to a portrayal of political and spiritual bondage.

The two last panels are on the short wall of the east wing and are visible through the two square piers at the end of that space. *Modern Human Sacrifice* (cf. *Ancient Human Sacrifice* earlier) shows an orator glorifying war, accompanied by a brass band and flags. Before him, draped in a flag, lies the unknown sacrifice to the war, the skeletonized dead soldier. His feet face the spectator; his body is hidden under a heap of wreaths; and in the background are a war memorial and flags.

The other panel shows *Christ Destroying His Cross* (fig. 43). The militant Christ represents an aroused and fighting spirituality towering above the

43

OROZCO. *Christ Destroying His Cross*. FRESCO. EAST WING, BAKER LIBRARY.

heaped-up and destroyed religious symbols of all ages—Greek, Buddhist, and especially Christian—which He apparently repudiates as not genuine. This impressive figure, with its staring eyes, blue-streaked face, reddish hair and beard, has a yellowish torso tinted with orange, green, blue, purple, and purple-gray from the awesome head to the horribly torn legs below. In pose and aggressive emotionality it reminds us of Piero della Francesca's *Resurrection of Christ*. Its drawing and contained spirituality suggest the eleventh-century Byzantine mosaics of Daphni and later examples at Mt. Athos. The spirit of this Christ is that of an avenging judge or Pantocrator (ruler of the universe) who here returns to earth to find His Cross misused, to find in the broken tools of destruction evidences of wars fought in His name. He has therefore destroyed the Cross, and now confronts the spectator with a frightening and questioning look. Thus the series is brought to a close.

The three additional panels in the central vestibule may have been intended to tie together the entire project in a kind of spiritual climax. Here Orozco represents *Modern Industrial Man*, an ideologically significant figure through whom the new civilization prophesied by Quetzalcoatl might perhaps be achieved. Although composed without benefit of direct light, these panels have a very successful decorative quality. The dark figures are seen against modulated green backgrounds and reddish metal structures. The side portions offer semi-allegorical arrangements of iron and steel construction, while the central section shows a reclining worker against an architectural background, utilizing his leisure time to read. Though they are deliberately less dynamic in mood and arrangement, these panels have a feeling of quiet sorrow typical of Orozco at his best.

During the course of this job (summer, 1932) and again after its completion, Orozco visited Europe. By February 1934, he had returned to Mexico to take his place in a new political and aesthetic configuration.

Siqueiros

1924 to 1934

X

The years between the Preparatoria dismissals in 1924 and the end of the Calles period in 1934 also mark a coming of age for Siqueiros. From the meager fragments that comprise his work of the previous period Siqueiros extended his activity during this phase—when politics and the labor movement monopolized most of his time—to include additional murals, a considerable number of easel pictures, and a quantity of graphics. While Rivera shifted back and forth between a passive and an active political role and Orozco defined his Revolutionary concepts in the paintings already examined, Siqueiros, driven first from the capital and finally from Mexico itself, remained a constant factor in the social evolution of that country and its art. It was in those years also that his new theories and techniques found their initial application.

With the completion of the first murals at the Preparatoria, Siqueiros and a number of associates left for Guadalajara. There he worked for some time as assistant to Amado de la Cueva and Carlos Orozco Romero on a contract for decoration of the University and State Capitol buildings. Meanwhile, Governor Zuno (sponsor of the 1919 Congress of Soldier Artists) also commissioned a new house for himself; Guerrero did most of the decorative work and Zuno himself participated. These people, together with the followers of Siqueiros who had accompanied him to Guadalajara (e.g. Roberto Reyes Pérez), could have created an artistic movement in that city. But Siqueiros lost interest, at least for the time being, and his dynamic energy and leadership were channeled into the social struggle, which he felt was the only way of guaranteeing the artist a place in society.

For a while Siqueiros was involved in this short-lived local renaissance; he worked under de la Cueva at the University, made designs for the workmen who were carving furniture and doors in Zuno's house, and drew up plans for a market building. When, shortly after the University project had begun, de la Cueva was killed in a motorcycle accident and a few months later Zuno was overthrown, Siqueiros was once more out of work as an artist.

During this time Siqueiros had helped direct the miners' strike at Cinco Minas and had assisted in establishing the Miners' Syndicate in various parts of the state of Jalisco. In this connection he published a paper

44

SIQUEIROS. *Proletarian Mother*. OIL

called *El Martillo* (The Hammer), with drawings, poems, and stories contributed by workers. By 1927 he was so active in the labor movement that he was chairman of a delegation of Mexican miners to an international congress in Moscow. (Rivera was in Moscow that same year, showing the Soviets how to paint revolutionary pictures.) The following year Siqueiros became Secretary General of the Confederación Sindical Unitaria de México, and took a leading role in all the important strike movements. In 1929, while a delegate of the Mexican unions to the Continental Workers Congress at Montevideo, he got to Buenos Aires, where he was soon arrested and expelled from Argentina.

In 1930, as a result of participation in a rather violent May Day demonstration, he was imprisoned for about a year in Mexico City. During this period and the following year, which was spent under police surveillance in Taxco, Siqueiros returned to his art. First there was the series of thirteen woodcuts published in 1931 in Taxco by William Spratling. Here also Siqueiros came into contact with Sergei Eisenstein, the Soviet film director then at work on his famous *Que Viva México!* (issued in emasculated form in 1933 as *Thunder over Mexico*). From this unusual personality, Siqueiros acquired his interest in the motion-picture camera and its aesthetics, as well as a concern with the relation of psychology, chemistry, and biology to the plastic arts—all very important for his later development. George Gershwin, the brilliant United States composer, was also in Taxco at this time, as was Hart Crane, the poet. Siqueiros's portrait of the composer at the piano was done in 1936; his 1931 portrait of Crane was later slashed to bits by the poet in a fit of despondency.

The paintings done during these few years run parallel with Siqueiros's absorption of influences from *pulquería* paintings and other folk arts, and continue to show the previously mentioned effect of Aztec masks, with their highly polished surfaces. These works exhibit, in addition, the fruits of Siqueiros's six years as labor organizer—for example, the well-known oil, *Proletarian Mother* (fig. 44) of 1929. Here one may compare the features of the sculpturesquely modeled mother with those of the men carrying the coffin in the earlier *Burial of a Worker* (see fig. 13). There is also an extension from specifically Revolutionary themes to others that deal with everyday life raised to a high level of social and pictorial significance. Little anonymous forms bend over the eyeless mother in her magnificent sorrow and tension; the entire group is enclosed within the encroaching walls, to which the rhythms of the encircling arms and heads offer a powerful counter-movement. These general subjects of 1929–31, such as the *Peasant Mother*, the *Portrait of a Dead Child*, or the *Proletarian Mother*, have a monumental tragedy of their own. They sum up the sorrow of the Mexican people in a new and simpler way.

In 1932, continuing differences with the Mexican government caused Siqueiros to leave the country. He went to Los Angeles, where, in the course of teaching a mural-painting class at the Chouinard Art School, he did his *Meeting in the Street*, a painting that has since disintegrated, owing to the poor materials used. This mural was designed by Siqueiros and was carried out by a group of assistants and pupils—the first example of the Siqueiros painting team, or *equipo*. Among these are a number who have since acquired their own importance as artists: Millard Sheets, Paul Sample, Barse Miller, Merrell Gage, Phil Paradise, Tom Beggs, and others.

In this project the spray gun was brought into play to project Siqueiros's fresco paints on a cement-and-sand base, which dried much more rapidly than the traditional lime-and-sand combination. Existing reproductions of this mural[1] show massive figures and heads that give an impression of sorrow and force. An orator on his soapbox harangues the worker audience listening from their scaffold and from the roof of the building on which they are working. He faces his listeners, who are spread out before him in a kind of *Street Scene* set, giving the work a somewhat staged and theatrical character that takes a good deal away from it, as does the too heavy genre quality.

The 1932 mural[2] in the patio of the Dudley Murphy residence in Santa Monica shows how the Mexican Revolution had turned against itself by the time of Calles. This *Portrait of Mexico*, in the home of a movie director, is dominated by a huge receding pyramid with two women and a child on its steps. At the left a 'Revolutionary' peasant-soldier, with a mask (hypocrisy) hanging from his neck and a cluster of money bags at his feet, clearly reveals the face of ex-President Calles, then the power behind the Mexican government.

During that same year Siqueiros executed a mural for the Plaza Art Center in Los Angeles on a dark cement ground, again with the spray gun and this time with a team of thirty-five United States painters. This third example of outdoor-mural painting, done on a space forty-eight feet by ninety feet, begins to point toward a realization that most of the earlier Mexican murals, inside semi-public buildings such as the Preparatoria or the Ministry of Education, were not being seen by 'the people,' for whom they were presumably intended. *Tropical America*, done in five months with Duco (du Pont Company) industrial paint on Portland cement, was the result of Siqueiros's introduction to the industrial techniques of the United States, which apparently gave him an element lacking in his art up to that point.

Having begun to feel the ostensibly 'archaic' quality of Mexican mural art (according to him, the use of traditional media in traditional buildings), he reasoned that the new language of art, a worker's language,

---

[1] 'California Group Studies Fresco Technique with Siqueiros,' *Art Digest*, N.Y., vol. 6, no. 19, 1 Aug. 1932, p. 13.

[2] 'White Walls and a Fresco in California,' *Arts & Decoration*, vol. 41, no. 2, June 1934.

should be expressed in the materials of the modern world. He turned to outdoor murals, paintings in weather-resistant pigments on either white or natural-colored cement, instead of the traditional slow-drying fresco base. Using a film projector for the outlines and an airbrush for the large surfaces and for modeling the various details—since the cement dried so rapidly—he advanced during 1932 to his most characteristic methods and techniques, to the procedures that differentiate him so sharply from most of his contemporaries. Still lacking at this time was a satisfactory outdoor paint that would withstand rain and sun.

The Plaza Art Center mural showed a crucified peon, a United States eagle perched aggressively at the top of the cross, and a group of Mexicans standing below, shooting at the eagle. The ensuing scandal caused the mural to be whitewashed over, and Siqueiros to leave Los Angeles. From a design point of view, this mural marked a serious advance over earlier works in the counterpoint of rectangular and curved areas and the subordination of the figure to its geometrical background. It was also important as one of the first instances of Siqueiros's later characteristic recessive pyramid, seen much more vividly in the Chillán murals (see fig. 94). We may notice, incidentally, the brusque directness with which Siqueiros challenged the maltreatment of Mexicans in the United States, in contrast to the contemporaneous blandness of the also Marxist Rivera in San Francisco or the symbolic criticism of Orozco at Pomona.

In 1933 Siqueiros was in Argentina to give lectures on Mexican painting. Since the country was already under military dictatorship, the painter spent a short period in jail, but was then permitted to do a mural in the residence of Don Natalio Botana, editor of *La Critica*, in the town of Don Torquato. This work, the so-called *Plastic Study*,[3] brings the painter closer to his mature approach by the addition of silicate paints on dry cement (an important step forward in the realization of impermeable media) and by the use of a curved concave surface. With the latter innovation there begins to emerge Siqueiros's tremendous interest in achieving a certain dynamics of movement that will allow the spectator to participate from within the spaces of the mural by means of its more active, i.e. curved, surfaces. This highly stylized work, with its strongly moving female nudes, its primitive masks and sea shells, was done with the aid of a number of Argentinian artists.

This phase of the painter's life ended with his violent attack on the Rivera New Workers School murals as a 'betrayal of Marxism' (see above, Chap. VIII). Siqueiros also attacked the diluted Renaissancism of Rivera's painting, its lack of originality and ignoring of modern media. Those media Siqueiros himself was developing during the latter part of that period, and he continued to develop them from then on.

---

[3] Illustrated in the monograph, *Siqueiros*, Instituto Nacional de Bellas Artes, Mexico, 1951, fig. 37.

XI | Mural Versus Easel Painting
1924 to 1934

The abrupt termination of the first government mural projects in 1924, the dissolution of the Syndicate in 1925, and the general swing to the right during the 1924–34 Calles period furnish the background for the new non-Revolutionary easel painting of that era.

Although Mexican painting had been 'modernized' to a slight extent during the early Revolutionary years through adoption of the Impressionist methods of Ramos Martínez, the rapid growth of a socially conscious mural art with its specific representational problems arrested that development. Instead of a continuing awareness of the modern school of Paris, there was the powerful and lasting impact of the Rivera school of Revolutionary art. During these early years Orozco was pointing toward a personally evolved Expressionism, without knowledge (so far as we can tell) of its Central European counterpart; the mature art of Siqueiros still lay in the future.

Shut off from the kind of outside influence that was operative in the United States during this period, Mexico, because of its Revolutionary problems and its ever-growing nationalism, remained an aesthetic island. This nationalism, plus the Syndicate belief that easel painting had outlived itself, combined to keep post-Impressionist, Cubist, Fauve, and other contemporary influences out of Mexico. These factors are perhaps also responsible for the fact that there is no museum of modern art in Mexico today. Indeed, until recently there have been very few art galleries. Foreign influences came in—if at all—through illustrated magazines and color reproductions, whenever available.

Against this background of aesthetic isolation we come to the 1924–34 period, when the mural movement was forcibly repressed (with exceptions as mentioned) and the artistic momentum had to find a different outlet. During the late 'twenties a literary group called Los Contemporaneos (The Contemporaries) was formed, with the idea of combating Mexicanism and trying to arouse interest in an international rather than a nationalist culture. In the review of the same name that they published from 1928 to 1931 were included essays and verses by such outstanding figures as Celestino Gorostiza, J. Torres Bodet (a future Minister of Education and Director General of UNESCO), Xavier Villaurrutia (distinguished Tamayo biographer), and Jorge Cuesta. There were offerings by such noteworthy foreign writers as T. S. Eliot, Langston Hughes, Paul Valéry, and Rainer Maria Rilke.

In art The Contemporaries reproduced the works of Picasso, Braque, di Chirico, and others among the Europeans (Villaurrutia said that di Chirico had been the greatest influence in his life, an influence he apparently transmitted to his friend Agustín Lazo). Among Mexican painters, they featured the work of Manuel Rodríguez Lozano, who was influenced by Picasso's classical drawing and the Purist movement; Carlos Mérida, increasingly drawn to the abstract Expressionism of Klee; Agustín Lazo and Carlos Orozco Romero, both influenced by Surrealism; Gabriel Fernández Ledesma, an eclectic modernist; Julio Castellanos, clearly affected by the neo-Classicism of France and Italy during the 'twenties; and Rufino Tamayo, perhaps the outstanding easel painter of Mexico. Tamayo combines with his Mexican-derived background a number of elements stemming from Matisse, Braque, and Picasso; he brings these various factors together in an extremely personal and poetic manner.

Although it is difficult to select from the variegated European influences any one type to characterize Mexican painting during this epoch, the art of Julio Castellanos and that of Agustín Lazo typify a monumental and classically oriented form which seems to predominate. Sometimes this form takes on a Surrealist flavor, as in the distinctive works of Orozco Romero; elsewhere it assumes a more poetic quality, as in Lazo, a solemn hieratic character as in Castellanos, or a mystical essence as in Rodríguez Lozano. But all these men place definite emphasis on the large, isolated, and quiet form (unlike the increasingly abstract and decorative tendencies of Mérida and Tamayo) which may be compared with that of a second monumentalist group of painters in another part of Mexico.

This latter group, known as Bohemia, in the city of Guadalajara, belongs to the same historical period. It includes among its founders such personalities as José Guadalupe Zuno, ex-governor of Jalisco and patron of the arts, and among later members Raúl Anguiano and Jesús Guerrero Galván. These painters were influenced by a rather important German book devoted to New Objectivity or Magic Realism, Franz Roh's *Nach-Expressionismus*, published in Leipzig in 1925 and presented in Spanish as *Realismo Mágico: post-expressionismo* in 1927. From this formulation of a clearly delineated three-dimensional form in an aura of disillusionment, from the comparable neo-Classicism of Picasso and others in France and the *valori plastici* painters of contemporary Italy, came the chief impulse for Mexican easel painting of the late 'twenties and the 'thirties.

We may envisage this intellectual reaction against muralism in Mexico as also partaking of the bitter wine of postwar—in their case post-Revolutionary, or Calles period—disenchantment. Undoubtedly many of these men, especially those in Los Contemporaneos, objected to what seemed to them the stridency of Mexican Revolutionary art. But it is worth noticing that many, including Mérida, Tamayo, Castellanos, and Rodríguez Lozano, had been teachers in the open-air schools in the early 'twenties. Moreover, none of them ever lost sight of his ancient heritage, however much influenced by modern French and other forms of painting.

The monumentalism of Julio Castellanos, for example, with all its reminiscences of European postwar classicism, has a specific Mexican quality as well. His first magnificent nude compositions, dating between 1928 and 1933, show typical Mexican physical forms but no desire on the part of the artist to create picturesque folk types. They betray a poetic melancholy and a plastic definition that represent his and Mexico's version of this international style. Castellanos, who was a follower of Rodríguez Lozano, is important not only for his successful formulation of Mexican Magic Realism but also as a teacher who has influenced many younger men and fostered public art consciousness. One of his best-known paintings, *The Dialogue* (Philadelphia Museum, fig. 45), illustrates in a touching manner the mixture of strong form and controlled poetic feeling.

Along the same lines Manuel Rodríguez Lozano, a little older than his pupil, represents a similar interest in monumental form of a generally Mexicanist but nonpolitical character. We may distinguish between earlier works of this type (from the 'twenties and early 'thirties) and his more formalized Picasso-influenced linear paintings since the middle 'thirties, when he began to develop his own brand of mysticism. This is clearly exemplified in the 1945 mural, *What Have They Done to the People*, painted for the residence of Francisco Sergio Iturbe (Orozco's patron on the House of Tiles mural). Rodríguez Lozano's style has proceeded along the same general path evident in the disturbing mural *Pietà* in the Mexico City Penitentiary and a considerable number of completely personal easel paintings, such as the 1947 *The Parting* (artist's collection, fig. 46). Here his somewhat strained symbolic quality emerges in the starkly designed white horse and blue-garbed man approached by women with mystic gestures, the upper portions of their figures in white, the lower sections in blue or green. The greater part of this picture has a grayish-black background to reinforce its emotional purpose.

Jesús Guerrero Galván may be included in this monumentalized-form group; since the late 'twenties he has produced a number of rather sweetly colored and poetic compositions. Like Castellanos he contributes to the second wave of mural painting in the 'thirties, imparting to his murals the same general quality found in his easel pictures, e.g. the *Image of Mexico* (1950, Dallas Museum of Fine Arts. fig. 47). The gentle poetry of the self-contained figure with two sleeping children about her is augmented by the equally mild colors—gray-blues, violets, and reddish ochres. Guerrero Galván's painting of the 'thirties exhibits a somewhat

45

CASTELLANOS. *The Dialogue*. OIL.
PHILADELPHIA MUSEUM OF ART.
COLL. MR. & MRS. HENRY CLIFFORD, RADNOR, PA.

more formal and sculpturesque quality than is found in many of his later easel works, which tend increasingly toward the decorative. His 1942 mural at the University of New Mexico, *Union of the Americas Joined by Liberty*, and the 1952 work in the National Electrical Commission Building near Chapultepec Park in Mexico City still show the adherence to the classicism of Picasso characteristic of the late 'twenties.

On the Surrealist side is the influential Carlos Orozco Romero, who came to Mexico City in 1925 after a year of European travel. With Carlos Mérida he directed the Galería de Arte Moderno, which can be credited with the first important exhibitions of the work of José Clemente Orozco

123

46
RODRÍGUEZ LOZANO. *The Parting*. OIL.
MEXICO CITY, COLL. THE PAINTER.

and Rufino Tamayo. Since the early 'thirties both Orozco Romero and
Tamayo have been doing French-influenced figure painting in which
color and abstract form have been of paramount importance. By the
middle 'thirties Orozco Romero had added a Surrealist humor and
fantasy that give his work its unique quality in the Mexican school, e.g.
Los Hilos (1939, National Institute of Fine Arts, fig. 48). Here imaginative
forms, deep space penetration, and vivid coloristic expression are brought
together. (Apart from the Contemporaneos group is the formal Surrealist
work of the late Frida Kahlo, which is closely related to the European

124

47

tradition and in many instances shows structural ability of a high order.)

To the degree that Magic Realism verges on Surrealist expression, Agustín Lazo may be linked with the latter group. A talented scenic designer as well as painter, he contributed during 1931–2 a series of brilliant designs for the Teatro de Orientación, which was under the direction of Celestino Gorostiza of the Contemporaneos. Here, as in their magazine, this company of intellectuals, by presenting the works of Pirandello, Giraudoux, Molnar, and other non-Mexican playwrights, did a great deal to diversify the cultural interests of their country.

48

OROZCO ROMERO. *Los Hilos*. OIL.
MEXICO CITY, INSTITUTO NACIONAL
DE BELLAS ARTES.

To the Surrealism of Orozco Romero and Lazo must be added the Abstract Surrealism of Carlos Mérida, which belongs to the same epoch and general development in the late 'twenties and early 'thirties. After early training in the studios of Paris (Van Dongen and Modigliani), the Guatemalan Mérida came to the United States during the First World War, and developed here his first series of folklore pictures. These were shown in Mexico in 1921 and had tremendous impact and subsequent influence on the growing nativist movement.

After his association with the Syndicate and its dissolution in 1925, Mérida went back to Europe in 1927, where he produced his famous *Images de Guatemala*. At this point his earlier nativist style, e.g. the lyrically primitivistic *Farm Hands* of 1924, changed in the direction of an increasingly abstract and Surrealist formulation. In the well-known *Profiles*

126

49
MÉRIDA. *Watercolor no. 29.*
WATER COLOR, 1932.
NEW YORK, THE WELDON COLL.

watercolor he juxtaposed a number of outlined figures—similar to those in his earlier works—around one large profiled head that suggests Aztec painting. By the early 'thirties his watercolors had lost much of their relationship to concrete forms and move first in the direction of Kandinsky in an emotive play of nonobjective forms and then toward Klee with a humorous and evocative arrangement of more concrete shapes (fig. 49). Mérida has had great influence as an example and as a teacher. He has led a constant series of experimental developments that have perpetuated among Mexicans the idea of painting as painting.

Before Mérida turned away from folkloric painting during the 'thirties, Rufino Tamayo seems to have been the first to bring up the question of easel painting and to have advanced the idea of painting for its own sake. Born of Zapotec parents in Oaxaca in southwestern Mexico, Tamayo passed his childhood in the tropics—a fact that, in the words of Villaurrutia, 'filled his hands with color.'[1] When he lost his parents, he came to Mexico City to live with an aunt, who worked as a fruit seller. In helping at this work, he received vivid formal and coloristic impressions of the excitingly tinted and arranged fruits that appear so often in his later paintings in strong shapes and brilliant hues.

In 1917 Tamayo went to study at the Academy of San Carlos, where he was in the group with Agustín Lazo, Antonio Ruiz, Francisco Díaz de León, Gabriel Fernández Ledesma, and Julio Castellanos. He was a special friend of Lazo, with whom he worked out a good many mutual problems, especially those related to modern European painting, toward which they were drawn through illustrations in books and magazines. Many of these artists were to become part of the Contemporaneos group later. Tamayo left the Academy in 1918 to study on his own, and in 1921 was appointed head of the Department of Ethnographic Drawing in the National Museum of Archaeology. He was only twenty-one when he was again exposed to the precolonial material he had experienced as a child in Oaxaca. His teaching in the open-air schools during the 'twenties has already been mentioned.

The first important paintings by Tamayo during the middle 'twenties were exhibited at his first one-man show, in Mexico City in 1926—in an empty store on the Avenida Madero, since there were apparently no galleries at the time. They present a blend of simple, everyday themes with French techniques. Fauve still-life arrangements alternate with monumentalized figure pieces that relate Tamayo to the general postwar classicism of his contemporaries. These works may be exemplified by the *Still Life* in the collection of Stanley Marcus in Dallas (1928, fig. 50), featuring the beloved fruits painted with reference to Braque and arranged with the symmetry characteristic of Mexican fruit vendors in the markets. The artist's intention here and in all his subsequent works is to organize the two-dimensional picture surface in the manner we have come to recognize as 'modern' but with his own resonant and personal color quality, which was still comparatively dark at that time. The more classical works of this period may be illustrated by the monumental brooding *Self-Portrait* of 1931 in the Salo Hale collection.

Whereas Revolutionary painters consciously refer to the ancient arts of Mexico, Tamayo has tended to depend more on his personal experiences with handicrafts of today, such as the colorful and cleverly distorted *Judas* figures with their brilliant colors applied to papier-mâché.[2] Their elongated bodies and tiny heads, their angular planes are echoed especially in the latter-day works of Tamayo.

But the difference between Tamayo and the social painters is far more

---

[1] *Tamayo—20 años de su labor artística*, Instituto Nacional de Bellas Artes, Mexico, 1948.

[2] Beautiful examples are reproduced in *Espacios*, no. 3, Spring, 1949, in an article by Diego Rivera ('Los Judas'), an ardent collector of these forms.

50

TAMAYO. *Still Life*. OIL.
DALLAS, TEXAS,
COLL. STANLEY MARCUS.

PHOTO JOSÉ VERDE

profound; it is a basic difference of aesthetic purpose and the very meaning of art. His belief in absolute values of form and color is expressed in
the following words:

It seems to me that to pretend that its (i.e. painting's) value is derived from other elements, particularly from ideological content which is
not otherwise related to plastic content, cannot but be considered a fal-
lacy which can temporarily deceive the unwary, but which Time, ruthless
enemy of everything specious, will undertake to refute.[3]

It is significant that as early as 1929 Tamayo is greeted by anti-Rev-
olutionary critics as the 'leader of a new Mexican school of painting'[4]
and as the symbol of a counter-Revolutionary trend. Such critics felt that

---

[3] In the same issue of *Espacios*, 'Unas palabras de Rufino Tamayo.'
[4] Jorge Montaño, 'Rufino Tamayo: Leader of a New Mexican School of
Painting,' *Mexican Life*, Nov. 1929.

129

the Mexican Revolution was properly a revolution of the middle class and not of the proletariat, and that the art direction of Tamayo and his associates represented an acknowledgment of the final stabilization of the movement. For periodicals devoted to the interests of the Calles regime and those of foreign capital in Mexico, this view was not too surprising. Writers in these journals hailed what they called the 'failure' of the Syndicate as a sign of the fact that the Revolution was misdirected in its earlier phases. They believed, further, that the Mexican artistic Revolution was no revolution but really 'pseudo-communistic' and that the peasants shown in those early paintings are a 'cross between Morelos Zapatistas and Russian moujiks.'[5]

Some Mexican artists have become the favorites of the reactionaries as they have escaped into the safe paths of linear mysticism or decorative charm. This is scarcely true of Tamayo, however, whose art remains progressive in essence just as his feeling for Mexico and its people is continually expressed in his own indigenous manner, as well as by constant reference to current ideas. Thus his water-color sketch for a government mural commission that was not executed, *The Conquest of Mexico* (1932), is a poetic and evocative interpretation of a scene that had been handled in a much more representational way by the Riveristas. Here the painter uses for the first time the idea of the colonial horseman. This theme, later developed as a centaur by Siqueiros, reflects the superstitious fear of the Indians, who had never seen horses and who thought of the rider as growing out of the animal.

Just as he gives tremendous pictorial interest to this theme, Tamayo also presents *Juárez* in 1932 (Inés Amor collection), a *Glorification of Zapata* (Miguel Covarrubias collection), *Call to Revolution* (private collection, Mexico City), and two versions of the *Workers' Rhythm*, one in the Carrillo Gil collection (see fig. 51), the other also privately owned—all but the *Juárez* done in 1935. Mention of the existence of these and similar works is intended not to underline Tamayo's activity in this area but to show that he does possess Revolutionary awareness. More important, these paintings are further evidence of his plastic handling of everyday as well as ordinary aesthetic themes within the Fauve, Cubist, or other disciplines. These products of the 'thirties mark the beginning of his first 'bright period,' in addition to a new feeling for spatial relationships which came through a direct and first-time contact with original works of modern art, when he took his first show to New York and stayed there from late 1926 to mid-1928. There is a considerable feeling for backward and forward movement in pictures of this era, typified by the first *Workers' Rhythm* (fig. 51), in which the dominant blues and blue-grays are played off against the brown bodies, black trees, and effective yellow moon in the upper left-hand corner.

---

[5] Guillermo Rivas, 'More Walls to Paint,' *Mexican Life*, Dec. 1930.

51

TAMAYO. *Workers' Rhythm*. OIL. MEXICO CITY, COLL. DR. A. CARRILLO GIL.

During the 'thirties also, Tamayo evolved a deeply spatial type of picture, such as the *New York from a Terrace* (1938), which conveys the sense of lonesomeness and distance often found in Surrealist pictures, but again with a personal handling of material or ideas taken from outside sources. This work has its own poetic quality, like many others of the late 'thirties, though without their frequent reference to the Mexican milieu in landscape, figures, costumes, and so on. The conception of space is not entirely that of the Europeans. Here space, while vast and penetrating, does not hint at endlessness, but is rather a carefully defined plastic entity with a beginning and an end, within which Tamayo's characters play their parts.

The pictures of this period begin to show the warm but thinly brushed-on and smooth colors that are absorbed into the fabric of the canvas: light-blue, pink, and rose tonalities that give his paintings their Mexican quality in spite of generalized themes. The added accents of yellow, black, or brown, the subtle transitions from one intensity to another within a generally limited palette, lend Tamayo's work its peculiar sensitivity and distinction. Whether applied to easel painting, in which he was the leading spirit from 1926 on, or to mural painting, which he has practiced from time to time, this subtlety of tone and hue, this delicate balance of intensities of the same color, is retained. Against the deliberate primitivism of his forms, these almost imperceptible shifts offer an interesting contrast, a quiet but effective aesthetic tension.

However outstanding Tamayo's contribution—and it can be argued that he is the foremost painter of the Mexican school in the modern sense —the fact remains that he has been an outside element in the Mexican situation. Because of lack of encouragement in his own country, where the growing group of collectors has concentrated for the most part on the work of the 'big three' (who have also been favored in the granting of government commissions), Tamayo finally decided in 1938 to shift the center of his activities to New York. For the next decade and more he spent the major part of each year there, the summers in Mexico.

During the years preceding this decision, there had always been the hope of achieving a success at home. In 1929 he joined Rivera (who had become director of the Academy of San Carlos) in an attempt to improve the teaching methods there, but the early resignation of the older man under double pressures from left and right cut short this activity in 1930. The following year Tamayo was appointed to a small Council for the Fine Arts within the Ministry of Education, and in 1932 he became one of the many short-lived chiefs of the Department of Plastic Arts. His attempt to improve art teaching in the elementary schools was brought to a stop by the end of the Abelardo Rodríguez administration under Calles. Tamayo's last important work during this period of change was the unfinished series of mural decorations in 1933 for the Conservatory of Music in Mexico City, of which the gigantesque and somber central figure of *Music* is a powerful echo of the precolonial experiences of the painter. Other figures include a nude *Intuition*, a clothed *Intelligence*, *Humanity*, *Song*, and so on.

With the new administration of President Cárdenas, the emphasis was once again on socially significant ideas and actions. The exiled Revolutionary artists began to flock back, and there was little hope for Tamayo's kind of art in Mexico—at least for the time being. After a brief stay in New York in 1936, where he had gone as a delegate from the L.E.A.R. (League of Revolutionary Writers and Artists) together with Siqueiros and Orozco, he decided in 1938 to remain there. His development during the subsequent years and his return to Mexico to become once more part of the movement belong to a later phase of Mexican easel and mural painting.

132

The Cárdenas Period

1934 to 1940

XII

In the last months of the dying Calles era, the final year of Abelardo Rodríguez's term of office, a number of distinct improvements were made in Mexico as public sentiment grew against the more blatant reactionary measures. Agrarian reform was re-established on a large scale. The progressive Narciso Bassols was made Minister of Education, to the considerable benefit of Mexican art. And a candidate acceptable to the liberal elements was agreed to by Calles as the next president: Lázaro Cárdenas.

From Calles's point of view, Cárdenas was the ideal candidate. He enjoyed the support of the army, labor, and farm elements, and although a cabinet member, was not considered a mere puppet. But if the Iron Man of Mexico thought he had secured another figurehead president, he was soon disillusioned, for Cárdenas even before his July 1934 election took his job very seriously. In the seven months preceding the *pro forma* election, Cárdenas traveled more than 18,000 miles by car, mule, train, and foot, 'campaigning' up and down Mexico and penetrating into corners of the land no politician had ever before visited. He simply wanted to find out what was going on and what was bothering his future constituents; and if he appeared to many of them as an incarnation of Quetzalcoatl, a god come to bring once more the benefits of civilization, it is not altogether surprising.

In view of the misunderstandings in both Mexico and the United States concerning Cárdenas's political philosophy, it is worth quoting from one of the hundreds of speeches made during this incredible journey:

The main road of the new phase of the Revolution is the march of Mexico toward socialism, a movement which departs equally from the anachronistic norms of classical liberalism and from those which are proper to communism that is undergoing an experiment in Soviet Russia. It departs from individualist liberalism, because this system cannot give rise to anything but the exploitation of man by man, to the unrestrained absorption of natural resources and to individual egoisms. It departs from state communism, because our people are not the kind to adopt a system which deprives them of the full enjoyment of their efforts, nor do they want to substitute the individual boss with the boss state.[1]

After the election, Cárdenas showed his sympathy for the workers by encouraging strikers in 1935, by pushing agrarian reform with such energy that certain Callista properties were taken over, and by daring to close down illegal gambling establishments owned by the followers of Calles. When Calles threatened to take measures against him, Cárdenas responded with disconcerting rapidity by firing the majority of his Calles-picked cabinet and replacing them with a reform group. The first bloodless revolution in the history of Mexico had taken place before anyone was aware of what was happening. Opportunists swarmed from Calles to Cárdenas, while in the provinces Callista governors fell like overripe fruit as laborers and peasants demonstrated against them. In 1936 a last attempt on the part of Calles and his old friend Morones to unseat Cárdenas resulted merely in their being quietly sent across the border into the United States, where Don Plutarco complained to reporters that Mexico was becoming a dictatorship of the proletariat.

Cárdenas proceeded to eliminate the last Calles elements from his cabinet and to tour the country again, inviting suggestions and permitting free press and political criticism. His greatest support came from a re-organized and strengthened labor movement which in 1936 under Lombardo Toledano had formed the C.T.M. (Confederación de Trabajadores Mexicanos), an industrial-union arrangement similar to the C.I.O. in the United States. A skillful politician, however, the president kept the peasants, labor, and the army apart. The peasant groups were organized into a national league, with their militia armed as a check on the army; regular army wages and morale were improved, especially for the rank and file; and labor was encouraged to build up its own organization—but none of these groups had too much power. The grip of the professional lawyer-politicians on national affairs was weakened by the reorganization of the old P. N. R., the government party. Renamed the P.R.M. (Party of the Mexican Revolution), it now admitted peasant and union delegates and did away with dues for officeholders.

In the reformist environment of the new administration, cultural and artistic organizations were formed to express the direction of the new Revolutionary program and to support it: the L.E.A.R. (League of Revolutionary Writers and Artists) and then the Workshop of Popular Graphic Art (Taller de Gráfica Popular). As for the reforms themselves, they featured an aggressive redistribution of the land; by 1940, this amounted to twice as much as all the previous governments together had been able to accomplish. Large co-operative farms were established with grants of seeds and machinery. New schools and consumer co-operatives

---

[1] Todd Downing, *The Mexican Earth*, Doubleday Doran & Co., N.Y., 1940, p. 286.

were also set up, and in general the living standards of the farm and factory population were considerably raised.

Most spectacular was the successful assertion of Mexico's sovereignty over its own natural resources, culminating in the 1938 expropriation of the oil companies, which had refused to abide by government regulations, paying unsatisfactory wages and selling Mexican oil at a higher price in Mexico than in other countries. The great furor this step aroused in the United States was equaled by the jubilation of the people of Mexico—including many artists, to whom this event offered a heroic theme. But the calm attitude of the Roosevelt administration, which refused to be stampeded into violent reprisal, resulted in a negotiated settlement. Yet the boycott of Mexican oil organized by the oil companies compelled the Cárdenas government to trade oil for machinery with fascist Germany, Italy, and Japan, an unenviable position for the only Western Hemisphere government that had actively supported the Loyalists in Spain during the civil war of 1936–9. The world-wide activities of the Nazis brought the growth of fascist-minded groups in Mexico, while the eventual Franco victory in Spain encouraged a certain amount of Falangist activity.

Not only had Cárdenas shipped arms to Spain but he now welcomed the Loyalist refugees in flight from Franco. That this was not because of alleged Stalinist sympathies is seen in the fact that he also gave asylum to that arch enemy of the Soviet government, Leon Trotsky. Yet even the milder conservatives in Mexico claimed not only that the president's policies were economically unsound (a great deal of money was spent on rural schools and co-operative farms) but also that the communists had too much influence in the administration. But this time most of the opposition was willing to wait for the next election instead of sounding the call to revolt—a distinct advance for Mexico.

Cárdenas himself was not a communist. This appears very clear from all the available facts and from various public acts, including his refusal to recognize the Soviet Union. He was inclined toward a modified socialism in which the workers would own the factories on a profit-sharing basis. At the same time it must be recognized that in this period of new Revolutionary ferment and general Popular Front activity the left would surely make definite advances. Nowhere is this more evident than in the cultural realm, which, even under the limited program of 1920–24, had been far ahead of the government. During this later period, however, a systematic organizing of the nation's cultural leaders and the fight against fascism both at home and abroad put the more radical writers and artists into an advantageous position. The situation is mirrored in the award of important government commissions to left-wing individuals and the denial of similar opportunities to those who were not part of that pattern. On a positive level, it is seen in the murals for the new schools in the Federal District and the widespread activity of the Workshop of Popular Graphic Art. The other side is reflected in the ambiguous position of

Diego Rivera, who did few murals at this time, and in the fact that most of Orozco's activity during the Cárdenas administration was in Guadalajara rather than in Mexico City, under state rather than federal sponsorship. In the case of Tamayo, the situation led, as we have seen, to his abandoning Mexico for the United States.

In 1934 the renewed activity of politico-cultural groups like the earlier Syndicate emerged in the organization of the L.E.A.R. by Leopoldo Méndez, Pablo O'Higgins, and others, to unite antifascist intellectuals.[2] Painters, it should be remembered, started this group; the same painting community is still the most vital part of a Mexican cultural scene in which literature, theater, or music of a comparable quality is relatively rare.

In 1930 and 1931, under the Calles regime, the more radical artists had had to work underground; they were harassed by the police, and their posters were regularly torn down. With the toleration exhibited in the Cárdenas period, it became possible for a group of artists to gather in the studio of the United States-born Pablo O'Higgins (former Rivera assistant) to plan a new art movement for the masses through the L.E.A.R. This group included O'Higgins, Méndez, Alfredo Zalce, Antonio Pujol, and Angel Bracho. They soon found in the recently completed Abelardo Rodríguez Market a series of walls that would fit their purpose, i.e. an area that was really public and unlike the earlier off-the-street walls of the Preparatoria, the Ministry of Education, and so on. In 1934 they started on this assignment, which was perhaps the first co-operative painting job done in Mexico; as already mentioned, Siqueiros had directed a number of team projects in the United States a few years earlier. (During this later period, however, Siqueiros was head of the League against War and Fascism, doing relatively little painting and no murals.)

The market project was carried out under the aegis of the government Central Department, with Rivera as the ostensible technical supervisor, although he does not seem to have functioned at all. Among those active in the work were the Mexicans Bracho, Pujol, Ramón Alva Guadarrama, Miguel Tzab, Raúl Gamboa, and Pedro Rendón, and the 'North-Americans' O'Higgins and Grace and Marion Greenwood. However appealing the idea of a collective art enterprise may be, the fact remains that the Abelardo Rodríguez murals are by and large among the least effective projects of this kind. With the possible exception of Pujol's panel on the dangers of mining—showing a frightened but militant miner dropping down into the pit—other murals here leave much to be desired both in drawing (generally inferior Rivera) and in color. More successful as a L.E.A.R. group project is the 1936 collective mural done in the entrance hallways of the government printing office, the Talleres Gráficos de la Nación, by O'Higgins, Méndez, Zalce, and Fernando Gamboa.

That same year the L.E.A.R. sent as delegates to the First American

---

[2] Verna Millán, op. cit.

Artists Congress in New York Siqueiros, Orozco, and Tamayo.[3] In 1937, as a result of the infusion of fresh blood into the L.E.A.R. through Spanish refugee intellectuals, there was held the Congress of Mexican Artists, the first of its kind in Mexico; it was particularly significant at that stage of the Spanish civil war, since the Loyalists received the Congress's full support. In this activity as in its other ones, the L.E.A.R. was led by the artists. Indeed it is claimed that the inclusion of writers in the organization was ultimately its ruin, presumably because these idealists were inclined more to talk than to action, Another factor was that by 1935 more of them had government jobs—but not as writers.

Yet in spite of this disparity between professional painters for whom contracts were signed by L.E.A.R. and intellectualist writers who would discuss Revolutionary problems but do nothing about them, the organization filled such an important need that it became an unofficial but powerful clearing house for all cultural activities. Its magazine, *Frente a Frente*, was printed gratis at the government printing plant, and important sympathizers contributed generously of their money. By the end of 1937, however, the latter dropped away, and since there was no arrangement for dues, there were no funds to carry on. The opportunist politicians who had used L.E.A.R. when they needed it also disappeared; and careerists within the organization had done a great deal of harm by taking advantage of its position to further their own interests. In November 1938 the League dissolved, but it had already been supplanted by the Workshop for Popular Graphic Art, strictly an artists' organization, which was formed in 1937.

The Workshop, or Taller, as it is generally known, was consciously organized to continue the traditions first of the Syndicate and then of the L.E.A.R.[4] Under the leadership of Méndez, O'Higgins, and Luis Arenal and encouraged by Siqueiros, the founding members also included Bracho, Pujol, Zalce, Ignacio Aguirre, Raúl Anguiano, Jesús Escobedo, Everardo Ramírez, and Gonzalo de la Paz Pérez. Within a relatively short time the Taller numbered sixteen members, their activity symbolically centered about an old lithographic press labeled 'Paris, 1871,' which is believed to have been used by the Paris Commune.

The activities of the Taller have been communal in every way, including group criticism in which all work is reviewed by the members as a whole, their criteria being primarily dramatic effectiveness of message rather than the formal concepts that generally characterize modern art. This is necessarily the case for the kinds of projects undertaken by the group. These include their first poster in 1937 greeting the newly formed C.T.M. (Federation of Mexican Workers); the caricatures dealing with the 1938 expropriation of foreign-owned oil fields; the illustrated popular

---

[3] See bibliography under American Artists Congress.
[4] See their *T G P México* album, La Estampa Mexicana, Mexico, 1949.

calendars done for the Workers' University; the 1938 and 1939 posters against fascism; and the series of prints entitled *The Spain of Franco*. Day by day they reacted to the tumultuous political events of that time throughout the world, turning out thousands of colored handbills with the words of the traditional *corridos*, or popular songs, or with the Posada-derived *calaveras* (skeleton figures) that have long been used effectively for popularizing picture messages to the people.

Inevitably these artists brought to a climax the tradition of graphic art, so strong in Mexico since the liberal and anticlerical movements of the late nineteenth century and continued first in the prints published by Vanegas Arroyo through the Posada period and then in the periodicals of the Revolutionary period proper: *La Vanguardia*, *El Machete*, *El Libertador*, and others. In addition to these traditional and Revolutionary sources, the members of the Taller feel themselves influenced by José Clemente Orozco as the great graphic master of modern Mexico, whose general style has become the basis for the work of many younger graphic men. It has been seen how during the 'thirties Orozco moved from a monumental classical form to a more Expressionistic, dissolved type of painting, stressing the whiplash stroke and the dynamically moving figure, using the brush almost as a colored pencil. Through this work (California, Dartmouth, Palacio de Bellas Artes, see fig. 56) and through his lithographs beginning in 1926 and his etchings beginning in 1935, Orozco had a great deal indeed to offer the members of the Taller.

This affinity is revealed at its most effective in an outstanding member of the Taller, Leopoldo Méndez (b. 1902). His tragic memorial to the two hundred school-teachers murdered by religious fanatics in the rural districts, the series of seven lithographs in *In the Name of Christ*, is one of the most moving creations of modern Mexican art. Produced in 1939, the little volume consists of seven scenes of the murders committed by the Cristeros, with adjoining newpaper or other comment on the event. The scene showing the brutal attack on *profesor* Arnulfo Sosa Portillo (fig. 52) has on the opposite page a summary from *El Universal* of 7 April 1937. This tells how a mob of armed men attacked a small village, committing the usual depredations, and after setting fire to the school killed the teacher with their machetes. His body was found in the city hall, where he had fled for shelter but where he had been abandoned by the fleeing municipal authorities. In a lithograph of this kind Méndez is probably at his dynamic best, with a rare intensity of movement and linear expressiveness.

He is also effective in the somber tragedy of the later *Deportation to Death* (1943). This linoleum cut is part of *The Black Book of Nazi Terror in Europe*,[5] a project in which the artists of the Taller added drawings and engravings to one hundred and forty photographs and official records

---

[5] *El Libro Negro del Terror Nazi en Europa*, El Libro Libre, Mexico, 1943.

52

MÉNDEZ. *The Assassination of Profesor Arnulfo Sosa Portillo.*
LITHOGRAPH FROM *En Nombre de Cristo . . .*

gathered by leading antifascist refugee intellectuals in Mexico. Here the huddled masses of frightened humanity, reminiscent of Orozco, are revealed in Méndez's brilliant light and dark contrasts. Their unending tragedy is symbolized by a deeply receding perspective of freight cars carrying the doomed Jews to their death.

On a somewhat different level, the work of the 'North-American' Pablo O'Higgins (b. 1904) in the Taller—as distinct from his early and some-what Riveresque mural painting—veers from a poetic, melancholy feeling for the poor of Mexico, e.g. *A Dog's Life* (lithograph, 1938) or the touching *Man of the Twentieth Century* (lithograph, 1943), to a more overt social expression. In his Posada-inspired *Calavera de la Justicia* (linoleum cut, 1951, fig. 53) a figure dressed in cap and gown (the judge stereotype)

53

O'HIGGINS. *Calavera de la Justicia.* LINOLEUM CUT.

PHOTO COURTESY TALLER DE GRÁFICA POPULAR

54

ARENAL. *Head of an Indian Woman*. LITHOGRAPH.
COLL. THE AUTHOR.

dances with the skeleton whore (presumably subverted justice) on a banner labeled 'Rights of the Working Class.' This is typical of the satirical illustrations done by the group in general. (It is interesting that O'Higgins was co-editor of a monograph on Posada published by Mexican Folkways in 1937.)

Although a good deal of Taller activity is concerned with group projects of a political nature, there are individual plates which, while distinctly propagandistic in tone, are done in the tradition of the fine-arts print. Some of the best work of the Taller members is to be found in this latter category, including plates that often have no specific topical purpose but which retain a broad humanistic quality and social sympathy.

The sculpturesque *Head of an Indian Woman* (fig. 54) by Luis Arenal (b. 1908) suggests the magnificent three-dimensionality of Siqueiros's

55

MORA. *Miner*. LITHOGRAPH.

forms. Arenal had worked with the older painter on the Chouinard School murals in Los Angeles. On his return to Mexico, he involved himself in the League against War and Fascism and became one of the founders of the L.E.A.R. Sent to New York in 1936 as one of the delegates to the Artists Congress, he remained to paint a mural in Bellevue Hospital and to join the Siqueiros Experimental Workshop set up in New York in 1936 to study new media. Later that year he was back in Mexico as one of the founders of the Taller. Although primarily interested in large forms of the *Indian Woman* type, Arenal has also done sensitive landscape rendering, such as the *Indians of Guerrero* (lithograph, 1943).[6]

The Bolivian Roberto Berdecio (b. 1910) arrived in Mexico in 1934. He became a member of L.E.A.R. and was sent with the 1936 delegation to New York, where he worked in the Siqueiros Workshop with Arenal and Pujol. Berdecio shows a sense of plastic organization that places him apart from many of the other Taller artists. His delicate *Head of a Girl* (1947), for example, is a sensitively beautiful lithographic drawing that may well owe something to Siqueiros, but the poetry of line is entirely his own. The *Tepoztlán* lithograph of the same year is a subtle study in surface textures and curvilinear rhythms for their own artistic qualities.

A combination of effective compositional values and human interest is achieved in Francisco Mora's *Miner* (lithograph, 1945, fig. 55). Light and dark contrasts help establish depth, while the contrasting oval and angular rhythms of the primary planes give interest to this bent figure emerging from the earth. Mora (b. 1922) is one of the younger members of the Taller.

Alfredo Zalce (b. 1908), a leading painter in Mexico today, worked as an art educator from 1930 to 1934. He was liaison man for L.E.A.R., and opened his own Cultural Missions areas in the provinces during 1935–40. A founding member of the Taller, he has contributed such notable works as the well-known series of *Estampas de Yucatán* (1945), illustrated by *The Fisherman* (lithograph, 1945), whose beautiful simplicity is equaled only by its primitive strength and directness. It is in some ways one of the finest prints produced by this variegated group of Mexican artists, with their American and European members, sympathizers, and occasional visiting artists (cf. fig. 109).

Other notable members of the group include Pujol, Aguirre, Anguiano, Bracho, Escobedo, José Chávez Morado, Francisco Dosamantes, Arturo García Bustos, Isidoro Ocampo, and Antonio Villagra C. Many of them have made contributions of value to the development of Mexican art: Villagra with his archaeological work in Bonampak; Anguiano, Chávez Morado, Aguirre, Pujol, and others, who have distinguished themselves in painting as well as graphics and other fields. Although we may perhaps speak of a Taller style, especially as applied to propaganda work (e.g. Aguirre's *Zapata*), each of these men has something personal to say, something that with varying degrees of effectiveness reflects the dynamics of the age of Cárdenas and the momentum it generated into the period following.

---

[6] This and other Taller prints are reproduced in the *T G P México* cited previously.

56

OROZCO. *Katharsis*, central portion. FRESCO. PALACIO DE BELLAS ARTES, MEXICO CITY.

The relative artistic positions of Mexico's leading painters change considerably during the period from 1934 to 1940. In the mural, Orozco emerges as the outstanding figure—first because of the intrinsic quality of his stupendous works, second because of the influence he begins to exert on the younger men, particularly the graphic artists but also some of the muralists. In easel painting, Tamayo appears as the leader of the non-Revolutionary group, while Siqueiros, in spite of his many outside activities, produces enough of his typical sculpturesque figures to dominate the politically oriented side of this art. At the same time Siqueiros finally hits his stride in mural painting with the exciting staircase in the Electricians Union building. Rivera's murals during this six-year period include one new government commission, in the Palacio de Bellas Artes. Then, after the completion of the long-delayed staircase project in the National Palace, his mural activity is confined to the abortive Hotel Reforma affair. From 1936 to 1940 his work is limited to easel pictures: imaginative landscapes, meticulous portraits, the series of studies of a well-known United States Negro woman dancer, and a number of fine genre pieces.

Orozco's great murals of this period begin with a large rectangular wall area in the Palacio de Bellas Artes (1934). It is a bloody picture of the violent conflict between modern man and the chaotic mechanized world that surrounds and tries to overwhelm him (fig. 56). By the same token, it is a well-integrated and well-composed symbol of the eternal struggle between men, of wars and especially of class wars, of the oppression of the poor by the rich.

In Dartmouth the philosophical position of Orozco seemed pessimistic, even hopeless, with Christ returning to destroy His Cross. Here in the Palacio mural, which the painter calls *Katharsis*, or purgation, there is a solution through purging or destruction of this horrible world. This is also typical of the solution the German Expressionists gave in an earlier period, before the First World War. In contrast to the rational and optimistic *Man at the Crossroads* by Rivera on the same floor of this building (also 1934), Orozco's *Katharsis* (it has also been called *Strife* and *Modern Civilization*) is a flaming symbol of the tortured and unhappy state of mankind.

Like the earlier *Prometheus* and the slightly later Guadalajara murals, the work is dominated by powerful diagonal thrusts. The two struggling central figures lean to the left and set the mood of the entire piece. One is a nude man (brown, flecked with green and black); his head is seen as part of a group of heads at the immediate left; the upper part of his body emerges against the red flames of revolt that complete the top of the wall. The other is a clothed figure into whose white-shirted back the first man is plunging a dagger. A powerful nude brown leg thrusts to the right and is braced against a steel girder to accentuate diagonal movement and to isolate the two horrible female heads at the lower right of the mural, part of a group of caricatures along the lower section of the wall that symbolize lechery and decadence. Between these two heads and the third full-length whore at the left are two diagonally placed rifles that parallel the struggling men in the center.

These women are derived only in part from the early caricature style of the Preparatoria, and represent a long evolution in drawing and print studies of this allegorical problem. The laughing female figure lying full length is the climax of these studies; compositionally, it closes the un-balanced receding pyramid of the center of the mural. A brown-haired, gold-toothed creature at the right gives way to the yellow-green hair and red face of the center caricature; then comes the vicious full-length figure at the left. The upper part of this body is in rich, sensuous reddish-pink; the lower part, from the belly down, is in a Toulouse-Lautrec color of evil greenish-tan.

We may consider the central portion of this painting either as a series of diagonals (the flexed legs of the whore, the men's backs, the down-pointed guns) or as an inclined pyramid, at either side of which appear contrasting gray-colored symbols of machinery that oppress man. Man-kind is seen immediately adjacent to this machinery both in the form of oppressed and dead people (upper and lower right and lower left) and in the form of those rebelling against the mechanized world. The latter force is represented in the powerful leftward movement of the naked protagonist of revolt who kills the clothed man amid the broken and falling rifles. From his outthrust diagonal leg that rejects the girder on which an open safe rests, the action moves symbolically left against the flaming fires of revolt, with the adjoining figures—those in rebellion against society—raising clenched fists. The symbolic groups of the defeated and the rebellious fall away from the main pyramid into the corners or parallel its diagonalities.

The main tonalities of this wall are the red of the background flames, the flag of the upper right-hand corner, the red tones in the women's bodies and in the center guns; the gray of the machinery that oppresses

57

OROZCO. FRESCO. DOME AND WALL OF LECTURE
HALL, UNIVERSITY OF GUADALAJARA.

humanity; the green of the lower part of the great whore's body, the hair
of the second whore, and occasional green accents as on the body of the
main protagonist.

This mural remains the only significant work accomplished by Orozco
in the capital during the Cárdenas period. Whether because of increasing
political pressures or because of accidental circumstances, the bulk of
Orozco's work at this time was done in Guadalajara between 1936 and
1939, ending with a portable mural in 1940 for the Museum of Modern
Art exhibition in New York.

His murals of 1923–6 and the easel and graphic works up to 1930 had
stressed the dignity of man and had emphasized (as in the Revolutionary
drawings) a certain compassionate quality. About 1930 he turned to a
new form of expression. First in the Pomona mural (1930) and then in
the Dartmouth work (1932–4) he shifted to an art of Expressionistic and /
or symbolic terror, showing the cruelties and hungers of the world. In
general, these works and the later Palacio and Guadalajara murals

58

OROZCO. *The Scientist* and portion
of *The Worker*. FRESCO.
DOME OF LECTURE HALL,
UNIVERSITY OF GUADALAJARA.

betray a far more pessimistic outlook, in which the bestial power of the
world's attacks on man and his own disillusionment at its cruelties seem
to be increasingly stressed.

Called to Guadalajara in 1936 by Governor C. Everardo Topete of
Jalisco, Orozco first painted the dome and end wall of the auditorium at
the University. The dome, forty-six feet in diameter and seventy-two
feet from the ground to its top, shows four allegorical male figures representing *Creative Man*: the scientist-thinker, the worker, the teacher, and
the rebel fighting for a new world (fig. 57). These are fitted into the
shape of the dome; portions of the forms overlap and fuse, in order to
effect the joining. A rich warmth emanates from this part of the building
because of the reddish tonalities that bathe it.

The four-headed *Scientist* (fig. 58), looking in various directions, holds
a compass in one hand and a ruler in the other and is surrounded by
symbols of mathematics, anatomy, and other branches of investigative

science. In the serene figure of the *Teacher*, with a hand raised in the traditional gesture of exposition, many people recognize Vicente Lombardo Toledano, after whom it is supposed to have been modeled.

The *Worker* is another portrait, this time of Orozco himself, with features altered and with two hands instead of one (Orozco had lost one hand in a childhood accident). Standing stark upright in effective foreshortening, the *Worker* is seen before a series of curved metallic forms representing the machine. The final figure here is the *Rebel*, shown upside down with his head at the foot of the *Worker*, a rope tied around his neck and his feet pointing to the skies. A red flag wrapped around his left hand unfolds to enframe the upraised hand of the adjacent *Teacher*. Color in this dome is dominantly brick-red touched with greenish shadows, sepia, black, and white areas, except for the completely red flag. The background is a lavender-purple.

In powerful contrast to the intellectuality and relative serenity of the dome is the flat wall beneath and its side panels, all with darker tonalities in black, gray, and brown and showing again the idea of an oppressed mankind. This area (fig. 59) is a logical development from the previous

59

OROZCO. FRESCO. MAIN WALL OF LECTURE HALL, UNIVERSITY OF GUADALAJARA.

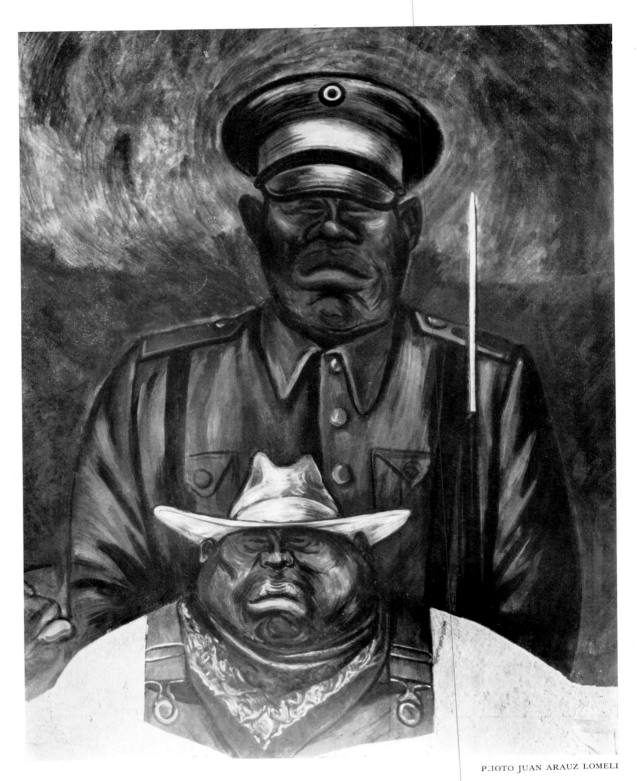

60

OROZCO. *False Leaders and their Allies*, detail. FRESCO.
LEFT SIDE WALL, LECTURE HALL, UNIVERSITY OF GUADALAJARA.

Palacio de Bellas Artes mural, in both composition and theme. Its subject is once more the revolt of man, this time against the false prophets that mislead him into continued hunger and suffering. Here two main diagonals dominate: first the gray-overalled 'labor leaders' with their pious texts, who shrink to the left, one individual bracing his leg to the right as in the Palacio; and then the magnificently pitiful symbol of a tortured human being, on the ground and leaning to the right. The false leaders, the representatives of the 'labor millionaires,' shrink from the uprising of the agonized sufferers, who are arranged in a rectangle on the upper-right portion of the wall and are revealed against the familiar symbolic flames of a world in revolt.

The fire that separates the hungry masses and their well-fed torturers pours over into the left-hand panel to serve as a background. There it lends a feeling of burning unrest to the brutal power and arrogance of the workers of the 'white syndicates' and their soldier allies (fig. 60). On the right side, the mass of gaunt fleshless figures is directly related to the pathetic misery symbolized by the right-hand panel (fig. 61). Here three figures, one standing, one kneeling in a begging pose, and the third a starved child lying on the ground, sum up the pathos of Orozco's intention in a continuous linear flow arranged in a curved, panel-like pattern.

Formally this building offers a more compact and concentrated impression than do the other Guadalajara works, partly because of the way in which the dome and walls are related architectonically and partly because the upward movement in the walls is climaxed by the soaring figures of the cupola. Moreover, the loosely painted and crowded back wall is framed by the relatively solid and less crowded compositions of the sides and dome. Yet the figure style of all the various areas is looser and more graphic than ever before. The masses of people with the usual apocalyptic intent of Orozco suggest El Greco and Tintoretto; their white highlights and black outlines are a particular feature of the work.

At no point before this and very seldom thereafter was Orozco able to achieve the degree of pathos found in these gaunt dematerialized forms, these ideographs of suffering. Every face and form is its own excuse for being, from the frightening bandaged figure lying in the foreground of the center wall to the individual heads framed by the waving arms in the background. From this point on, Orozco's Expressionist manner is fully formed, to be applied with variations in the other Guadalajara buildings and during the next period in Mexico City.

Ideologically, this auditorium represents a clearer and more direct statement than the still symbolic Palacio mural. There is a clear contrast between the creative character of the cupola themes, emphasizing the good that can be accomplished by education and by scientific research, and the destructive character of the walls below, with their demagoguery and resultant hunger. Yet at no point does Orozco come out for a

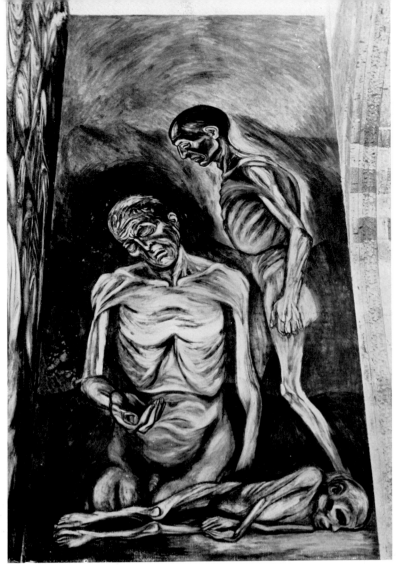

61

OROZCO. *The Victims*. FRESCO.
RIGHT SIDE WALL, LECTURE HALL,
UNIVERSITY OF GUADALAJARA.

positive political program (unlike Rivera with his idealistic-Marxist point of view). He gives us instead a strong negativistic and mystical feeling of unqualified opposition to those elements that are harmful to his people.

The next project in Guadalajara, the 1937 murals of the Government Palace (Palacio del Gobierno), although more direct in theme than the University paintings, still leaves a great deal unexplained. The murals are in a seventeenth-century building dominated by a huge staircase which leads up from the courtyard and on which the murals have been placed. On the ceiling vault of this stairway, the saga of the Mexican struggle begins with the gigantic black-coated figure of the priest Hidalgo y Costilla (see Frontispiece), who in 1810, at the town of Dolores, launched the Independence movement with the famous *grito*, or Cry of

Dolores. The great torch in his hand reaches down into the main wall below, where the seething masses of people, led into revolt by his cry, struggle and die against a background of swirling red banners, as though they were inflamed by that torch.

On the left wall adjoining this vault Orozco fires his heaviest guns at Mexico's traditional despotisms—the organized Church and the military cliques that combined to keep the people down. This section is known as *The Religious Phantasms in Alliance with Militarism* (fig. 62). Awesome and terrifying, the symbols take shape first in the red flag-draped central figure of an invisible soldier, from whom greenish-gray serpents emerge to crush a helpless naked form at the right whose head is obscured by a serpent spewing out endless guns to kill the people in the center wall. At the left of the soldier the gray-black figure of a bishop, also with invisible face, stands beneath a mighty purple-brown Cross looming against the sky, and moves forward as implacably as his soldier-companion (fig. 63). One serpent-covered arm points toward a death's head, while the other hand holds an enormous yellowish candle. Cross, priest, and candle effect a diagonal rightward movement down the stairs and toward the mass of people on the main wall whom they oppress.

62

OROZCO. *Religious Phantasms in Alliance with Militarism.* FRESCO.
LEFT STAIRCASE WALL, GOVERNMENT PALACE, GUADALAJARA.

PHOTO JULIO

63

OROZCO. *Religious Phantasms in Alliance with Militarism*, detail. FRESCO.
LEFT STAIRCASE WALL, GOVERNMENT PALACE, GUADALAJARA.

On the opposite side of the staircase is a more complicated and grotesque arrangement, *The Carnival of the Ideologies* (fig. 64), symbols of the political ideologies that mislead the people with their juggled slogans. One, for example, shows a puppet holding a hammer and sickle and controlled by a sinister Soviet caricature (fig. 65); another portrays a figure with a combination swastika-sickle attached to its head and

154

PHOTO JULIO

PHOTO JUAN ARAUZ LOMELI

64
OROZCO. *Carnival of the Ideologies.*
FRESCO. RIGHT STAIRCASE WALL,
GOVERNMENT PALACE, GUADALAJARA.

65
OROZCO. *Carnival of the Ideologies,*
detail. FRESCO. RIGHT STAIRCASE WALL,
GOVERNMENT PALACE, GUADALAJARA.

holding a pair of detached arms which he causes to shake hands. Confronting the Soviet puppet-master is a trio of fascist symbols: a Japanese waving a pair of dummy clenched fists, an animal-like caricature of Mussolini with arm extended in salute, and a figure of Hitler wearing an armband with swastika and star and a Phrygian liberty cap. Other areas are devoted to symbols of clerical fascism, a caricature of Marx, and a number of less readable symbols. The general intent and impression are completely antitotalitarian, with the various ideologies leering and mocking at one another. More interesting from the point of view of content than of form, this is perhaps the least well-organized portion of the murals in the Palacio del Gobierno.

Over the balcony arches on the wall opposite the main section are *The Outcasts* (fig. 66). Figures are fitted into the spandrels between the arches

66

OROZCO. *The Outcasts*, detail. FRESCO.
NORTH WALL, OPPOSITE PRINCIPAL WALL, GOVERNMENT PALACE, GUADALAJARA.

PHOTO JUAN ARAUZ LOMELI

and are also shown lying down near the haunch of the central arch. They are frightened, agonized, and graphically painted forms, dark-contoured and highlighted in the new expressive Orozco technique.

On coming up these stairs the initial impact—made by the brown-skinned mystical face of Hidalgo y Costilla framed by the wavelike tufts of white hair and rising out of the dark mass of his frock coat—is simply overwhelming. Although this first overhead impression is the most dramatic, the best view of the work as a whole is from the patio balcony above, from the railing facing the gigantic figure of the patriot priest, which also allows a complete view of the two side walls. Center and side sections of this mural are joined in a number of ways. As mentioned before, the serpent on the left wall spews weapons into the lower-right corner of its panel and across into the lower portion of the main wall, where they move in steel-gray tones into the mass of struggling revolutionaries. Here and there a figure in the main section appears with a sword buried in its back or throat.

In general, the amalgamation of the three sections is due first to a continuous gray-black tonality through their lower areas, strong touches of red throughout, and a less apparent series of purple touches. Second, and just as important, is the dynamic and Expressionistic movement of the various groups of figures, which grows from left to right throughout the left and center walls and then meets a series of opposing movements coming from the right-hand wall. A third unifying element is the over-all use of loose curvilinear strokes for form articulation, for distortion of shape, and for individual detail. Also, the upper sections of the three areas are joined rather loosely by purple-lavender patches in the upper left and right of the center panel which pour over into the side walls.

But the most significant unifying element is the mystic form of the great priest emerging from this welter of line and color like a Christ in a Last Judgment, setting in motion the awful events pictured and calling humanity to account.[1] As in many other Orozco frescoes, there is constant contrast between the vast anonymous mass and the idealistic individual, between chaos and idealism.

The climax of Orozco's efforts in Guadalajara and one of the outstanding monuments of Mexican painting is the series of murals in the chapel of the Cabañas Orphanage (Hospicio Cabañas), where in 1938–9 the artist covered some 1200 square meters. These involve a dome, a supporting drum, four pendentives, eight vaults, and fourteen panels, in addition to various small fragments. Architecturally this was perhaps the most advantageous space that had ever been offered to Orozco, for even though

---

[1] An interesting comparison may be made with a 1919 woodcut, *Hate Burns, War Rages*, by the German Expressionist Ernst Barlach, reproduced in *Art News*, Dec. 1955, p. 38.

it did not permit the single and immediate impact of the University auditorium, the very spaciousness of the simply built old chapel, with its well-defined wall and vault areas, allowed him to work out his most satisfactory large-scale mural. Whereas in the Dartmouth murals he had been forced to devise connecting elements, a not always satisfactory or successful procedure, here everything was laid out and waiting to be painted. The building presents a cross plan with a cupola over the crossing, a series of vaults over the nave and in the arms of the crossing, together with lunettes of various kinds.

As always, Orozco visualized his murals in historical and didactic terms, working toward a humanistic idea. Here, as at Dartmouth, the theme is the origin and development of the Americas and the world. Once more the painter seems to look with a certain disapproval on the facts and their evil features, and offers his characteristic soaring spiritual answer, this time in the dome (fig. 67). On the vaults and the walls below are scenes from the history of Mexico since the Conquest; the cruelty of colonial times is equated with the mechanistic oppression of our own day, the compassionate note again added by the good Franciscans. Over these, in the pendentives supporting the dome, is a series of abstract figures symbolizing the Revolution; above them on the drum a succession of constructive forms represent occupations; and finally in the dome over a second and windowed drum is the climax of the building, *The Elements*. Here in the portrayal of Earth, Air, Water, and Fire, we arrive at another Orozco representation of the aspirations of mankind, as the flaming symbol of *Fire* rises prophetically upward.

The crossing paintings deal with the barbaric precolonial aspect of Mexican history. In one arm of the crossing is the gunmetal-blue Coatlique, a mother of Aztec gods, worshipped in the vault overhead, with scenes of Aztec sacrifice on either side. In the other arm of the crossing, a nude figure is torn between Aztec and Christian gods and is flanked by Conquest scenes below. At each end of the nave and the crossing arms, a pair of symbolic figures refers to the advent of modern Western civilization: the Aztec warrior and the white man, two Franciscans, a writer (Cervantes) and a painter (El Greco), and so on.

The most important areas painted in this building, aside from the dome, are the vaults of the nave (three on each side of the dome) and the parallel paired panels in the walls underneath these. The vaults constitute a series of references to the Conquest period of the sixteenth century, and show in the order named *The Mystic Spain of Philip II*, *Warrior Spain*, *The Conversion of the Indians* (these on one side of the dome). The other arm of the nave shows *Cortez and Victory*, *War Scenes*, and *The Mechanical Horse* in the corresponding vault areas.

Perhaps the most effective single figure in this part of the building is that of *Philip II and the Cross* in the first vault (fig. 68), a gigantesque, scowling, ruffed Spaniard in gray-black supporting a large reddish-tinted

67

OROZCO. FRESCO. DOME,
HOSPICIO CABAÑAS, GUADALAJARA.

Cross, the entire scene against a bright-blue background. Immediately adjacent is a group of machinelike Spaniards on two-headed horses running down the Indians and waving the banner of Castile and León. The next two vaults offer a contrast: on one side of the dome, the compassionate Franciscan in the *Conversion* scene, with the Indian kneeling at his feet and a plaque bearing the ABCD in the background; on the other side, the figure of Cortez, the man of iron, bitter and unyielding. This mechanized black-brown figure stands out from a scene of butchery against a somber greenish background. Next to Cortez, another vault shows a group of semi-mechanical Spaniards in the act of conquering, while at the end of the nave away from the dome is the *Mechanical Horse*, half-animal, half-machine, with a chain tail, crawling over girders that crush people. The brick-red background again bears the symbols of León and Castile.

159

68

OROZCO. *Philip II and the Cross,*
vault section. FRESCO.
HOSPICIO CABAÑAS,
GUADALAJARA.

In the wall panels directly under the nave vaults, the painter has arranged a series of complementary pairs of thematic material: the unknown primitive state and the Conquest, the tragic and the ridiculous, the man of science and the man of religion—all emphasizing the contrast between prehistoric and modern civilization. To these contrapuntal pairs in one arm of the nave, he has added a series in the other arm contrasting and comparing the forces of charity and those of despotism: charity versus dictatorship, sorrowing humanity and the militarized masses.[2]

---

[2] These titles are from Justino Fernández, *José Clemente Orozco: forma e idea,* Porrua, Mexico, 1942.

160

First comes a group of frightening and savage leaders known as *The Dictators*, who set in motion columns of highly abstract marchers waving gray-green banners, the leaders in contrasting green and brick red. Then come *The Militarized Masses*, with endless columns of robotlike forms moving from background to foreground and turning right at the end into the next panel, *Despotism*. Here the little mannikins are met by a huge man-form, its head cut off by the side of the panel; the figure is dressed in jackboots and belted shirt and holds a knout in its fist. All three of the panels on this side have strands of barbed wire in the foreground, a continuous accent underlining Orozco's reference to the imprisoned human spirit.

Directly across the aisle is another trio of panels. A group of dark-brown anonymous *Demagogues* (opposite *Despotism*) stands on a series of platforms, waving their arms against the gray background. This is followed by a mass of figures symbolizing *Sorrowing Humanity*, in violet-gray with black outlines against a background of sharply angled buildings with façades in orange and reddish purple. This melancholy crowd moves left into the next panel to meet the founder of the Hospicio Cabañas, Archbishop Juan Cruz Ruiz de Cabañas y Crespo (1752–1824), who stands in a blue doorway that is part of an orange building continued out of the previous panel. In his luminous purple robes, he blesses three little orphan girls and three women who kneel before him.

In the other arm of the nave, the series of wall panels begins with a flying mass of apocalyptic horsemen, black and brown symbols of *The Tragic*; the horses but not the riders are visible as they move over the square roofs of a town. In the next panel, *The Religious*, a church tower emerges over the city roofs—this is Guadalajara and its Church of San Felipe. The third section features a group of heroic armored figures seen through a vivid blue stylized sentry box, and represents *The Conquered*.

Across the way from these three representations is *The Unknown* (opposite *The Tragic*), a powerful orange-colored architectural symbol offering a wall and column section through which is partly visible the imminently triumphant Spaniard against the red and yellow banner of Spain, while on the near side appears the hooded blue figure of a sorrowing Mexico. Opposite *The Religious* is *The Scientific*, a gigantic metal wheel rolling forward over the ruins of Aztec civilization in the yellow-red sunrise of a new day. The third and last section in this group is a less effective series of architectural forms symbolizing *The Baroque*, placed opposite *The Conquered*.

Although individually effective and poetically powerful, these panels must be considered as they were planned, together and in the context of the architecture. Moreover, each side of the nave has its own organized meaning, with one wall opposed to or complementing the other.

From this carefully balanced didactic and allegorical material, we look upward to the pendentives (see fig. 67), with their brown-green-black nudes, their highly Expressionistic drawing, and white highlights. Above these are the rectangular divisions of the drum with various similarly colored figures representing the constructive activities of mankind: e.g. a pair of hands molding a vase, a stone carver working on a head, or a symbol of architecture.

On the climactic dome, in tones ranging from stone gray to vivid flaming red, Orozco has achieved what is perhaps his greatest single composition. More effective than the dome of the University, this arrangement involves first the three reclining figures in blackish gray around the base of the dome, representing Earth, Water, and Air. Moving upward is the flying, flame-wrapped figure of Fire, a marvelously foreshortened conception, with reddish-brown body and reddish-yellow flames enframed by the ring of dark arms belonging to the figures below (fig. 69). Although it is customary to give these figures the titles indicated, it is perhaps more justifiable to think of this cupola as a summing up not only of the meaning of this building but of Orozco's philosophy as a whole. Here mankind is seen in its barest essence, two of its proponents on the ground frantically struggling for mastery, a third looking upward to the prophecy of the future, the lambent symbol of man rising above his environment, dematerialized in form but humanized in spirit. Here, without the aid of the conventional and traditional symbols, Orozco has again created his own world of meaning, his own distillations of a great and overpowering feeling for mankind. From the historicity of the nave with its torment and horror, through the apocalyptic vision of the vaults and the pendentives, he carries us into the blazing firmament of the dome, into his own version of a Heaven where man is finally raised from the ground into the realm of the spirit. Together with the Riveras at Chapingo and the Siqueiros works at Chillán in Chile (1942), these paintings of Orozco must rank with the greatest murals produced in the Americas.

In 1940 Orozco accepted another mural commission, this time for the Gabino Ortiz Library in Jiquilpan in the state of Michoacán, where the retiring president, General Lázaro Cárdenas, wished to make a suitable gift to his native city. Here a former chapel was converted into a library, offering a long nave and a curved apse for the painter's purposes. Unfortunately, however, the nave walls seemed to Orozco somewhat too long for the curved, pointed apse in the rear. To avoid overbalancing the design, he chose to paint the apse in his characteristic flaming colors and the side panels in an almost exclusively black and white arrangement that makes them look like monumental lithographs. As in the Guadalajara Hospicio and University murals, he again balanced historical narrative (the wall panels) with a symbolic and climactic moment (the apse).

The black and white rectangular panels on the side walls, some of which are touched with vivid spots of red in the Revolutionary banners, represent a high point in the abstract emotional direction in which we have seen Orozco's art moving since Pomona. Some are primarily representational: *Las Acordadas*, with the bound Indian dragged behind his oppressor's horse; *The Executed* against the wall; *Brute Forces*, with powerful horses surging over inert humanity, and so on. On the other hand, there are panels such as *The Masses* (fig. 70)—there are two of these—in which Orozco, in a partly nonfigurative manner, unleashes his despair and anger at the unreasoning power and brutality of revolutions in

69

OROZCO. *Fire*, dome detail. FRESCO. HOSPICIO CABAÑAS, GUADALAJARA.

70

OROZCO. *The Masses*. FRESCO.
SIDE WALL, GABINO ORTIZ LIBRARY, JIQUILPAN.

symbols that are all screaming mouths, red flags, and violence. Comparing his early drawings of the Revolution (see figs. 34, 35) with the black and white style of Jiquilpan, we can see the distance Orozco has traveled along the road of emotive abstraction. During the 'forties, with the murals in the Hospital of Jesus, the logical climax of this development will be reached.

Balancing the long walls of black and white panels are a painting over the front entrance door and the work covering the apse in the rear. The former shows two tigers (the so-called Mexican *tigre* is actually a jaguar), one on each side of the doorway; they are climbing a giant cactus bush, while above them two horrible travesties of female Liberty symbols stretch a snake-headed ribbon across the top of the door.

On the far side of the building in the curve of the pointed apse is an *Allegory of Mexico* (fig. 71) in which Orozco features the proud figure of an Indian woman in reddish brown riding on the brown-black tiger of

164

Mexico. The latter is covered with a vivid red cloth and moves through green cactus. With the tiger stretching across the lower part of the panel, the strong bolt-upright figure of the woman becomes part of a pyramid that includes in magnificent three-dimensional fashion the snake-and-eagle symbol of Mexico. This symbol protects proud Mexico from another tiger trying to get around the pyramid to attack the woman and her mount. This second tiger is a voracious, hungry beast that symbolizes the menace of imperialism. It comes sweeping forward parallel with the left-hand curve of the arch and passes by its instigator, the winged, derby-hatted figure at the left. To the right are the guardians of Mexico's rights (Law, Liberty, Justice)—three women with crowns and rifles representing the combination of idealism and force necessary to maintain the freedom and independence of that country.

The entire scene is shown before a huge Mexican flag in red, white,

71

OROZCO. *Allegory of Mexico*. FRESCO. GABINO ORTIZ LIBRARY, JIQUILPAN.

and green, which occupies all of the upper background and blends with the green of the cactus below, the red of the woman riding the tiger, and other portions of the wall. Here is Mexico in 1940, having gained a certain measure of freedom and a better way of life—a Mexico that must be constantly on guard to preserve these gains lest they be despoiled by the greedy at home and abroad.

The portable mural for the Twenty Centuries of Mexican Art exhibition in 1940 at the Museum of Modern Art in New York was carried out while Orozco was in the midst of the Jiquilpan commission. Shortly after he had begun to work in the Gabino Ortiz Library, the painter was called to the United States. Working for the most part before museum visitors, he executed a six-part fresco within ten days, between 21 June and 30 June. The interchangeable sections of the *Dive Bomber* are so conceived that they can be arranged in any number of schemes, Orozco himself preferring six of the many possible patterns. The brochure published by the Museum of Modern Art at that time, *Orozco 'Explains,'*[3] does no such thing, as the quotation marks in the title indicate. It describes, rather, the technical procedures utilized, and has a number of generalized statements from the artist on the nature of painting and the relationship of the symbolic painter to the public which demands 'program notes' for his works. 'The public,' says Orozco, 'refuses TO SEE painting. They want TO HEAR painting. They don't care for the show itself, they prefer TO LISTEN to the barker outside. Free lectures every hour for the blind, around the Museum. This way, please.'

Certain things, however, are clear about the *Dive Bomber*. It is topical in a general way, like the contemporaneous Jiquilpan work warning Mexico of renewed dangers to its liberties. Here, a year after the outbreak of the Second World War and only a week after the tragic fall of France before the mechanized might of the Nazis with their dive bombers and tanks, Orozco presents a symbol of the dangers of machine aggression. Stylistically this work is a logical outgrowth of the earlier mechanical symbols utilized by the painter in the Hospicio murals and at Dartmouth, where the *Machine Age* perhaps came closest to the bleak inhumanity of the scene in the Modern Museum. The Dartmouth panel, however, had been meant at worst as a denunciation of the tyranny of the machine, a tyranny from which man in the Palacio and the Hospicio murals tried to escape, and did escape finally. But whatever hopeful elements were present in those two works disappear in the *Dive Bomber*, from whose ruined and twisted machine parts the legs of a solitary human being protrude, crushed by the metallic demons that have killed each other as well.

In the terms of mid-1940, the *Dive Bomber* is a vivid, accurate report of the fear and the spiritual state of mankind.

---

[3] Bulletin of The Museum of Modern Art, no. 4, vol. VII, Aug. 1940.

Siqueiros

1934 to 1940

XIV

Siqueiros's return to Mexico in 1934 was not merely a matter of resuming or attempting to resume his mural work, as was the case with Orozco and Rivera. For Siqueiros, the business of painting could not be dissociated from the class struggle. In 1934 he became president of the militant League against War and Fascism, involving himself in further difficulties with the police. At the same time he held his first New York exhibition at the Delphic Studios of Alma Reed.

The following year came the public controversy with Rivera on the nature of Revolutionary art, a continuation of the battle that had begun in New York in 1933 over the New Workers School murals. For Siqueiros this was really an attack against all the muralists of the Mexican school, particularly against their continued use of the fresco medium and their ever-present need for archaeological material and folkloristic elements. 'We may be able,' said Siqueiros at this time, 'to play a revolutionary hymn on a church organ, but it is not really an adequate instrument for such a purpose; the fresco, at least technically speaking, does not correspond to the formal and organic quality of architecture ... of our time; we must turn to the physical and chemical sciences of our time, to materials that correspond to industry, that is to the society of which we are a part.'

To this attitude, deriving from his technological experiences in the United States, Siqueiros added the idea that buildings should no longer be chosen for decoration solely for aesthetic reasons. 'We must turn,' he said, 'from older colonial ideas to the new public architecture; in this area it is appropriate to consider the execution of exterior murals, toward the street and facing the passing multitudes.'[1]

Although Siqueiros was not then doing any murals, he had already applied some of these principles in his since destroyed Los Angeles works and in the Buenos Aires example. For easel painting, he consistently used the Duco paint medium (a du Pont trade name for all pyroxilin paints) adapted from industrial procedures such as the spray-painting of automobiles. Although it was at first fashionable to decry the 'impermanence' and 'inadequacy' of this medium, Siqueiros was able to demonstrate as

---

[1] 70 *Obras Recientes de David Alfaro Siqueiros*, pp. 20–21.

early as 1935 the plasticity of the pyroxilin technique in such pictures as the *Portrait of María Asúnsolo* (María Asúnsolo collection)[2] and many other figure paintings of the time. Here with the synthetic lacquer paint is achieved a sculpturesque solidity, especially in the masklike face and the powerfully modeled arms and hands, with their special textures and resonant dark tonalities. This monumentality and three-dimensional movement of form are also conveyed in a number of the lithographs of this period, especially the well-known *Self-Portrait* (fig. 72), which seems to leap from the picture space. The strong forward-moving accents of the curly hair, the line of the ear, the curve of the nose, and the movements of the shadows on the face underline the outgoing and fiery glance of this romantic conception of the artist's own features.

---

[2] 20 *Centuries of Mexican Art*, The Museum of Modern Art, New York, 1940, p. 164.

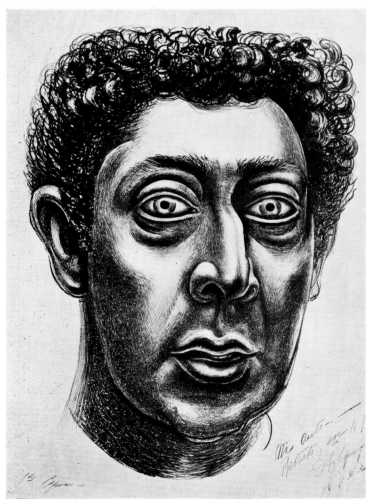

PHOTO GUILLERMO ZAMORA

72

SIQUEIROS. *Self Portrait*. LITHOGRAPH. MEXICO CITY, COLL. THE ARTIST.

In 1936 Siqueiros went to New York as a delegate to the American Artists Congress, where he delivered a paper on *The Mexican Experience in Art*. The L.E.A.R. point of view expressed in this paper reiterated an attitude previously stated by Siqueiros himself, that revolutionary art was not merely a matter of content or theme but also a problem of form—a point on which he parted company from the didactic Rivera and his elaborate preachments. Siqueiros also spoke of the need for art forms that could reach the greatest number of people, e.g. print media. Important among the ideas offered was that of seeking new types of buildings for murals instead of the official buildings that were far removed from the masses.

After the Congress, Siqueiros founded the Experimental Workshop in New York in 1936, known as the Siqueiros Experimental Workshop to those who carried it on after he left for the Spanish civil war. The basic purpose of this association was to investigate modern materials and instruments as well as the subjective elements involved in artistic creation, and here Siqueiros made the final shift from oils to pyroxilin and other new materials. He realized more fully than ever before the richness of form and the depth that could be achieved through the quick-drying glazes of pyroxilin paint. The addition of fibers, sawdust, marble dust, and so on, gave a heavy impasto to the works and added to the flexibility of the basic Duco medium.

Its concern with the elements proper to modern painting, both spiritual and technical, gave the Experimental Workshop a special importance, particularly among the more radical artists in New York. During the few years of its existence, among its adherents were a good many members of the later Taller de Gráfica Popular, including Arenal, Berdecio, and Pujol, all important for subsequent graphic works. Also active in the Workshop was José L. Gutiérrez, who was to make significant contributions to the development and application of ethyl silicate and vinylite paints. Although it is difficult to assay the specific effect of the Workshop on American art at this point, Siqueiros's paintings of 1936 had their influence—e.g. *Collective Suicide*, *Birth of Fascism*, *Stop the War*, or simpler but equally moving single figures such as *The Frightened Child*, *Negro Woman*, the already mentioned lithograph, *Self-Portrait*, and so on.

In addition to new media and appropriate ideas for revolutionary painting (to paint what one sees with all the conviction at one's command, whether battles, beggars, or boys at play), Siqueiros also worked on the possible aids to be derived from the still camera and the motion-picture camera. These, he felt, could increase space elements, especially volumes in space, achieve complex movements, and generally further the mobile idea conceived after his contact with Eisenstein, an idea he had first attempted to work out in the Buenos Aires mural. He believed that the camera (both still and moving) could be the basis of a new realism and that it could make possible the combination of objectivity and subjectivity necessary for that purpose.

An example of this consciousness of the camera effect is the well-known *Echo of a Scream* (1937, Museum of Modern Art). Siqueiros must have been tremendously affected, as many others had been, by the heart-wrenching pathos of the newsreel shot showing an almost naked Chinese baby seated in the midst of a wrecked railroad track and screaming, after one of the Japanese bombardments of invaded China. In this pyroxilin painting it is as though the scream issuing from the mouth of the abandoned child grows larger, unbearably larger, until in its vividly seen double image it spreads into the entire upper part of the picture and echoes out into space.

Since the end of 1936 Siqueiros had intended to go to Spain as a pictorial propagandist for the Loyalist forces. When he arrived there in 1937, he found himself engaged in regular military activities, taking part in a number of important campaigns and rising to the rank of Colonel. By 1939 he was back in Mexico, where he founded a pro-Loyalist review called *Documental*, and engaged in other antifascist activities against the older Spanish inhabitants of Mexico. Again he was attacked by the conservative press, this time as *El Coronelazo* (The Big Colonel), a sarcastic appellation he has used with great pride since then. This spate of activity ended with another brief jail sentence.

But he was painting as well, first for his show at the Pierre Matisse Gallery in New York (three of these pictures were bought for the Modern Museum) and then for his one important mural project of the period. In the Electrical Workers Union in Mexico City he worked with a team consisting of Luis Arenal, Antonio Pujol, José Renau, and a group of Mexican and United States assistants on a mural called *The Trial of Fascism* (fig. 73).

Done in pyroxilin on the three walls and ceiling of a rather small staircase, Siqueiros's exposition of the presumable steps from capitalism to monopoly to imperialism to fascism to war was projected with his new modern techniques. The approximately one hundred square meters of this enclosure were painted with the aid of a still camera for some of the sketches, an electric stereopticon to project the drawings as they were made for transfer, and a spray gun for applying the paint to the wall surface. As in the *Echo of a Scream* and many other works from this point on, we see immediately the relation between the painting and specific photographic and documentary material from newspapers, magazines, et cetera.

The full-scale view of this mural shows in the center a group of photographically painted, dead child-victims of the Spanish civil war, placed in the maw of some horrible machine, also seen with the same relentless clarity. Immediately overhead is the distorted dive bomber that brought death and destruction to these children and that is about to engulf Europe (fig. 74).

To left and right of the central scene are two gas-masked and helmeted

73

SIQUEIROS. *Trial of Fascism.* PYROXILIN.
ELECTRICAL WORKERS UNION, MEXICO CITY.

groups of the 'fascists.' The Tokyo-Rome-Berlin fascists stand at the right—with a tiny photographic rendition of a weeping Chinese mother and her dead child painted near the Japanese representative. At the left of the central child-swallowing machine is a group of three nonmilitary figures, this time the democratic nations that are at that moment allegedly yielding to fascism in their several ways: Britain, France, and the United

74

SIQUEIROS. *Trial of Fascism*, detail. PYROXILIN. ELECTRICAL WORKERS UNION, MEXICO CITY.

States, identified, like the first trio, by little flags that have been projected on them by the stereopticon and painted on as transparencies. The British figure is dressed in the wing collar and spats that suggest Chamberlain, the French symbol is that of a paunchy and Laval-like figure, while the United States is shown as an informally dressed person with a number of lynched Negroes hanging close by. To the left of these representatives of the democracies, the painter has indicated a burning parliament building whose pediment motto, 'Liberté, Egalité, Fraternité,' is partly obscured by a film-projected outline of a money bag. On the steps we see similar transparencies of little people scurrying about.

172

75

SIQUEIROS. *Trial of Fascism*,
detail. PYROXILIN.
ELECTRICAL WORKERS UNION,
MEXICO CITY.

PHOTO COURTESY THE PAINTER

To the extreme left and right of this outspoken view of the modern political scene, Siqueiros has placed two enlarged and contrasting symbols.
On the right the figure of a determined man of the people, who has only
a rifle and courage to defend himself and his country (a vivid idealized
portrayal of the Spanish and other nonprofessional soldiers), points his
weapon diagonally across to the other side of the mural, toward the arch-
symbol of the fascist demagogue (fig. 75). There at the far left on the side
wall stands a puppet figure fixed to a mechanical device for raising and
lowering it in the pulpit. It is a two-headed, multi-armed figure with the
face of a vulture, one arm waving a torch, another waving a kind of
baton, and the third holding a tiny pansy (a reference to Hitler's ambigu-

ous sex). It stands before a microphone and sets into motion the waves of tiny figures that stream from the wall opening in the rear. These move toward the podium of the ranting speaker, swing sharply right, and then wheel inward to the parliament building they are about to overwhelm. In the rear of the mural, similar endless groups of mannikins move in rigid formation across the wall surface, furnishing a background for a projected image of a poor weeping woman and her little daughter amid dynamically overlapping Futurist planes of light. The entire composition, from the Hitler caricature at the left to the fighting worker at the right, is set on a platform above a menacing below-ground mechanical maze that forms the basis of Siqueiros's conception of the development from capitalism to war.

These wall surfaces show a spatial treatment never before felt in any mural. The spectator finds himself surrounded by movements and double views of all kinds as he is enveloped by the four-sided space box formed by the three walls and the overhead area. From the front, the mural gives a series of perspective impressions that is markedly altered as we look left or right. The figure of Hitler, for example, has more than the usual number of arms and heads, so that he can be seen from different points of view. Such a device lends to the mural as a whole a quality of movement that enables us to move comfortably through the spatial complex, always able to see a coherent picture and not limited to the frontal visualization point. This may be tested by simply turning the image of Hitler's vulture head on its side, which will give an entirely new but equally complete configuration of that head.

Also taken into account is the relation between the walls and the ceiling. These areas are fused by Siqueiros's dynamic perspective distortions that bring them together in a new kind of unified action. The eye moves through these spaces like a motion-picture camera, catching one view here, another there, seeing some things in sharp focus, others as though after-images still remained. The spectator is forced into an entirely new method of looking, absorbing, and understanding that becomes increasingly appropriate for the artist's exhortatory purposes.

Here in the mural of the Electrical Workers Union, Siqueiros has achieved his first complete synthesis of modern techniques and political ideas. It marks the end of a period of experimentation dating back to the Los Angeles mural, and is already a fully formed technique that will be applied with growing effectiveness during the next period, which produces the full flowering of his neo-Realism.

In 1940 Siqueiros became involved in the unfortunate Trotsky affair which resulted in the death of Trotsky's secretary. For his alleged part in this situation, the painter was jailed for a short time and, though 'freed and legally absolved,' was forced to go into exile. While Mexico was not for him for the time being, there were still many things he could do elsewhere in art and in politics.

Rivera's progress during this period is less spectacular and creative than that of either Orozco or Siqueiros. His work represents rather a continuation of the didactic and decorative line laid out earlier in his career, although far less actively than before. Rivera still had the most impressive reputation of all the Revolutionary painters, but his equivocal political position, already visible in the struggle at the Academy in 1930 and climaxed during this period by his sponsorship of Trotsky, made him *persona non grata* to the increasingly powerful leftist intellectuals.

His two government projects of this era both rank as completions of 'unfinished business.' The Palacio de Bellas Artes mural of 1934 was a more or less faithful reconstitution of the painting destroyed by Rockefeller Center authorities the previous year (fig. 76). Similarly, the final wall had to be done in the National Palace stairway; this had been waiting since Rivera left for San Francisco in 1930. Once these two commissions were out of the way, Rivera's role in the mural movement became a subordinate one for some time, confined to the Hotel Reforma commission, which was never made available to the public on its original site, and to the mural done for the San Francisco World's Fair in 1940. His easel paintings, on the other hand, were quite plentiful, ranging over a wide field of subject matter and reflecting his general aesthetic qualities with often greater effectiveness than the wall paintings of the time.

Man at the Crossroads is the title generally given to the 1934 expository mural on the third floor of the Palacio de Bellas Artes, just opposite the Orozco *Katharsis* of that same year. No greater contrast of intent and purpose could be imagined. The Orozco work emphasizes purgation, human suffering, and even the destruction of the world as a prelude to its improvement, as well as dynamic Expressionism of color, composition, and form distortion. The Rivera work, on the other hand, is almost classical in the Renaissance sense; its forms are carefully balanced, one group against another around a carefully and quietly worked out X shape and a vertical axis running from top to bottom. Color here, as in most of Rivera's work, is bland; it offers a compositionally unifying element in a light green that pervades the entire work. There are vivid touches of blue-green also. While these colors undoubtedly help to hold the composition together, they do not animate or set anything in motion. They have no emotional force whatsoever, in contrast to the general coloristic purpose in Orozco.

76

RIVERA. *Man at the Crossroads*. FRESCO.
PALACIO DE BELLAS ARTES, MEXICO CITY.

In the same way we may contrast the meaning of the diagonals here and in the Orozco work. Here they are used for purposes of unification, balance, and dialectic, as they help to oppose millionaires to workers, capitalist armies at the upper left to workers' armies at the upper right, the world of nature below to the world of the machine above, and so on. In Orozco, on the other hand, the diagonals create an asymmetrical effect that moves the eye diagonally up and down and side to side in a deliberately disturbing fashion, bringing the various parts of the composition into a state of dynamic rather than static balance.

The greatest contrast between the two works, however, is in their respective intellectual and social attitudes. Rivera's, however static, is crystal-clear and logical, everything put into its proper place, with a beginning and an end. The worker placed at the crossroads, holding in his strong right hand the lever that will determine the future, is given a definite choice: the world of socialism at his left or the world of capitalism at his right. These are symbolized first by the group of workers of all ages around the (previously controversial) figure of Lenin. Balancing it on the other side is a night-club scene with the (actually abstemious) John D. Rockefeller, Jr., holding a champagne glass in one hand and the slim fingers of a young lady in the other—a gratuitous but understandable gibe from the bitter Diego. In the upper sections is the same contrast: the workers with their red banners yelling before the Kremlin wall versus the anonymous menacing soldiers of the capitalist world.

At the extreme left and right are two sections that were separate panels in Radio City. These are now incorporated into the main design through a pair of enormous magnifying glasses that offer the people portrayed at either end of the wall a view into Rivera's future. Workers and children of all races and ages look through these magnifiers into the alternative worlds envisaged by the painter. Out of the left-hand section emerges the gray, sculptured figure of Religion, rising handless from a mass of unemployed and visible against a panorama of Wall Street. The workers are harassed by mounted police and then by the masked and helmeted figures of war, the inevitable consequence of these circumstances. From the right-hand section rises the gray, headless figure of Fascism conquered by the socialist groups portrayed here. The upper portion shows the ordered ranks of the present Soviet leadership and their followers, a not too attractive-appearing group that includes Stalin, while in the lower section Marx, Engels, and Trotsky urge the workers of the world to 'unite in the IVth International.'

As for the young worker in the center of the mural, he has at his command the resources of nature and those of the machine age to help him determine his future—either to the right or to the left. The pious, Gros-like look of the Heaven-directed eyes is in line with previously noted Rivera expression, and underlines a general hopefulness that is in strong contrast to the fatalism of Orozco and the direct activism of Siqueiros.

Rivera has been very specific here, using the telescope in the center to symbolize man's looking toward infinite space and the microscope to denote the tiniest forms on earth. The diagonal from lower left to upper right contains the movements of the planets and the nebulae, while the other diagonal shows the forms revealed by the microscope.

Orozco, on the other hand, is far less interested in telling a story or preaching a political sermon; his chief concerns are his symbols of human anguish and his own pessimism. Siqueiros, in another fashion, offers an optimistic attitude; it is however, an optimism springing not merely from doctrinal faith in the future but also from a profound belief that much can be accomplished through struggle.

The Rivera Palacio mural is basically the same as that in Radio City, with a number of relatively unimportant changes. These include the incorporation of the side sections into the main body of the mural, the change in the night-club scene to add the figure of Mr. Rockefeller, and the addition of Trotsky and Marx. Like the 1935 final staircase wall in the National Palace, the Palacio mural underlines the changed political climate at the end of the Calles period and the beginning of the Cárdenas regime.

After the relative compositional calm of the Palacio painting, the left-hand staircase wall in the National Palace has a violence of mood and a directness of personal reference that suggest the New Workers School paintings of 1933. We must make the same reservation, however, that the things and people he attacks are no longer in a position to strike back very effectively. The villain of this mural wall is the Calles administration, with all its venality and corruption, its murder of *agraristas*, its unscrupulous demagogic politicians, its resistance to progress in any form. But Calles had already been thoroughly discredited by the progressive Cárdenas administration, and it was now quite clear that the Calles forces were in check.

In all fairness to Rivera, it is entirely possible that what was intended here was to show the iniquities of the previous administration (which he had attacked on the rear wall by implication some years earlier; see chap. VIII) and the triumph of justice in the new period. Being a professed Marxist, Rivera was bound to show this triumph in terms of the Marxist revolution, as indicated in a banner held by Marx at the very top of the wall: '. . .it is not a question of reforming the society of today but rather of forming a new society.' This is the climactic point in Diego's narrative, which presents the sinister trio of Banker (Calles), Army, and Church in a rectangular space from which lines radiate to their respective henchmen: the National Socialists, strikebreakers, peon murderers, demagogues, and so on. From the toil, suffering, and religious subjection of the Mexican people, these persons pump an endless flow of gold coins that passes through the religious shrine below. This is a serious and violent indictment of a situation from which Mexico had not then (or even later) freed

78

RIVERA. *Agustín Lorenzo*. FRESCO.
PANEL FOR HOTEL REFORMA,
MEXICO CITY.

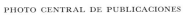

77

RIVERA. *Fiesta*. FRESCO.
PANEL FOR HOTEL REFORMA,
MEXICO CITY.

itself, but the Marxist answer does not necessarily represent that of the Cárdenas government. The uncompromising call to further revolution may be taken as Rivera's refusal to countenance reformism, an attitude which may be justified from the point of view of international Marxism but which in the light of the current situation in Mexico appears extremely visionary.

The third and final mural project of the period was for the Hotel Reforma on the elegant Paseo de la Reforma, a hotel designed primarily for the tourist trade (as indeed were the murals themselves). This was another of the *causes célèbres* in which Rivera has involved himself from time to time. Here he designed a set of four movable mural panels presumably concerned with popular festivals, particularly those of Huexotzingo, but with more or less obvious comments on the contemporary situation, which soon led to removal of the panels from the hotel.

One section is a simple colorful representation of festival dances in ancient Indian and nineteenth-century French occupation costumes, to which no one could object on political grounds. The second is a satire on tourism and features a rather gangly woman in the background and two black donkeys, one writing and one holding money bags, a reference to the anticlerical *Caprichos* of Goya and intended here for a similar purpose. A third panel (fig. 77) is another mask festival, with a huge puppetlike figure emerging against waving flags; its curious face is a combination of Calles, Hitler, and Roosevelt, and reinforces the impression of Diego's intransigence. Beneath this, a masked general in charro costume swings a whip that somehow takes the form of a sickle, while at the right a pig-faced soldier dances with a peasant girl. Perhaps the most effective portion of the panel is the yellow Straw Man at the lower right. The would-be satire on dictatorship intended by the large composite figure above, with its tiny banner combining the emblems of the United States, Japan, Nazi Germany, and England, leaves something to be desired both as composition and as symbolism.

The most dramatic and again a completely uncontroversial panel in this commission shows the guerrilla leader Agustín Lorenzo as a dashing equestrian figure followed by some of his companions and striking out lustily at the French zouaves of Louis Napoleon, whose symbol is seen in the outline at the upper right (fig. 78). The green-cloaked rider on a blue-gray horse makes a striking combination with the red and blue of the French soldiers' costumes. More interesting, this picture, unlike most of Rivera's works of any period, has a flair and excitement that are quite new.

When the murals were first put up, it became evident that Rivera had deliberately satirized the Archbishop of Mexico and a well-known Mexican general (apart from the implications of the 'Dictator'). When the Hotel Reforma management had a number of changes made in these offending portions, Rivera in righteous wrath initiated a strike of the

79

RIVERA. *Mother and Child*. TEMPERA AND OIL. NEW YORK, COLL. MRS. JAMES HENK.

PHOTO CENTRAL DE PUBLICACIONES

Wall Painters Union, of which he was a member. The result was the sale of the panels to a leading book and picture dealer, who left them on view at the Galería de Arte Mexicano. Rivera got very little money out of this project but had the satisfaction of being once more the center of a politico-artistic controversy.

For the next few years, 1936–40, his activities were confined to easel paintings. The portraits, which seem to be so popular and desirable, are by no means brilliant studies. His poetic landscapes, on the other hand, have a fine, firm, and imaginative quality that makes them worthy of the painter's talent. In the same way, the much-heralded primitive dances, e.g. *Dance of the Earth*,[1] mildly interesting for their linear design, are an unassimilated departure from Rivera's basic qualities. These are revealed far more sympathetically and with great effect in such paintings as the *Mother and Child* (fig. 79, 1935, Mrs. James Henk collection, New York) or the *Scavenger* of the same year in the Earlham College collection at Richmond, Indiana. In these works, in various water-colors, drawings, and lithographs of the same general content, Rivera reveals himself once again as a master draftsman and capable of tremendous lyrical feeling. Although historically Rivera has great significance in the mural movement, one may wonder if artistically these smaller and more modest works are not just as important.

Apparently in exile from the main Mexican mural development during this period, Rivera's first chance in a half a decade came in 1940 with a commission from San Francisco Junior College for the Golden Gate International Exposition that year. In keeping with his variously expressed ideas on the need for combining the art forms of the South (Mexico primarily) with the machine civilization of the North, he painted a series of five longitudinal panels (about twenty-five meters wide by about seven meters high). One of these shows on its left side a series of forms inspired by the Aztec goddess Coatlique and on the right others derived from the machine age, while before them a group of sculptors is carving out the future. At the bottom a benign Diego extends the hand of Pan-American friendship to a charming young woman, apparently Paulette Goddard, the film actress (cf. the San Francisco Luncheon Club mural showing Helen Wills as the symbol of California).

Other panels are concerned with the development of Mexican and United States civilization and contain portraits of significant historical figures such as Lincoln, Washington, et cetera, and artists such as Ryder. In San Francisco, Rivera no longer felt it necessary to include the United States in his list of dictator nations—times had changed. He now set up a trio consisting of Hitler, Mussolini, and Stalin. After this work, three years would pass before Rivera would do a mural again.

---

[1] Illustrated in 20 *Centuries of Mexican Art*, p. 173.

The Mexican School of Painting

1934 to 1940

The general situation in Mexican art during this period—apart from the contributions of the now 'big four'[1]—is reflected in the already indicated group activity of both the L.E.A.R. and the Taller de Gráfica Popular and in the work of a number of individuals of equally marked social tendencies.

The not altogether successful group project at the Abelardo Rodríguez Market in 1934–5 involved future Taller members Bracho, O'Higgins, and Pujol (as well as other painters) in an often clumsy and generally Riveresque type of art filled with Revolutionary clichés that became increasingly typical as this period wore on. In many subsequent cases, the Rivera-derived decorativeness was supplemented by a stiff monumentality based on the early Orozcos of the Preparatory School. This may be seen, for example, in the joint project at the National Printing Office (Talleres Gráficos de la Nación) in 1936, where O'Higgins together with Méndez, Zalce, and Fernando Gamboa did a series of murals that marks a considerable advance over the Rodríguez Market, to the degree that there were fewer individuals involved and more of Orozco fire than Rivera decoration.

Many schools were decorated in the Federal District during this period and later, and they represent the same balance of the qualities of the two masters. This mixture was already apparent in the 1933 murals previously mentioned (except for the more independent contribution of Castellanos) and remains evident until the late 'forties in such works as the O'Higgins-Méndez mural in Maternity Clinic No. 1 of the Social Security Administration (1946–7). In cases such as this one, the artists have managed to exorcise Riverism by admitting more of the Orozco influence, which has penetrated also through their individual work in different media; and above all, they have achieved a more dynamic social approach.

The experience of Pablo O'Higgins, for example, illustrates this process of an overwhelming Rivera influence changing to something else. Coming to Mexico in 1924 at the end of the first 'golden age,' he worked as Rivera's assistant at Chapingo and in the Ministry of Education from

---

[1] Including Tamayo.

1925 to 1927. After two years as a cultural worker in Durango and a year of teaching drawing in the elementary schools, he spent 1931–2 in Soviet Russia on a scholarship. Returning to Mexico, he participated in the 1933 new mural movement and in the 1934–5 joint murals at the Abelardo Rodríguez Market. At this point his style began to depart from the deeply inculcated Rivera method, and by the time he arrived at the National Printing Office he had turned in the new direction. Between that assignment and the murals of the 'forties, he engaged in a good deal of graphic work, underwent strong influences from Orozco, and became a leader in the radical art movement of the Cárdenas period.

With the single exception of Siqueiros, Leopoldo Méndez is perhaps the most significant radical artist of the Cárdenas era. He has worked in the mural field only in association with others (e.g. the Talleres Gráficos or Maternity Clinic No. 1). In the one case where he seems to have worked alone, in the Assembly Hall of UNESCO at Mexico City in 1947, he enlarged woodcuts to giant scale as wall decorations—a brilliant tour de force but with very little relation to painting.

Among individual artists not hitherto mentioned whose style and content reflect the general Revolutionary character of the 1934–40 period, we may cite Antonio Ruiz (b. 1897). After a period in Hollywood working on sets for Universal Films, Ruiz returned to Mexico in 1929 and applied the great precision and accuracy of style developed in his colonial movie sets to the everyday themes and Revolutionary subjects of the Cárdenas period. His well-known *Street Meeting* of 1935 is an example of one of the many facets of the socially conscious art movement in the 'thirties, utilizing basically conservative techniques with radical subject matter. Ruiz is also important for his work in the Mexican theater, especially plays for children, and for the fact that some of his work, including the *Street Meeting*, is closely related to popular painting of the nineteenth century.

Parallel with Ruiz, at least technically, is the talented architect-painter Juan O'Gorman, who has already been mentioned in connection with the short-lived Rivera administration at the Academy of San Carlos in 1929–30. At that time also, O'Gorman built the Rivera house in Coyoacán, one of the first modern residences in Mexico and an important point of departure for modern architecture in that country.

One of O'Gorman's most interesting contributions to the Mexican mural movement lies in the since removed frescoes in the waiting room of the Mexico City airport. These were done under the patronage of General Francisco Múgica, author of the celebrated Articles 27 and 123 in the 1917 Constitution and Minister of Communications under Cárdenas. In view of the convictions of both sponsor and artist, it is scarcely surprising that these panels contained the violent anti-Church, anti-fascist statements they did. Working between 1937 and 1938, O'Gorman produced a fine philosophical if somewhat sarcastic summary of flying,

DESPUES DE INVENTADA
LA AVIACION,-DE LOS
VUELOS MILAGROSOS
AL CIELO NO QUEDA
MAS QUE EL VACILON.

CASTIGO DE
MUERTE A QUIEN
TRATE DE VOLAR

80

O'GORMAN. *History of Religion*. FRESCO. PAINTED IN WAITING ROOM
OF MEXICO CITY AIRPORT AND DESTROYED IN 1939.

religion, history, and so on, a work of art quite different in spirit and form from the usual run of Mexican murals during this period (fig. 80).

Coloristically the panels were by no means startling; they displayed O'Gorman's usual color gamut, including bright red, greens, and blues, which stand out in small areas. But this pleasant color arrangement is in strong contrast to a clear, precise drawing, a deliberately cold, hard realism of delineation that is quietly merciless in its effect. The clergy of yesterday and today in the left-hand corner are shown with the same sardonic humor as the superstitious colonial nobility in the lower right, while all around are little touches of religious scenes of flying figures: Ascensions, Elijah's chariot, et cetera. Needless to say, the Church was not happy about this work. The companion panel contains a number of small historical spots, many of them contemporary and equally mordant, however controlled in form. One of these bits shows a series of serpents emerging from the top of O'Gorman's characteristic fantastic architectural painting, two of the snakes with the heads of Mussolini and Hitler.

By 1938, with the expropriation of foreign oil concessions and the need for disposing of Mexico's oil to fascist nations, who were the only ones willing to break the boycott of England and the United States, the Axis powers were at least temporarily in the category of friendly nations. In addition, following the defeat of the Spanish Loyalists in 1939, increasing pressures were felt from fascist and Falangist-minded groups. Thus the offending political panels of O'Gorman were destroyed. Only a small part of the original eighty-five square meters of fresco—the central and highly detailed *History of Aviation* (1937)—was permitted to exist in the face of the extreme right-wing pressure. This remaining portion is now in the Palacio de Bellas Artes in Mexico City.

But O'Gorman continued to paint, producing easel pictures with the same dry, meticulous, but highly imaginative and personal style. In 1941–2 he did an impressively large (fifteen meters by twelve and a half meters) mural in the Gertrudis Bocanegra Library at Pátzcuaro. Here he has given a history of one thousand years in the three-story-high panel which must rank among the most elaborate wall decorations ever to be painted. It is a narrative history of the state of Michoacán—where the city of Pátzcuaro is located—from pre-Conquest times down to the Revolution; Zapata, Morelos, and the great folk heroine, Gertrudis Bocanegra, are included.

O'Gorman is one of the few Mexican painters to devote himself to landscape; he has produced such work as the well-organized and textur-ally sensitive *Los Remedios* of 1943, the *View of Chalma*, and many others. Here, as in his mural paintings, is evident the meticulous draftsmanship of the architecturally trained person as well as the influence of foreign artists such as Rousseau, the German New Objectivist Kanoldt, the *pulquería* painters of his own country, and Rivera (especially in color). O'Gorman's is a strange dream world, often without people, in which the

186

eye is free to roam back and forth in the firm but gentle establishment of pictorial and textural balance that marks the painter's work.

Both by virtue of his critical and historical murals and through his great contribution to the architecture of the 'thirties, O'Gorman came to occupy a foremost place among his contemporaries. In 1928, he built for his father the first functional house in Mexico (Rivera's was done the following year). In the middle 'thirties, as head of the Department of Construction in the Ministry of Public Instruction (1932–5), he was in charge of building thirty new schools, and assumed the leadership in an architecture that has since become one of Mexico's important links to the progress of the Western world. Not only were new schools built, many with murals (a few painted with the help of O'Gorman), but there was also a great deal of rebuilding of older schools. O'Gorman helped to organize the architectural curriculum of the new Polytechnical Institute; and in 1935 he turned seriously to painting the kind of works we have cited, pictures that have the clear imprint of his own quiet, sensitive, but compelling personality. His 1952 Library Building decorations at the gigantic new University City are among the most recent developments in Mexican art.

XVII | The War and Postwar Periods

The end of the six-year Cárdenas administration brought with it increasing pressures from the Nazi and the Franco elements in Mexico. In part this was a local reaction against the Revolutionary program of the regime, but even more it came because of the world political situation. In these circumstances O'Gorman's antifascist, anti-Church murals at the Central Airport were destroyed in 1939, an act traceable as much to the general swing to the right as to the ambiguous situation of a government that could not afford to offend nominally friendly powers. The growing conflict between left and right in Mexico was summarized in the 1937 Orozco murals in the Guadalajara Government Palace, with the *Carnival of the Ideologies*; the first victory of the Nazis was portrayed in his *Dive Bomber* of 1940.

In the face of these mounting tensions, especially the imminence of a world-wide war, Cárdenas realized that it was time to consolidate the gains of his administration instead of trying for further advances. The resulting nomination and election of the more conservative General Manuel Avila Camacho brought into office a man who immediately changed the direction of Mexican development from left to center—and even to right. Even the un-Revolutionary Avila Camacho, however, was not satisfactory to many elements in Mexico at this time, and for a while counter-revolution was a definite possibility. Camacho managed to keep things on an even keel with the calming aid of Cárdenas, his own public profession of religious belief, and the support of the United States, which sent its vice-president, Henry A. Wallace, to the inauguration in December 1940.

Although there were several drastic slow-downs in the Revolutionary course Cárdenas had been following, the Mexico of 1940 had traveled a long way from the Mexico of twenty years before. Land distribution had stopped, but a good deal of emphasis was placed on making the *ejidos* (communal farms) more efficient. The labor movement, though no longer closely allied with the government and now under more conservative leadership, was still an important factor in national life. The schools stopped teaching socialism and attacking the Church; but the appointment of Jaime Torres Bodet to the Ministry of Education in 1944 marked the beginning of a remarkably effective campaign against illiteracy, in the course of which more than a million and a half Mexicans learned to read—no mean achievement. Similar swings back from center to left of center were made that year in the fields of social security and agrarian reform. In general, however, the trend was from agrarian reform toward industrial expansion during the Camacho regime and the following Alemán period.

This resulted from the two basic problems of the early 'forties in Mexico: the participation of that country in World War II and the increasingly close association with the United States, one issue strongly bound to the other. The Good Neighbor policy undertaken by the Roosevelt administration, the Wallace visit, and the final adjudication of the oil dispute put Mexico squarely on the side of the antifascist nations. Mexico's growing importance in the community of Latin-American nations was symbolized by the election of Lombardo Toledano to head the Confederation of Latin-American Workers and by Mexico's leading role in the Rio de Janeiro Pan-American Conference in 1942. Thus she was able to organize the nations of Central and South America in defense of the Western Hemisphere.

An interesting side light on this situation was the commissioning of Siqueiros to decorate the Escuela México in Chile in 1941 after that country had suffered an unusually severe earthquake. Finished in 1942, this monumental work, with its remarkably apposite title, *Death to the Invader*, furnished an important link in the ties that Mexico was trying to forge in Latin America, especially with Chile, which under the influence of Argentina had held back from full participation in the decisions of the Rio conference. After completion of this project, Siqueiros traveled throughout Latin America to mobilize the artists of many different countries in the fight against fascism. His 1944 mural in the Palacio de Bellas Artes in Mexico City, *The New Democracy*, was another powerful antifascist statement.

In the case of Orozco, the period began with the Supreme Court murals in 1940–41, a strong pro-Revolutionary statement in which he pointed out the need to safeguard Mexico's natural resources. His Hospital de Jesús murals in 1942–4 reflect the general world-war situation in their apocalyptic frenzy and destructive mood. Rivera, on the other hand, did not react to the crisis of the times. His 1943 murals in the Institute of Cardiology are simply a history of cardiology, however attractive. The 1945–50 walls in the National Palace are a meticulous and decorative narration of ancient Mexico; a new set done in the Hotel Reforma in 1943 merit no comment here; while the Hotel del Prado commission of 1947–8, *Dream on a Sunday Afternoon in the Central Alameda*, offers the old Rivera with romantic overtones.

Mexico's chief contribution to the war effort proper was along the lines of production and supply, furnishing agricultural products, textiles, minerals, and various types of manufactured goods. This resulted in a tremendous increase in industrial activity and, as in other countries during this period, a serious inflation also. Although some people were enriched through the extensive purchases by the United States in Mexico, the majority suffered from high prices and scarcity of goods as wages lagged far behind the rise in prices. By the end of the Camacho administration in 1946, business had made remarkable strides with the aid of government subsidies and exemptions of all kinds, while left-wing activities were correspondingly weak—in deference to the war effort. The right-wing Sinarquists, who were equally anti-Soviet and anti-United States, made considerable headway.

Under the next president, Miguel Alemán, the first civilian president since Madero, Mexico continued to follow this course of industrialization. Government became linked to business, as it now definitely turned from the agrarian revolt to the Industrial Revolution. Mexico was hurrying to catch up with other nations and, while the emphasis was primarily on development of material resources and encouragement of native industry, there were also impressive projects in irrigation, soil conservation, and education. One of the most significant educational accomplishments of the Alemán administration, in addition to building many schools in various areas, was the planning and construction of the giant University City on the outskirts of Mexico City. This Ciudad Universitaria, with its many modern buildings effectively arranged and designed, is the location of mural decorations by Siqueiros, Rivera, O'Gorman, and Chávez Morado, some in paint, others in mosaic, but all out of doors.

The turn toward mechanization and industrialization during this period (1946–52) is paralleled in the arts by such works as the Orozco machine-art mural at the National School for Teachers in 1947; the many murals by Jorge González Camarena in banks, office buildings, and even a brewery; and the 1952 Siqueiros mural in the Instituto Politécnico Nacional, *Man the Master and Not the Slave of Technology.* In 1945, Siqueiros, who had been interested since the 'thirties in the development of industrial materials for art, persuaded Minister of Education Torres Bodet[1] to establish a division of Chemical Research for Plastics[2] in the National Polytechnic Institute, for the use of both artists and industry. Here, under the able leadership of the painter and former Siqueiros Workshop member José L. Gutiérrez, modern materials such as vinylite, pyroxilin, and ethyl silicate were adapted for the benefit of the art world.

The growth of business and industry in Mexico brought a new middle class, for whom art has inevitably become the symbol of social importance.

---

[1] 70 *Obras Recientes de Siqueiros,* p. 31.
[2] Taller de Ensaye de Materiales de Pinturas y Plásticos.

During the 'forties, therefore, private galleries began to appear in numbers for the first time as the necessary intermediary between this new public and the easel painter and independent print-maker. For this body of artists, the government during the Alemán administration (1950) organized the Salón de la Plástica Mexicana and its branches, where artists could show their works free of charge and sell them without the customary commission fee.

The late and unusually rapid process of industrialization in Mexico has also caused the dislocation and social inequities typical of such situations. As a result, since the end of the Avila Camacho administration tendencies toward social reform are mirrored within the art world as well as in the labor movement, whose ranks are constantly enlarged as industry grows. The O'Higgins-Méndez mural in Maternity Hospital No. 1 of the Social Security Administration in 1946–7, the mural of González Camarena in the Social Security Building on the Paseo de la Reforma in 1950, the Siqueiros mural for the Polytechnical Institute in 1952, and many others are evidences of the reaction to this situation. These works reflect the effort of the government to extend to the Mexican people the benefits of social security, free medical care, increased educational opportunity, and so on—very real and tangible gains. At the same time, other works show the persistent feeling that business has acquired too much voice in government, that for the general-presidents of the previous era have been substituted the corporation lawyers of today. Thus left-wing artist groups of various kinds have become active again, groups such as the Taller and the recent National Front of Plastic Arts, headed by the veteran Goitia.[3] But their contribution, like that of the L.E.A.R. of the 'thirties, is primarily political rather than artistic. The great achievements of the war and postwar periods are still those of the outstanding independents, reacting to the times in their own ways: Orozco, Siqueiros, Tamayo, Rivera, and the younger men, who best represent Mexican art today.

---

[3] Frente Nacional de Artes Plásticas.

XVIII | Orozco
1940 to 1949

After completing his Jiquilpan mural for the outgoing president, Lázaro Cárdenas, Orozco began to work early in 1941 on the wall decorations of the newly built Supreme Court in Mexico City. He was given four large areas to paint in its main entrance hall, the so-called Hall of Lost Steps. One is behind the spectator as he comes up the stairs, one on each side of the large open space, and the fourth on the far wall, where columns partly obstruct the view.

It is this last area, opposite the staircase, that is confronted upon entering (fig. 81). The long rectangular space of this main mural is dominated by the Mexican tiger (or jaguar), its upper portion gray and black, its lower part lavender with black spots. With teeth bared, the ferocious animal, wrapped in the red-white-green national flag, leaps to the left in a powerful protective movement across the symbols of Mexico's underground wealth arranged directly below.

Scanning these symbols from the lower right, we see first a golden skeleton, its head that of a medieval moneylender type, its ribs containing the corpse of some fantastic beast that has died in the golden cage. This is the symbol of Mexico's *Gold.* Above it is the figure that denotes *Silver,* an elongated parody of the female body, a soulless, dessicated creature, as dead as the gold near which it is placed. On the lower left-hand side is *Iron,* represented by a series of metal fragments. Immediately above this is the dignified and impressive *Copper,* a male figure lying on its face, suggesting in a general way the ancient pre-Spanish inhabitants of Mexico. In the center, set directly between the two pairs of minerals, is a primeval headlike image representing *Oil,* whose teeth are metallic spouts from which the rich liquid flows in unending streams.

These five symbols move inward and outward in space, lending their poetically abstract forms to as unusual a conception as Orozco has ever offered. Yet in spite of the increasingly generalized and symbolic treatment of form, this mural is more specific in intent than the tiger composition at Jiquilpan. Here the painter apparently exhorts the Supreme Court to guard the subsoil wealth of Mexico, as they had recently done by invoking Article 27 of the Constitution in expropriation of the oil industry.

On the square wall over the staircase (all the others are rectangular)

Orozco reminds the judges of Article 123[1] guaranteeing the rights of labor (fig. 82). But this is no political speech, no picturesque appeal to so-called native values. It is rather a series of phantasms, representations in stridently nonnaturalistic terms of the violent—even vicious—struggle of mankind to fight its way out of one social dimension into another.

In the background is a reddish-brown, geometrically abstract, open building, through which vague shapes and faces appear like the ghosts of those who fought in the struggles of the past. The forms, in lavender and gray-green, vary in substantiality from complete dematerialization in the the background to the transparent and simian face on the left-hand upright of the building shape. This wraithlike symbol holds in its hand a solid pickax, which comes forward into the main body of the composition. Here the battle takes on a more tangible and climactic form. A file of bent-over gray-green and gray-blue figures (the oppressed) moves across the center of the panel between two pairs of struggling workers. There is one pair of straining figures in the upper right, whose movements carry us out of the picture. The other pair is in the immediate foreground. One of the latter is painted in lavender-gray, his face hidden in the enormous red flag, and the other in lavender-violet, his formless face suggesting the Jiquilpan *Masses* and blending into the equally faceless bent-over forms in the middleground—the humanity that continues to suffer during the fight for liberty.

---

[1] Fernández, *Orozco: forma e idea*, p. 107.

PHOTO LUIS MÁRQUEZ

81

OROZCO. *The National Riches*, detail.
FRESCO. SUPREME COURT,
MEXICO CITY.

82

OROZCO. *The Working-Class Movement.*
FRESCO. SUPREME COURT, MEXICO CITY.

83

OROZCO. *Justice*, detail. FRESCO. RIGHT-HAND WALL, SUPREME COURT, MEXICO CITY.

Series of verticals and horizontals, predominantly red, oppose the struggling forms of the workers, which are colored from lavender-green to lavender-gray to gray. Formalistically these figures, anticipated to some extent at Guadalajara, go even farther along the road of Expressionistic distortion, with the aid of Byzantine emaciation and elongation.

This rear panel is tied to the main one opposite it by the side murals, each of which surrounds a doorway in the center of its wall. Gigantic figures of Justice and Vengeance lean down at left and right of these doors to destroy or attack the invidious forces of dishonesty, treachery, et cetera. In the left-hand mural, from one side of the wall a colossal form sweeps out of the heavens with an ax in its hands to drive away a group of figures who are subverting justice. At the other side of the doorway, a red flame emanates from the lower part of the avenging figure, moving diagonally downward into a group of bandits who are tying up the people and stealing their resources. The thieves are in subdued gray tinted with green; the avenging figure is gray tinted with blue.

The right-hand wall is a companion piece, with a similar figure overhead attacking from both sides of the doorway (fig. 83). The left portion reveals true Justice with a torch thrust menacingly at a group of nude usurpers of governmental power (one with a Phrygian liberty cap) who

84

OROZCO. FRESCO. CHOIR VAULT AND REAR WALL.
CHAPEL OF JESÚS NAZARENO, MEXICO CITY.

85

OROZCO. *The Demon Tied.* FRESCO.
LEFT-HAND WALL ADJACENT TO CHOIR VAULT.
CHAPEL OF JESÚS NAZARENO, MEXICO CITY.

PHOTO LUIS MÁRQUEZ

are feverishly looking through books for justification of their illegal acts. The other end of this wall again shows the diagonal ray of fire, this time cutting into a group of masked men, including a terrified travestied Justice figure. On a pedestal at the rear, another figure of Justice leans back in its chair asleep and unaware of what is being done in its name. On both walls, the background elements at right and left include generalized shelves, walls, and so on, which bring the murals into conformity with the intervening doorways.

During the following year, 1942, Orozco began to paint the former church of the ancient Hospital de Jesús Nazareno, founded by Cortez early in the sixteenth century and said to be the first institution of its kind in America. Although Orozco worked on this building until 1944, he was able to complete only a few sections: the vault and walls of the choir, and the vault of the first section of the nave adjoining the choir. (Apparently the funds for the job ran out.)

The subject matter of these few murals is visionary and prophetic in character, not as Biblical illustrations but rather as a projection of Orozco's feeling concerning our own turbulent period of war and destruction (figs. 84, 85, 86). His personal symbols convey a powerful awareness of the anguished times in which we live. The most abstract form on the choir vault is that of Deity, with evangelists in a more figurative style flying about it. In a kind of symbolism and abstraction altogether different from that of the God form, he shows a near-by angel first tying a demon and then, on the other side, untying him. Two figures, male and female, at the base of the choir wall represent human sorrow. These are conceived in a simple Expressionistic manner (especially the woman), each placed before a geometrically constructed tomb, whose mechanical shape suggests the elements of the slightly later Normal School mural.

Examined more closely, this first section is seen to be a kind of Last Judgment. The colors are cool; gray, black, and green accents convey the feeling of mutability, of death itself. The light-green, abstract symbol of God (which seems derived from some Aztec glyph) is basically a rectangle with a T-form attached above it. Forceful in its geometrical rigidity, the whole element is made up of perspectivized slabs. One writer[2] claims that

---

[2] Cleve Gray, 'Orozco's Recent Frescoes,' *Art in America*, vol. 36, 1948, p. 137.

86

OROZCO. FRESCO. CHOIR VAULT, DETAIL OF RIGHT SIDE.
CHAPEL OF JESÚS NAZARENO, MEXICO CITY.

this is a precolonial ideograph very close in form to the actual glyph meaning 'the destruction of a city.' Whether or not this is so, the effect of the representation is that of a Romanesque Last Judgment in which, as here, flames (or rays of light) shoot out from the Deity. This impression is heightened by the four anthropomorphic evangelist symbols flying about the central God-glyph.

In keeping with Orozco's development since 1940, there is an advanced looseness of brushstroke; his work shows a genuine Expressionistic (and visionary) quality in this respect, as in the movement of the flying figures and in the flowing, tortured shapes of the two symbols of humanity. These latter curvilinear figures are in decided form and color contrast to the brutal rectangular tombs behind them. The two are on either side of a window at the foot of the choir wall.

On the side walls of the choir vault, the painter has placed the pair of highly suggestive allegories in which an angel ties a demon and, at the other side, liberates him. Here Orozco has worked out monstrous shapes of remarkable fantasy and strength, shapes completely personal and original. The monster's innumerable appendages are restrained for only a while and then freed again, all portrayed in the general greenish tonality of this choir vault.

In the adjacent vault, which is part of the four longitudinal nave sections, Orozco shifts to a hot color scheme, with reds and oranges added to the earlier grays and blacks, the whole effect more curvilinear than geometric. These nave vaults are about 40 feet across and about 30 feet deep. Had they been completed, they would have offered as impressive a group as Orozco ever produced.

This last vault section presents four apocalyptic beasts in black, tan, and brown: three horses and a jaguar (a traditional symbol of Mexico). The jaguar is ridden by the *Whore of the Apocalypse*, clear enough reference to what Orozco felt was being done to his country. She is a horribly caricatured reddish creature, similar in general effect to the repulsive female of the 1934 Palacio de Bellas Artes mural. This section of the Jesús murals is a terrifying vision of suffering, excess, and violent emotion of all kinds. A powerful arm thrusts a spear through several figures; other forms are seen with pieces of swords sticking out of them; mangled and decayed shapes abound. The motif of the sword-pierced human being occurs many times in Orozco's work, and the great chains seen here have also been used by him before to denote captivity. The barbed-wire areas suggest oppression and punishment for transgressions against man-made restrictions.

In spite of its incompleteness, the Jesús Hospital project represents another high point in Orozco's art and another new approach to the problem of human suffering and man's fate. Concerning this approach, Orozco is quoted as follows: '...having seen the torment of our times, comparable to apocalyptic punishment, I reinvented the demon, painting him in such form that it [this work] represented the renewal of Baroque art, and as the expression of the triumph of the human over itself, over the mechanized world of our times.'[3] Even in the fragmentary condition in which they were left at the painter's death and in spite of the unfortunate neglect that is allowing this great work to disappear, the Hospital de Jesús murals offer a spectacle of such imaginative and overpowering poetic force that they must be ranked among the artist's major achievements.

His next work, the *National Allegory*, was done in one of the most impressive buildings in Mexico City, the National School for Teachers (or Normal School). Built in 1947 by Mario Pani, the school includes a magnificent long open-air theater, bounded on each side by tiers of open balcony corridors and focusing on a stage backed by a six-story curved concrete wall, which was given to Orozco to paint. This formidable assignment, fifty-nine feet high and seventy-two feet across, made even more difficult because it was out of doors, brought Orozco into contact with the problem of the open-air mural for the first time. As we have already seen, this problem had engaged the attention of Siqueiros for some time. It had also been the subject of innumerable experiments in the Polytechnic Institute's division of Chemical Research for Plastics, whose professor, the painter José Gutiérrez, and chemist-technician Manuel Jiménez Rueda advised Orozco to use ethyl silicate for his outdoor job. Gutiérrez furnished the actual formula[4] by which the mixture of ethyl silicate, alcohol, water, and hydrochloric acid was prepared for use on this gigantic wall. The formula was based on Gutiérrez's own experience with this medium, dating back to 1938. In addition to this technical advice, Orozco received help from a team of assisting artists, which enabled him to accomplish the huge task by 1948 (exact dates were November 1947 to April 1948).

The parabola-shaped stage wall is anchored to the galleries at the sides of the open-air theater by gray and red columns (fig. 87). Horizontal thrusts from these galleries are repeated in strong horizontal lines throughout the mural. The intensive verticality of the tower looming behind the mural wall is repeated in equally distinct up-and-down elements in the painting, particularly in the central serpent form with its bent neck. In this way, as well as by the use of small metallic inlays on the surface of the work,[5] the integration of painting and architecture is brought about in a calculated and effective manner. The Baroque doorway at the bottom of the mural (from the old university) is brought within the symbolic meaning of the wall in general, and is worked into the curvilinear forms directly above it.

---

[3] Justino Fernández, 'El pintor de nuestro tiempo,' *Anales del instituto de investigaciones estéticas*, no. 16, 1948.

[4] *José Clemente Orozco, Sexta Exposición*, El Colegio Nacional, Mexico, 1948.

[5] Cf. Siqueiros in Chillán, 1941–2.

87

OROZCO. *National Allegory*. ETHYL SILICATE.
NATIONAL SCHOOL FOR TEACHERS, MEXICO CITY.

By these various means Orozco used the structural lines of the painting first to maintain the relation with the architectural design of the building and then to give life to the wall and its various sections. Although this mural is usually called 'abstract' in the school-of-Paris sense and does suggest certain spatial penetrations by such artists as the 'North-American' Stuart Davis (as in the upper right-hand section), the fact remains that this is as symbolic a representation as anything Orozco has done so far. He knows exactly what he wants to express and says:

Theme: National Allegory, with large geometric forms, stone and metal. In the center: the Eagle and the Serpent, a representation of Life and Death, a representation of the Mexican Earth. At the left, a man with his head in the clouds moves up a gigantic staircase; at the right a hand puts a block into place... The forms of the composition are so organized as to acknowledge and preserve the parabolic form of the wall and to be seen at any distance.[6]

At the right side of the mural (fig. 88) are symbols of the precolonial past, especially the blackish ruins at lower right. Above them at right

---

[6] *Orozco: Sexta Exposición.*

center, the brown hand of an Indian comes in from the side, grasping a gray block of stone that cuts through a series of lavender, red, gray, and blue elements. Above this hand are rectangular architectural forms in orange; resembling in a general way the outlines of an ancient pyramid, they also suggest the girders of modern construction as they change at the bottom into red shapes that move left.

The center of this great composition shows a vivid green serpent—native Mexico—living yet dying, its drooping neck clutched in the beak of the eagle emerging from the block forms at the upper right, and its lower body grasped in the buff-colored claw of the eagle. This central portion ends immediately below in the colonial doorway, the presence of which (together with the sword) symbolizes that other historical element in the history of Mexico, the Spanish, which combines with the Indian to evolve the basic Mexican formula.

This world, the Indian-Spanish, is attacked by gray-blue, pointed mechanical forms rushing in from the left and also by corkscrew-spiral gray-blue pipe shapes that represent modern mechanized life. Through the entire left-hand area man ascends, one foot on a kind of gray metal-form step, the other on the ground, while his head is hidden in the clouds above. The lower leg is still enveloped in materialistic steel elements from which he rises heavenward, another symbol of man's hopeful

88

OROZCO. *National Allegory.*
ETHYL SILICATE.
NATIONAL SCHOOL FOR
TEACHERS, MEXICO CITY.

future as he advances out of the material into the spiritual (cf. Hospicio Cabañas).

Compositionally this work is dominated by a series of verticals (the legs, the sword, the endless corkscrew, the serpent form, the up-and-down lines of the buildings at the right), against which a number of powerful horizontal parabolic movements work in opposition and balance. Chief of these are the metallic forms that come in from the left and the horizontal lines of the buildings at the right, which lead the eye across the entire composition. If we measure diagonally across the mural —and we are assured by Orozco that he calculated every line and color effect with great care—the lines drawn from corner to opposite corner meet at the precise point where the lower curvilinear metallic bar touches the body of the serpent.

The brilliant foreshortening of the dynamic elements coming from the left is perhaps the most effective of all Orozco's representations of mechanized force. The forms move powerfully right and yet are held in check by the equally dramatic verticals in the center and at left of center. Orozco's adaptation of the post-Cubist technique is as individual as his handling of Expressionist methods. It is an imaginative utilization of space techniques in which the interpenetration of planes appears in a new and personal manner; structural lines, for example, extend beyond the boundaries of the color areas they are supposed to define, creating a different kind of transparency and deeper space indications. In this way the eye is led through and allowed to penetrate areas in a constantly moving dynamic fashion quite different from the aesthetic of either the Futurist or the machine painters. There is a 'force line' that comes from the lower left in a wide sweeping parabola across the top center of the wall into the upper right, linking man's ascendancy and man's building power. But this is no mere substitute for movement; as it penetrates the various in-and-out-moving areas, it is part of the action of the wall.

We may say further that the mechanized forms—man, inswinging metal bars, spiral pipes, and the brown hand at the right—have a genuine symbolic quality that is the result of Orozco's pictorial and allegorical approach. Indeed it would be difficult to conceive of a mural destined for such a building in Mexico in which a 'form for form's sake' approach would be acceptable either to the artist or to the public, given the environmental factors already established.[7]

Orozco's use of metal pieces, indentations on the surface of the cement, and deliberate surface roughenings are part of a new technique that enriches mural painting in this period and in which both he and Siqueiros, especially the latter, play leading roles. Painting on an inward-curving surface has been one of Siqueiros's specialities, but never in the poetically abstract manner of Orozco here. Once before Orozco was confronted

[7] Perhaps the only purely formal instance is the Mérida decoration for the Juárez Housing Project (1949).

with the problem of painting in a completely modern building, the New School in New York. At that time, his style changed markedly and not necessarily for the better, in a stiff version of Hambidge's dynamic symmetry. Now, however, after the experience of many years' experimentation with machine forms on a different level (the Hospicio Cabañas, the *Dive Bomber*, et cetera), he came to this problem with a new point of view and a new understanding of what could be done with these elements.

Machining of form in this *National Allegory* influences the eagle and the serpent that represent Mexico, just as it does the brown hand at the right and the Coatlique face (from the Aztec mother goddess) above the serpent head, that represent the force of the dead past. On these shapes are superimposed the real mechanical factors—the curvilinear beams, the corkscrew forms, the various devices that overwhelm and obscure the older symbols. It is from these new elements that man rises to his hope of the future, but one group is balanced against the other, each keeping the other in a dynamic suspension from which better things may or may not come.

The overwhelming of the ancient by the modern is indicated also in the way in which the older symbols not only are mechanized in form but are given a roughness of surface and more distinct visibility by the indentation of lines throughout and by the addition of metallic elements to the figures themselves. Modern iron and steel fragments are placed about the outline of the body of the serpent and on the Coatlique mask in the upper center. But if this would give the feeling of an old world succumbing completely to the force of the new, the living-dying form of the serpent remains the central and dominant part of the composition, resisting the onslaughts of the metal pieces and surviving the piling of block on block. The future is unknown, but in the eyes of the painter, Mexico always remains.

In this National School for Teachers Orozco also did some fresco murals in the vestibule of the same building. They were painted in 1948 after the outside wall had been completed. Here he projected a series of black-outlined forms in grayish black occasionally touched with blue. These are seen on both sides of the vestibule against a dark-red background and below a three-dimensional architecture that projects inward and deepens the space of this narrow passageway. Two panels here show people waiting in line—poor, simple, even gaunt and ragged folk bringing their children to school. As they move forward, the mood changes from sadness and despair to hope; those in the front of each line have white highlights on their faces and the upper parts of their bodies. A symbolic abstract and buff-colored triangle of light illuminates them with the promise of a better future.

The last year and a half of Orozco's life was a period of constant activity and increased growth, of happy creativity and further public acknowledgment. During 1948, while assistants were carrying out his designs and ideas in the Normal School outdoor mural, he managed to find time for a long rectangular fresco in the National Historical Museum at Chapultepec Castle. Here, in an extraordinary composition known as *Juárez and the Reform*,[8] Orozco has reinterpreted the story of Juárez and the reforms he promulgated, in a characteristic vibrant and poetic symbolism (fig. 89).

What is new here is the way in which the enormous brown head emerges diagonally into the picture space against its red-pink background, flanked on either side by semi-nude soldiers in gray trousers and red-plumed caps. The soldiers at the left, before their BATALLON SUPREMOS PODERES banner, trample and hack at the recumbent clergy and at the mummified body of the Emperor Maximilian, which stretches across the lower part of the panel. This amazing conception of Maximilian (which may be compared with the dessicated symbols of Mexico's wealth in the Supreme Court murals) rests on a series of clerical, military, and royalist figures—including Napoleon III, who comes out of the lower right-hand corner. The soldier at the upper right whips at a clerical caricature with a torch of rebellion that illuminates his military cap inscribed with the significant number 57, symbolizing the Juárez constitution of 1857. The priest himself, hands tied behind his back, is a horrible travesty of a human being, with clawlike fingers and vulture beak.

The design of this mural is unusual in that it is based on a broad, upsweeping curve, in the midst of which the head of Juárez comes almost straight out toward the spectator, as though about to fall into the room, and yet holds its place in the picture space admirably. It is dynamic and monumentally controlled at the same time; the forward movement is balanced by the thrusts up and back. The vivid colors of the Mexican flag at the upper left leap out from the picture, as does the bright blue of Napoleon III at the lower right. These are also balancing and opposing political forces, as are the immensely plastic Juárez and the dessicated Maximilian below him.

Orozco's adaptation to the circumstances of each commission is seen again in this mural; the facial characteristics of both the French emperor and Maximilian are derived directly from historical documents in the museum itself, as are the face of Juárez, the uniforms of the soldiers, and the Mexican standards. In the national flag, however, Orozco has modified the actual colors, and has altered them into a more decorative and spatial agreement with the picture as a whole. (The same is true of his handling of the flag on the back wall of the Supreme Court.)

Toward the end of 1948, the busy Orozco undertook to decorate the concert hall of the newly built National Conservatory of Music. He was called away before he got very far with that project, and went to Guadalajara to paint the half-dome of the Chamber of Deputies in the Govern-

---

[8] Professor Fernández calls it *Juárez Reborn* in 'Obras recientes de Orozco,' *México en el Arte*, no. 6, Dec. 1948.

ment Palace, which became his last completed work (fig. 90). In the building where he had done the magnificent staircase with its figure of Hidalgo y Costilla, he returned to the Hidalgo theme, this time to celebrate the latter's decree abolishing slavery, which had been issued in that city. To this symbolic representation he added a number of other famous Mexican lawgivers in a composite tribute to the various acts of legislation that marked important steps in the progress of Mexico.

The technical problems here were rather serious, since the half-dome covering the chamber is directly overhead and is also connected to a flat, arched wall space below and at right angles to the spherical section. In

the half-dome proper, Orozco presents an idealistic half-length Hidalgo inscribing on a plaque the word LIBERTAD. Around him and emerging from the lower part of the sphere, there writhe in anguished motion three gigantic and Expressionistic yellow-brown nudes—the slaves. The one at the left waves a red banner and holds his blue-tinted sword across the word on the plaque, while at his side is the grayish-black mass of chains and barbed wire that symbolizes Mexico's slavery (cf. Jesús Hospital vault figures). The other two forms radiating from the base are tied to a similar figure, its back criss-crossed with the scars of whips, swung across the open space above the great patriot's head. These three slaves are bound together with chains, against which they struggle fiercely.

The center one of the trio has a head formed of two iron bands at right angles to each other, a chain riveted to its top and extending to the two figures to which it is attached. This effigy, the climax of many interesting studies of slavery that Orozco did during this period, has its manacled hands held out to Hidalgo as though demanding liberty. The resemblance here to a Siqueiros idea of a slightly earlier period (see fig. 100, the 1947 *Nuestra imagen actual*) is very interesting, although the actual form is still typically Orozco. The dynamics of this curved area, like that in the National School for Teachers, suggests in a general way the same influence. The background color of the vault is similar to part of the staircase Orozco had done some years earlier, and features a lavender-purple tonality.

The only way to get a proper view of this half-dome, aside from lying back in a chair, is to look at its reflection in the glass-topped speaker's table at the front of the room (when the legislature is not in session). This affords an adequate idea of the forms and of the dynamic thrusts of movement that surround the figure of Hidalgo. The conception of this area is different in many ways from that on the staircase, where a fanatic has set an earthquake in motion. Here Hidalgo is shown as a dreamy, albeit determined, type, around whom the tortured enslaved forms swirl, demanding to be set free. In the earlier mural the keynotes are violence, hysteria, and slaughter; here the key words are liberty and reform.

The deeds of other great reformers are shown on the flat wall below the dome. These men—Morelos, Juárez, and Carranza—although accompanied in two cases by the soldiers of their respective eras, appear in their legalistic and corrective aspects rather than as fighters. Against a large square plaque bearing the letters REFORMA, from left to right are Carranza, author of the great 1917 Constitution, Juárez, author of the Reform laws, and at the right Morelos, who serves here in his capacity of agrarian reformer.

This work, concluded in August 1949, was Orozco's last completed mural. The painter died a few weeks later, leaving unfinished the Hospital de Jesús murals and the recently undertaken decorations of the Alemán

90

OROZCO. *Hidalgo and the Liberation of Mexico*. FRESCO.
SENATE CHAMBER, GOVERNMENT PALACE, GUADALAJARA.

housing development, known as the Edificio Multifamiliar Presidente Alemán.

The period 1940–49 in the life of Orozco marked not only the production of the various murals examined here but also the creation of a number of distinguished easel paintings. There is more unevenness of quality in this area than in the murals, where Orozco's graphic basis is always helpful; in easel painting it tends in some cases to override the necessary function of color.

A picture such as the somber, low-keyed 1943 *Landscape in the Mountains* exemplifies the application of Orozco's Expressionistic and abstract style of the 'forties to a problem of landscape. Its particular virtue lies in the way the painter has conveyed the violent restlessness and agitation of this place without losing a sense of unity. The forms move violently to the right in most instances, yet are counteracted by contrary elements that provide a balancing force.

From 1943 to 1948, Orozco was given a special exhibition each year by the Colegio Nacional, in all of which his progress as a painter and his

91

OROZCO. *After the Battle*. OIL. MEXICO CITY, COLL. DR. A. CARRILLO GIL.

preparatory work for the various mural projects can be seen clearly. Each of these exhibitions seems to have had some basic idea behind it. In 1947, for example, Orozco presented the results of a year's work on the theme of the Conquest of Mexico, with texts derived from the early Spanish chroniclers. This series of canvases, known as *Los Teules*,[9] are violent and tortured representations of specific incidents from the Conquest. For instance, in the bloody *After the Battle* (fig. 91)[10] arrows are shown sticking through a horse's head and through a human hand in the lower left, while around them in diagonal arrangements the refuse of battle is piled in a tightly organized and horrifying composition. Heavy white-on-black accents and grays mark this scene and its grayish background, which shows all the furious intensity of some of Orozco's best mural work. One or two of the forms appear in a kind of grape color, in contrast to the morbidity of the total effect.

[9] The Man-gods, as the Indians at first called the Spaniards.
[10] See also *Time*, 5 Dec. 1955.

92

OROZCO. *Indian Pierced by a Lance.*
PYROXILIN ON MASONITE.
MEXICO CITY, COLL. SRA. MARGARITA
VALLADARES DE OROZCO.

In another scene, the *Paso del Puente*, he shows the Spanish horsemen plunging into the water. The figures of the men and horses take part in a scene of carnage and defeat that is seldom matched in paint. One of the most poignant studies of this 1947 series is the pyroxilin *Indian Pierced by a Lance*, a sensation of the 1950 Biennale in Venice (fig. 92). Here a soft amorphous form sinks left, it arms raised in supplication as the sharp weapon cuts diagonally through it. Again the white highlights appear, again the powerful and expressive draftsmanship that underlies so much of Orozco's work, and again the pathos that makes him unique among artists of the twentieth century.

His final Colegio Nacional exhibition in 1948 showed a series of sketches and studies for the mural works of 1946–8. One of these, apparently in preparation for the Guadalajara Chamber of Deputies, is the *Head of a Slave* (1948). A veiled form is bound to silence and imprisonment in two massive iron bands at right angles to each other, restrained physically by the enormous key dangling from them and spiritually by the rosary wrapped about the head.

In 1946 Orozco had been awarded the National Prize of Arts and Sciences, and the following year he was given a retrospective exhibition in the Palacio de Bellas Artes, an enormous show that marked his apotheosis as a living artist. When he died in September 1949, it was a day of national mourning and international regret. Whatever it may signify, he was the first painter to be buried in Mexico's pantheon, the Panteón Civil at Dolores, the village of Hidalgo. Although Orozco had been far from a public figure during his lifetime, in spite of the many honors heaped upon him toward the end, his passing unleashed a torrent of sorrow within every segment of the Mexican population, an outpouring that had to be experienced to be understood. From his colleagues Siqueiros and Rivera (who demanded that he be interred in the pantheon and stood as honor guard at his bier), through the black headlines of the newspapers, to the ordinary man in the street, all Mexico was moved.

Without political significance of any kind but with moral significance of the highest order, the passing of Orozco underlined the place of the artist in Mexico, both as an outstanding element in its intellectual life and as the custodian of its conscience. Throughout his life, Orozco had reminded Mexico of the blood bath of the Revolution, of the false leaders and their betrayal of the people, of the spiritual danger of mechanization, of the social menace of unscrupulous self-interest, and finally of the simple fact that man can aspire to better things.

The career of Siqueiros since 1940 has been a succession of significant applications of his theories of neo-Realism, first fully developed in the 1939 mural at the Electrical Workers Union in Mexico City. Some instances are less successful than others; some, such as the murals in Chile and those in the old Customs Building in Mexico, have surpassed the first example in this vein. Siqueiros has also done a good deal of easel painting, but in keeping with his strong belief in the superiority of mural over easel painting, he is unwilling to admit the importance of his own achievement in the latter medium. Even if it is true, as he claims, that all or most of these easel pictures are 'ideas' for murals not yet executed, they remain one of his greatest contributions to modern Mexican painting. As for the ever-growing number of mural projects since 1940, none perhaps is so important as the one in Chile.

In 1941 Siqueiros went to Chile, where, at the request of the Mexican ambassador, Octavio Reyes Spindola, he worked for an entire year on a set of murals in the provincial city of Chillán—a job of two hundred and fifty-nine square meters in the Escuela México. Some two years before, in January 1939, there had been a catastrophic earthquake in the southern part of Chile. In Chillán, the birthplace of Bernardo O'Higgins, the Chilean liberator, about fifteen hundred people had been killed in one of the greatest disasters in South American history. The Escuela México, part of the extensive rebuilding program, was formally opened on 25 March 1942, as a gift from the people of Mexico to the people of Chile. (It was also an important political symbol at a moment of crisis in the affairs of the Americas.) The Siqueiros murals are in the school library, which is named after Don Pedro Aguirre Cerda, former president of the Chilean Republic. The room with the paintings is known to the children as 'The Room of the Giants.'

The library is entered through a doorway in the middle of one of its long sides; the murals are seen to right and left on the narrow end walls, with a ceiling painting connecting the two. The rectangular shape of the room is modified by concave masonite panels mounted on armatures on the narrower walls. These concave areas are then connected with the flat ceiling by pinched-in corners, to form one continuous surface—a kind of curved box within a rectangular box. The mounting of the murals on armatures is designed to cut down future earthquake dangers to the paintings. Most important, these curved surfaces create a powerful optical illusion, a dynamic action that involves and envelopes the spectator as he walks through the room.

The one hundred and seventy-five square-meter ceiling together with the walls (each forty-two square meters) form an area of two hundred and fifty-nine square meters, conceived as a totality for greater movement and expressiveness. Each wall is concave with a camber, or curvature, of about sixty degrees, which increases the dynamic effect. The murals are painted on masonite with pyroxilin paints to give greater textural variety: rough, smooth, brilliant, opaque, et cetera, and to take advantage of the rough and luminous glazes the medium offers. This powerful composition, known as *Death to the Invader*, with its straining figures, its many-sided and superposed forms that increase the effect of spatial motion, is considerably different from all other Mexican murals, but it is a logical outgrowth of the 1939 cinematographic conception in the Electrical Workers Union.

One wall is devoted to Chile (fig. 93), the other to Mexico (figs. 94, 95). On the Chilean wall we see that country's struggles for independence and progress from the time of the Auracanian Indian Galvarino to the modern Recabarren; fallen figures represent the invaders. On the Mexican panel opposite is the form of an Aztec Indian, Cuauhtémoc the resister, bending backward with terrific energy and shooting his arrows at the symbolic fiery Cross overhead. At the feet of Cuauhtémoc lies the fallen invader, with an arrow in his chest. These two walls and the ceiling joining them are another fervid political allegory, a statement rendered in terms that Siqueiros calls 'pictorial eloquence,' part of the public art he has been trying to create.

Here Siqueiros has worked out illusionistic effects allowing for ocular adjustments and corrections which the human eye can make and which he intends it to make. For example, the Cross, the target of the Aztec in the Mexican panel, as it moves upward into the ceiling, is illusionistically painted. It is more or less normal in its proportions when seen close up and when we are facing the Mexican side, but it has an entirely different effect when we turn our backs and walk toward the Chilean wall. Now the Cross seems to stretch out endlessly along the surface of the ceiling. Similarly, in the Chilean panel a circular flame rises from the heads of the two main figures; as we go away from this wall, the flame seems to move along the ceiling toward the other side of the room.

The tremendous projection forward and the liberation of forms (e.g. the Aztec, whose back is curved as he shoots his arrows upward) seem to exist in a new kind of space created by the painter, a space that results from the multiplication of parts and the cinematic superposition of images that may be viewed from different angles. In the Chilean panel this is seen in the head of Galvarino, through which we may look to the head

93

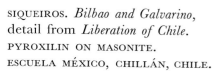

SIQUEIROS. *Bilbao and Galvarino*,
detail from *Liberation of Chile*.
PYROXILIN ON MASONITE.
ESCUELA MÉXICO, CHILLÁN, CHILE.

of his countryman Bilbao. Also, there is a curious doubling of feet in the lower right, as the intense and forcefully moving Indian comes forward waving his bloody arm stumps. These stumps, like the arms of the Aztec on the other wall, are rendered in a fluid form that increases the sense of movement. The simultaneous presentation of two feet or two arms gives a kind of Futurist dynamism wherever it occurs, as well as an increased number of possible viewing points. Superposing of forms is done through the use of the projector, while the airbrush permits rapid painting; the pyroxilin paint gives a wide range of surface variations in textural effects. All these things combine to increase the spatial dynamics of Siqueiros's technique.

The relation between the walls and the ceiling, their unified impact as a space continuum, is exemplified in the figure of the Aztec warrior, whose bow gives the illusion of existing on a flat surface (or at least on a vertical surface), but actually half of that bow is on the ceiling above the head of the warrior. On the Chilean side this same illusion is effected by the spears at the left and the flags at the right.[1] To these elements of

---

[1] For most of the details in connection with these murals, the author is indebted to the two excellent articles by Lincoln Kirstein in the *Magazine of Art*, Dec. 1943 & Jan. 1944.

94

SIQUEIROS. *The Liberation of Mexico.*
PYROXILIN ON MASONITE.
ESCUELA MÉXICO. CHILLÁN, CHILE.

95

SIQUEIROS. *Cuauhtémoc*, detail
from *Liberation of Mexico.*
PYROXILIN ON MASONITE.
ESCUELA MÉXICO, CHILLÁN, CHILE.

214

illusionism we must add the effect of the recessive pyramid on the Mexican side.

Once the many preliminary steps have been taken, especially the determination of the spatial composition (a process that requires a great deal of analysis),[2] the quick-drying pyroxilin paints and the spray gun enable the artist to paint as rapidly as he likes without waiting for each section to dry. The speed possibilities of this technique were dramatically illustrated by the painting of the upper left-hand part of the Mexican panel, showing Morelos, Hidalgo, and Zapata led by Adelita, the *soldadera* heroine of the Revolution. This section still lacked the last figure on the very morning of the official opening of the school. In half a day, while officials and other guests were on their way from Santiago, Siqueiros posed his wife, Angelica, as Adelita and completed the job before the ceremonies began.

The most powerful portion of the Chillán murals is the double figure on the Chilean side, with its mutilated gigantic Galvarino attached, Siamese-twin fashion, to Bilbao, the popular leader of a much later date. These paired figures, like the combination at the upper left of this panel (Lautaro, the organizer of the Auracanian Indians, and Recabarren, the famous labor leader), grow out of the same root. They are brought together in Siqueiros's dynamic time-space relationship. (In the 1937 *Echo of a Scream* and the 1939 Electrical Workers Union mural this device was also used effectively.) At the right side of the Chilean panel, the liberator O'Higgins holds a double banner, one part the original independence flag of Chile, the other its present flag. The two meet above the head of the spectator in a movement that takes us through time and space. Similarly on the Mexican panel a portrait of Juárez is superposed on that of Cárdenas. This is a wonderful psychological study as well, and a reminder that Siqueiros has other talents in addition to those of creating space and dynamism.

In these murals, more than in many other works, there is a deliberately strident quality. This is especially apparent in the Chilean wall, which gives a feeling of continuous anguish as the bleeding Galvarino, with his tortured and cut face, his angry screaming mouth, and horribly mutilated arms, falls forward and with his knees crushes the armor of the recumbent Spanish conqueror. As Galvarino falls onto this invader (who clutches a rosary in his hand), the action shatters an actual piece of mirror set into the curved surface of the wall beneath the armor. The mirror is broken and covered with paint, and represents the shattering of ancient superstitions such as the Indians' fear of the white man's mirror.

The story told in the Chillán murals is familiar enough to the observer of Mexican painting. It is the long struggle of the Indian against the

---

[2] See the painter's own *Como se pinta una mural*; also figs. 86 and 87 in the Siqueiros monograph of 1951.

invader and oppressor, against the white man's religion with its social connotations, and the final release through nineteenth-century liberalism and the revolutions of the twentieth century. Rivera, Orozco, and many others have told this tale countless times and in various ways. What is new here is the manner in which the narrative is projected, the movement of the figures, the motion inherent in the walls themselves (designed by the painter) and finally achieved by the deliberate distortions that enable the spectator to participate tactually and visually in the artist's experience. 'In my Chillán murals,' says Siqueiros, 'I have been able to move farther along the road of what we can call the objectivization [i.e. giving form] of the subjective, the pictorial objectivization of metaphors, mottoes, and so forth, for an art of political meaning. Cárdenas is the Juárez of his time, for example, through the clear and precise superposition of the two people and their respective politico-historical themes. The same is true for the solution relative to Bilbao and Galvarino.'[3]

Undoubtedly Chillán is a strong pro-Chilean, pro-Mexican statement and a powerful reaffirmation of national integrity for both countries. That it can be considered a strong anti-United States statement[4] is questionable on three grounds. First, there is no objective evidence within the murals to indicate this. More important, however, no socially conscious individual of Siqueiros's particular convictions would have made that kind of statement in the period after 22 June 1941 (the murals were finished in March 1942), when the invasion of the Soviet Union by the Germans brought, however temporarily, unified activity with the West in all areas, cultural and political. Finally, from the point of view of the Mexican government, which sponsored this project and which was engaged in trying to forge Pan-American unity, especially with Chile (then being influenced against the United States by Argentina), such an attitude would have been inadmissable.

In the same Escuela México, Siqueiros's long-time friend and associate Xavier Guerrero also did a series of somewhat Rivera-like murals: *Brotherhood, Human Feeling of the People* (the latter an enormous pair of very reminiscent hands), *Dynamic Human Labor* (a large Diego-esque woman), among others. Siqueiros's presence and influence in Chile is reflected in a mural done by three of his Chilean assistants (Erwin Wenner, José Venturelli, and Alipio Jaramillo) in the Alianza de Intelectuales in Santiago.

At Chillán a stage of Siqueiros's evolution is reached in which his style is decisively fixed along personal lines. He does not use relatively simple generalities of form or the lineally outlined figures of Rivera or the Expressionistic technique of Orozco. His is an individual and romantic realism in which paint, although broadly applied, is firm in texture and

[3] 70 *Obras Recientes*, p. 25.
[4] As maintained by Kirstein, op. cit.

96

SIQUEIROS. *Allegory of Racial Equality* (now destroyed).
PYROXILIN ON MASONITE.
PRIVATE RESIDENCE, HAVANA.

even tight in feeling. In order to avoid any possible monotony that might come from the mechanical means employed in applying it, he uses frequent scumblings of paint as well as applied textural devices. His palette at that point is somewhat limited, however, because of the relatively early stage in the development of pyroxilin paint, which was available in only one tone each of yellow, red, and blue, plus black and green.

In 1942 after the Chillán project Siqueiros produced a number of Duco portraits of women, and wrote a pamphlet called *Arte Civil*, in which he gave the Chileans a short summary of his technique and philosophy. The following year he traveled from Chile to Cuba, stopping on the way in Peru, Ecuador, Colombia, and Panama, giving talks on modern Mexican art and trying to mobilize the artists of those countries in the war against fascism. In most places he seems to have been helped by the authorities. Groups of War Artists were formed here and there who played an important role in wartime cultural propaganda.

Arriving in Cuba at the end of 1943, Siqueiros executed one fixed mural and two transportable ones. The first is called *Allegory of Racial Equality in Cuba* and was done for the residence of Sra. María Luisa Gómez Mena in Havana. A second mural, *Lincoln and Martí*, was painted for the

217

Cuban-American Center of Cultural Relations; and a third, *Dawn of Democracy*, in the Sevilla-Biltmore Hotel.

The *Allegory of Racial Equality* (fig. 96, now destroyed) was painted in a corridor facing the street, where three small concave walls and a flat ceiling offered a shell-like form. Here, in his now typical manner, Siqueiros brought together the curved surface of the wall and the flat surface of the ceiling through the downward-plunging figure of the Equality symbol, which moves from the straight to the curved surface with the usual dramatic distortions. The upper part of this violently moving figure appears from a distance to be vertical (as in the photograph), but when seen close on, it moves back into a space over the head of the spectator, who is then surrounded by its multiple lower limbs. The same effect pertains within the spatial area formed by the plastic Negro and white women at either side of the curved wall. These also offer certain illusionistic elements, such as the overlapping spherical forms for the breasts, which enable the spectator to see them from various points of view.

Painted in pyroxilin on masonite with Siqueiros's modern technical equipment, the *Allegory* has a pulsating, almost unendurable force, considering the relatively small space in which it was placed. Compositionally it offers an interesting combination of diagonal effects, the triangle formed by the arms of the Equality figure moving into the space between the upper parts of the women's bodies, whose knees come up from left and right to form the lower part of a clearly defined X shape. Aesthetically it is another example of the objectivization of subjective ideas.

Siqueiros's second mural in Havana, the *Lincoln and Martí*, was also done on a curved surface, while the *Dawn of Democracy* was projected on a flat surface. Both are executed in pyroxilin paint.

In 1944 Siqueiros returned to Mexico. Apparently not yet altogether secure politically, he installed himself quietly in the Mexico City home of his mother-in-law, where he worked on a new mural idea. In this building at Avenida Sonora No. 9 (which became for a short time the Centro de Arte Realista Moderno) Siqueiros produced his *Cuauhtémoc against the Myth*, a seventy-five meter square painting done on a concave surface joined to a plane surface and part of the ceiling (figs. 97, 98). The vertical surfaces consist of three areas: a back wall and two small side walls of unequal size, all part of an open staircase that has been amalgamated into the general design of the work, as can be seen in the lower portions of the centaur, which pour over onto the side of the stairway. (The painted sculptures beneath the stairs are the work of Luis Arenal.)

The interplay between curved and straight wall surfaces and the staircase itself offers Siqueiros an unusual opportunity to place the spectator within the moving spaces of the painting as he climbs the steps and, going up and along that area, is forced to take different views of the

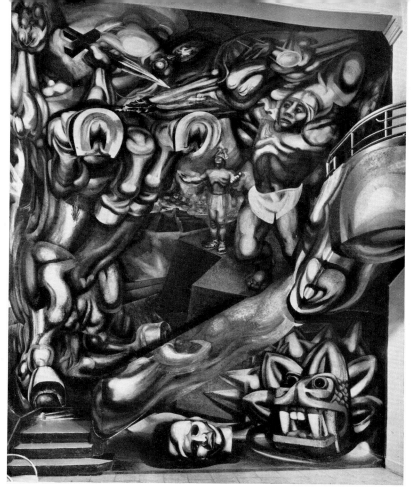

97

SIQUEIROS. *Cuauhtémoc against the Myth.*
PYROXILIN ON CELOTEX.
MEXICO CITY, SONORA NO. 9.

figures in the painting. The multiplication of parts, seen before primarily as a means for increasing dynamism of action, now emphasizes also the value of allowing the mural to be seen from different aspects. The spectator may move about, instead of having to maintain a static position with regard to the painting; he may 'scan' it, as with a motion-picture camera. Here at Sonora No. 9 there is no one place from which the mural can or should be seen—as in traditional murals—but rather a wide variety of viewing positions: coming toward it from the bottom, on the stairs at various points, from the balcony at the top, and from the balcony at the other side of the landing above. Here more than in any of the previous murals in which this technique was developed (Electrical Workers, Chillán, Havana), the feeling of constant and powerful movement is conveyed to the spectator.

The Cuauhtémoc mural symbolizes the heroism of the people. It contrasts Montezuma's pious acceptance of the colonial centaur with the powerful resistance offered at the right by Cuauhtémoc (cf. Chillán), who becomes the great and constant protagonist of Siqueiros's painting from now on, his symbol of a resisting Mexico. The centaur concept arises

219

from the fact that the horse had been unknown in the Western Hemisphere. The Aztecs thought the Spaniard on horseback was a kind of half-human, half-animal creature. This beast rears terrifyingly at the left, the artist having imparted an almost supernatural power to its enormous overwhelming form, with the red-tinted and bleeding underbelly and the multiple hooves that threaten the Indian at the top of the purple steps. The white—and therefore mythical—invader (cf. Quetzalcoatl story above) carries a spear-tipped Cross in one of his four arms; two of the others hold a rosary, as had the recumbent invader in the Chillán mural. His face is generalized and almost invisible; his personality is summed up in the menacing hooves that leap out at the Aztec and at the spectator, even moving across the lower part of the stairs, and in the waving arms with their symbols.

The Cuauhtémoc at the right comes into the mural in a violent and diagonal fashion suggesting the somewhat similar movement of the revolutionist at the right of the Electrical Workers Union mural. Cuauhtémoc is the avenger, the people's defender, with his many arms matching those of the enemy. These arms thrust various weapons at the centaur, one of them obsidian-tipped and dangerous-looking, while the arm that holds it also carries a beating heart, an extraordinarily poetic symbol.

98

SIQUEIROS. *Cuauhtémoc against the Myth*, detail. PYROXILIN ON CELOTEX. MEXICO CITY, SONORA NO. 9.

This highly Expressionistic work carries with it a violently emotive and imaginative feeling, an obsession treated a number of times before and since, but never with this amazing balance of gigantic fury and gentle steadfastness. Technically, it grows out of the Chillán and Havana works, bringing to bear the already seen multiplications of form, overlappings, different viewing points, sinuously curving and therefore more dynamic forms. In the relationship between the vertical rear and side walls and the horizontal ceiling we have another point of correspondence with the earlier works. Here the upper portions of both the centaur and the Cuauhtémoc, with their respective arms and weapons, move from the vertical to the horizontal plane as the spectator moves into the staircase area itself and finds these portions directly overhead.

As might have been expected, this mural, with its violation of traditional ideas in perspective, paint application, and color, did not meet with universal approval, and Siqueiros vigorously defended himself and his Centro de Arte Realista Moderno. He condemned all his colleagues who had 'not gone beyond the first romantic phase of the mural movement,' pointing out that only Orozco in his recent show at the Colegio Nacional had begun to use the new modern materials.

The work may be compared ideologically with Siqueiros's *Agony of the Colonial Centaur* (1947), a painting in pyroxilin on paper and masonite,[5] presumably done as a sketch for a mural in the Hotel del Prado that was never executed. Here a gigantic dead centaur lies with its legs curled up and encircling a tiny Aztec warrior in the foreground. Another and more directly comparable work is the well-known *Centaur of the Conquest* (1943, Don Marte R. Gómez collection),[6] in pyroxilin on masonite, which was made as a sketch for this Cuauhtémoc mural done the following year in Avenida Sonora.

The balance of mighty surging forms against tiny resolute figures is seen once more in another mural sketch, the *New Resurrection* (1947, fig. 99), designed for the Palacio del Gobierno in Chihuahua (the painter's native city) but not carried out. This conception involves a tiny militant figure emerging from a red-encircled vision of white clouds, yellow fire, and rock—man rising, as it were, from primordial chaos with a lance in his hands and fighting against the forces of confusion and darkness. The title and the use of the tiny crosses in the yellow center of the painting did much to make this picture unpopular with the clergy.

The middle 'forties mark a further ripening of Siqueiros's talents, as shown in the various applications of his new dynamic method of space painting and the increasing number of fine portraits, landscapes, and general figure compositions. His landscape style may be seen in the wonderfully plastic effects of the *New Resurrection* background, where every

[5] See fig. 177, Siqueiros monograph.
[6] See fig. 122, Siqueiros monograph.

form moves powerfully within the picture space and toward the spectator, and in which the effect of hard tangible substances is effectively conveyed. The feeling for rocky landscape is especially strong in these paintings, landscapes that convey here and in such works as the *Burning City* (1947) a sense of bitter desolation, an end-of-the-world quality, derived from their origin in the lava-covered Pedregal area outside Mexico City.

The figure paintings of this period, closely related to mural ideas in the artist's mind, show a greater variety than the landscapes, although not necessarily higher quality. They range from single figures to complex compositional arrangements, but in every case they retain the characteristic sculpturesque form that Siqueiros has achieved with his synthetic paints. Thus the flowing forms and the ideological content of his 1944 *Dawn of Mexico*, with its exultant references to the earlier expropriation of foreign oil concessions, are close to many of the mural designs; indeed the picture was conceived as a mural. *Our Present Image* (1947, fig. 100) is a climactic version of Siqueiros's constant attempts to project his figures out of the picture space at the spectator, while pushing enough of

99

SIQUEIROS. *New Resurrection.*
PYROXILIN ON MASONITE.
MEXICO CITY, COLL.
DR. A. CARRILLO GIL.

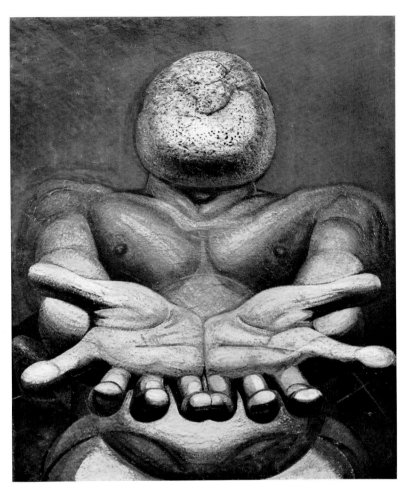

100

each figure back so that the balance is maintained in a carefully adjusted pulsating equality of movement. This symbol of the world today thrusts its hands out in appeal, while the utterly blank and featureless face with its roughly textured pyroxilin surface suggests Surrealist ideas (di Chirico, Grosz, and so on). But this is not a dreamlike shrinking away from the world; it is a violent affirmation of the fact that something must be done about the enforced anonymity of the average man and the world he represents.

In the outstanding collection of Dr. Alvar Carrillo Gil (just as notable for its excellent examples of Orozco works in all media), there are a number of contemporary Siqueiros easel paintings and sketches, including the *New Resurrection* landscape. In the realm of single-figure pieces, two works in particular exhibit an extraordinary plasticity. One of these is entitled *Head of Cuauhtémoc* (1947, fig. 101), a brown face with white contrasting highlights, the body a vivid warm red, with a striking

101
SIQUEIROS. *Head of Cuauhtémoc.*
PYROXILIN ON MASONITE.
MEXICO CITY, COLL.
DR. A. CARRILLO GIL.

lavender accent on the shirt; the entire background is in dark brown. This powerful physical presence carries with it an intense emotional overtone, generalized and yet inescapable.

The *Nude* of the same date (fig. 102) is one of a pair of female figures in light brown with yellow highlights. She is seated on a block of stone, with her back to the audience, and is pointing to the right. The other figure is held down by some restraining organic substance, is blindfolded (she is called *Faith*), and points in the other direction. They are companion pieces, one facing away from the spectator and pointing inward, the other facing toward the spectator and pointing outward. Both of these monumentalized and generalized forms, whatever their anecdotal purpose, show the powerful three-dimensionality of Siqueiros at its highest level, and this without the aid of optical illusions, multiplications, and so on.

Other striking easel paintings of the period, in the Carrillo Gil collection, include the *Death and Burial of Cain* (1947), a memorial to the cowardly death of Mussolini, who, in the Mexican proverb, 'died like a chicken.' He is shown here as a gigantic fowl in yellow-lavender, stripped of his feathers, while the people come to witness his death in huge crowds, rank on rank. There are also the poetic *Allegory of the Fatherland* (1946); the declamatory but effective *Orator* of 1948; a series of fine landscapes such as *Road to Vera Cruz* (1947); and the highly imaginative *Stratospheric Antenna* (1949), which is a lavender view of Mexico City, with bulbous brown forms above it and long vertical wires stretching into the air and supporting what look like panes of glass.[7]

Siqueiros's mural painting continues with the *New Democracy* (fig. 103), executed in 1945 for the Palacio de Bellas Artes in Mexico City, on the same floor as the murals by Rivera and Orozco. This event may be taken as proof of his final acceptance as a member of the 'big three.'

---

[7] See the splendid monograph on Siqueiros for illustrations of these. Instituto Nacional de Bellas Artes, Mexico, 1951.

102

SIQUEIROS. *Nude.* PYROXILIN.
MEXICO CITY,
COLL. DR. A. CARRILLO GIL.

PHOTO GUILLERMO ZAMORA

103

SIQUEIROS. *The New Democracy*. PYROXILIN.
PALACIO DE BELLAS ARTES, MEXICO CITY.

The main rectangular panel here is 60 square meters in area; each of the side panels is 20 meters square. *New Democracy* was intended by the artist to commemorate the anniversary of the Mexican Revolution (20 November) and the military victory of the democracies over fascism. Although the flat walls of the Palacio were not altogether suitable to Siqueiros's newly developed technique, which seemed to demand a curved surface, he succeeded even here in achieving not only the desired dynamic effect but one or two technical innovations as well. This mural was painted in the usual pyroxilin but on celotex covered with cotton cloth and with a more solid base than before, owing to the addition of various kinds of plant fiber for surface quality. Against these successes must be weighed the unfortunate visual circumstances that make it necessary for the spectator to view the paintings from across the wide and open space of the stairwell, which separates the narrow corridor sides of the hall. Even at this uncomfortable distance, the view is blocked by square columns directly in front of the walls.

The center panel of the *New Democracy*, called *Life and Death*, portrays the conquest of life over death symbolized by the defeat of the Nazi-fascists. Its principal figure is the perennially outgoing form that rushes

226

on the spectator, here a Liberty-capped, powerful female torso, two of its multiple arms still carrying the ball and chains of its slavery, a third the torch of liberty. The top of the painting continues on the projecting ledge overhead. The sensation of forward movement is so intense that the figure seems to be leaning out over the railing of the balcony corridor, straining toward us with anguished face, the body literally tearing itself from the concrete enclosure at the waist. In stark and dismal contrast to this rich tan form with its red bonnet is the dead gray figure projecting inward, with anonymous face, blood-stained hands, and Nazi helmet. This is the Death whom Liberty, or Life, has conquered, and it is fitted in at the right under the forward-moving arms of the female form to help carry our eyes back into the picture space and maintain its balance.

The chief color effects here are the strikingly contrasted red areas and the occasional touches of blue. In the lower part of the mural, gray tonalities are dominant as representing the darkness of oppression. Liberty herself bursts out of a gray-colored stone element which cracks and turns toward white and then into a reddish girdle about her waist; above this is the tan of the body and the climactic revolutionary red of the bonnet. This contrast of color for symbolic and ideological effect, i.e. from gray to red, is a common feature of the more recent works of Siqueiros.

The gray stone mass out of which Liberty tears herself resembles the top of a volcano, and in the background at the left, another such natural form is seen with a hole in its top, as though prefiguring a second visitation of this kind at some later date. Balancing the gray form of the dead Nazi, this second volcano can perhaps be taken to symbolize the imprisonment of mankind, which, like the volcano, has within it the imminent possibilities of explosion or revolution.

The two vertical side panels of the *New Democracy* show the *Massacre of the Civilian Population* at the left (fig. 104) and the *Torture of the People* at the right, testimonials to the barbarism of the Nazis toward the noncombatant inhabitants of invaded countries. In the first, Siqueiros has arranged a Mantegnesque composition with a corpse lying on its back at right angles to the front line of the picture. One leg points straight toward the spectator, the other is pulled back onto the first of a series of mounting steps that support the figure. Partly covering it is another corpse, lying face down, one leg cut off and the other parallel with the extended leg of the first figure. The total effect of these combined bodies is a mass of flowing, rounded forms beginning at the top of the steps and moving down to the front of the composition, where two leathery soles become visible, one pointing down, the other up, in a macabre opposition matched by the arrangement of the arms above.

The companion panel shows a single figure lying face down over a high stone block, hands tied together and back crisscrossed by the scars of whips. This scene is visualized as an upward-moving composition, portrayed slightly from the side to increase the sense of movement.

104

SIQUEIROS. *Massacre of the Civilian Population* from *The New Democracy*.
PYROXILIN. PALACIO DE BELLAS ARTES, MEXICO CITY.

In 1946 Siqueiros began working on a three hundred and sixty square-meter space in the old Customs Building of the Federal District, the mural to be called *Patricians and Patricides*. After a limited amount of work had been done, the job was suspended because of lack of funds until 1952–3, when it seemed once more that it would be carried out, but it has not yet been completed. The painting space consists of two walls and the ceiling of a wide, low vault over a staircase. As in the Palacio, the painter covered celotex with cloth, on which the pyroxilin was to be sprayed. Here again he favored curved surfaces, the combination of areas moving in different planes—the differences to be overcome by his illusionistic devices.

The general story Siqueiros is trying to tell is one of evil beings (plutocracy, tyranny, imperialism, and feudalism) attacked, overcome, and thrust into oblivion by revolutionary forces coming up from the opposite wall across the orange center of the vault. Swarming across the ceiling, the avengers emerge from blue-gray and red-yellow clouds, and plunge their daggers into the main forms: the brownish-yellow Imperialism and Feudalism, the former with his yellow imperial globe and scepter, the latter with the symbolic yellow-flamed candle of clericalism (fig. 105). Both look like demons, the first with gray devil's horns and the second with satanic gray ears and a face meant to caricature the Spanish dictator, Franco.

For Siqueiros this vault space presents more complex problems of visualization than many other works have had, since these murals are to be viewed from three different heights, at seven, nine, and fourteen meters respectively. He speaks of this work as post-Baroque in style, apparently referring to its emotive fury and to the fact that the original function of the wall surface is no longer operative but is subordinated to the various distortions that have been introduced.

During 1946 and 1947 Siqueiros completed some seventy easel pictures for his 1947 show in the Palacio de Bellas Artes, many of which have been referred to above.[8] At the same time he planned an exhibition at the Museum of Modern Art in New York, which in the changing political circumstances of the postwar period did not materialize.

In 1949 he organized a team of assistants and students for the planning and execution of a gigantic mural in the former Convento Santa Rosa at San Miguel de Allende, at that time being used as a United States veterans' art school. In this building he worked out a scheme with his team of painters and photographers to portray the life of Ignacio Allende, a great hero of the Independence movement, who had been born in that town. The project, which had begun as a pedagogical experiment, turned into a mural job with some twenty Mexican and United States team members working on an area about five hundred meters square. When

---

[8] 70 *Obras Recientes*.

105

SIQUEIROS. *Patricians and Patricides*, detail. PYROXILIN.
EX-CUSTOMS BUILDING, MEXICO CITY.

the director of this school got into financial difficulties, the place was
closed and the work stopped.

In 1951 Siqueiros was called back to the Palacio for another commission,
this time for a pair of panels dealing with the general theme of *Cuauhtémoc
Reborn*, one showing him tortured by the Spaniards, the other standing
beside the colonial centaur he has finally killed. The first panel portrays
the brave Indian and a companion enduring torture by fire applied to
their feet. The gold-yellow flames blend with gray-gold on the Spaniards'
armor and turn to red-gold on the bodies of the Indians themselves. Bil-
lowing clouds of gray smoke in the background signify the burning Indian
cities. The watching women have bleeding faces, and a little child is seen
with hands cut off. The only feeling of movement comes in the waving
arms of one of these women, whose reddish-gold robe (reflecting the
fire) stands in fine contrast to the blue worn by another woman. In
general the color treatment here seems far better than in many of Si-

queiros's works, but the composition and quality of movement are on an entirely different and less effective level. Here, and in the second panel showing the reborn Cuauhtémoc who has overcome the centaur, the effect is more one of easel painting than of mural.

In 1951 there also appeared the magnificent monograph on Siqueiros published by the National Institute of Fine Arts as a tribute to his winning second prize at the Venice Biennale of 1950. In an international assemblage of art, where the venerable Henri Matisse was given first honors for the work of a lifetime, Siqueiros was awarded the 500,000 lire prize donated by the Museum of São Paulo in Brazil.

The year 1952 was one of the most active in the painter's career. Two mural projects were completed by autumn, one in a new building of the Instituto Politécnico, the other in Hospital No. 1 of the Seguro Social. Half a dozen other projects were begun at the University City that year, and the painter also began to reconsider his Treasury Department mural, abandoned in 1946, in the old Customs Building.

The Politécnico mural is called *Man the Master and Not the Slave of Technology* (fig. 106), a long, horizontal, and relatively low rectangle in concave form like a section of a cylinder. Here a series of diagonals radiates outward from the figure of the man, which is in the exact center of the panel; they give an illusion of forward curvature as well as

106

SIQUEIROS. *Man the Master and Not the Slave of Technology.*
PYROXILIN ON ALUMINUM. INSTITUTO POLITÉCNICO, MEXICO CITY.

107

SIQUEIROS. *Man the Master and Not the Slave of Technology*, left view.
PYROXILIN ON ALUMINUM. INSTITUTO POLITÉCNICO, MEXICO CITY.

inward bending. The painting itself is done in pyroxilin on an aluminum surface placed on a thick plywood frame, the entire arrangement mounted on metal bars attached to the columns of an outdoor loggia.

In the center of the composition is the Worker, nude to the waist and wearing blue trousers. He stands on a pedestal like an orator and points with one hand to the blood-red sun coming over the horizon (the glorious future), while with the other he holds the symbol of the atomic age. The left side of the panel is dominated by enormous circular red and gold wheels on a diagonally thrusting gray shaft that connects the deep center with the lower left of the panel. This side with its symbol of the sun represents 'man free'; the right side, with its gigantic foot, leg, and arm imprisoned in the machine, the wrist grasped by a powerful hand coming from the right, represents 'man the captive of the machine.' Over this end the painter has placed the moon as a sign of darkness, with the colors predominantly low-keyed (grays, browns, and flesh tones) in contrast to the symbolic left, with its vivid red, yellow, and red-yellow against a blue background.

Although not so exciting as many of his earlier works, or as satisfying from either a symbolic or an ideological point of view, this panel exemplifies the oft-repeated Siqueiros dictum that 'the normal transit of the spectator in a given topography determines the pictorial composition within it.' In other words, when the spectator moves, he sets in motion this rhythmic architectural machine; when he stops, the machine stops, too. The aim is to provide a 'normal' view from any vantage point. Thus, from the front a head or other similar object may appear oval in shape, but seen from the side this painted oval would ordinarily shrink too much. It is therefore necessary to amplify the oval to a circle or even to a horizontal ellipse so that it will retain a proper shape when seen from the side, as in the machine elements at the left of this mural. But in order to leave intact the normalcy of the front view, the necessary distortions are made to look from the front like shadows, draperies, or parts of other contiguous figures, as appropriate in each case. In this way, the mural makes sense from any angle. The figure first appears in its ordinary aspect from the front with the added shadows, and so on, seen as such; and then the same elements become part of the figure as it narrows in a side view, and keep it normal in spite of the change.

Here, for example, we can see the extremely elliptical shape of the wheels and end of the driving shaft in a front view (see fig. 106); but viewed from the left, they become narrower and return to circular unshadowed forms (fig. 107). Another good illustration of this may be seen in the long rectangular mural of the 1952 Rectoría (Administration Building) in the University City (see fig. 124). Heads appear round (with shadows) from the front; these shadows become part of the narrowing figures as we move to either side, and keep them in normal proportion.

The mural in Hospital No. 1 of the Social Security Administration, begun in 1952 and finished in 1954, is 310 meters square and is called *Song to Life and Health*.[9] It is painted in vinylite on a curving iron structure to which first celotex and then canvas have been attached. The curve of the wall blends into the curve of the ceiling.

In the left part of the mural, an unprotected worker falls victim to an industrial accident. From this same side and dominating the entire composition, a huge Sun Man comes plunging down in the already established Siqueiros dynamics in which the figure seems to follow as the spectator shifts his position. The artist himself explains a figure of this

[9] See *Time*, 13 April 1953.

type as being held in place while the spectator moves about—in opposition to the cinematic technique in which the spectator is fixed in one place and the images move about him. Thus the legs of the giant figure, which appear to recede so violently, are actually about seven meters in front of the Sun Man's head and are painted illusionistically on the ceiling overhead, as in Chillán. At the right are towering buildings of various countries, dominated by a huge red star, the symbol of proletarian revolt. In the center a group of women comes forward carrying the sheaves of prosperity.

Although the symbolism and ideology of this mural offer nothing unusual, the work is interestingly done in relation to the architecture. The rectangular room space is glass-walled on one long side and has a straight, blank wall on the other long side. The curved ceiling and short far wall, which are connected pictorially by the flying figure, form the only area of painting. On the short entrance wall, instead of another mural section, the painter has set up a non-glare mirror which dramatically reflects the painted surfaces in the room. In this respect, certainly, if not in the painting itself, a new facet of Siqueiros's dynamism has been brought into view.

During the same period (1953) the artist completed a square mural for the University of Morelia, depicting the excommunication and the shooting of Hidalgo. In 1955 he received a commission to do the 'world's largest mural' (4500 square feet)[10] for a sports stadium in Warsaw, Poland.

With the death of Orozco, Siqueiros emerged in the 1950's as the outstanding living muralist in Mexico and one of its pre-eminent easel painters as well. Some of his most recent works, however, have not measured up to the standard of the Electrical Workers mural or of those in Chillán. This cannot be attributed to any flagging of Revolutionary ardor on his part, for Siqueiros is still the ideological leader of the artistic left and as intransigent as ever. But the conflict between these feelings and the growing public acceptance of his work is apparent in the rather inconclusive and generalized ideology of the Politécnico and University City murals—a conflict visible in the work of other leftist artists as well. These men, including Siqueiros, are faced by the paradox of opposing the government (and being shot at in a May Day parade) and at the same time working for it in an official capacity.

Whatever the disagreement with Siqueiros's social philosophy, many things for which he has fought in mural art are gradually coming to pass. Today he speaks of mural painting as having reached its second stage in Mexico through modern rather than traditional buildings, a dynamic rather than a static surface, and turning to exteriors rather than confining murals as before in the interiors of buildings. A goodly share of the credit for these changes belongs to Siqueiros.

---

[10] *Time*, 5 Dec. 1955. Cf. *New York Times*, 11 Dec. 1955.

Rivera
Since 1940
XX

The first important commissions to come to Rivera in Mexico since the 1936 portable panels in the Hotel Reforma appear in 1943: two walls in the Institute of Cardiology and a primarily decorative composition for Ciro's night club in the Hotel Reforma.

In the two movable panels of the Institute, Rivera has worked out a pleasing and colorful arrangement of historical personages involved in the development of medical knowledge, especially of the heart. The left panel, as one enters the building, is a reddish work conditioned by the flames emerging from the burning of Michael Servetus by the Calvinists in 1553 (upper left); these red-gold tonalities affect the rest of the wall. Below this scene of burning, at the lower left, the painter shows earlier events in the life of this discoverer of pulmonary circulation and martyr in the cause of free thought. The rest of the panel consists of portraits of famous scientists, whose dates and personalities highlight the history of anatomy and the function of the heart as far back as the ancient Greeks.

The right-hand wall, dated 1944, is dominated by a lavender tonality and also shows famous figures in the history of cardiology, with reddish faces like those on the opposite wall. Both walls have rectangular grisaille panels appended below which contain typical Rivera references to the past. Here they deal with the practice of medicine among primitive and oriental peoples, and may be compared in general effect to the gray panels that supplement the murals in the corridor of the National Palace.

Both walls in the Institute are decoratively effective and pleasant—and very little cluttered, considering the number of figures represented on each side. The compositional use of a spiral-stair arrangement, along which the figures are placed, helps to keep the effect simple.

In 1944 Rivera returned to the National Palace to work on a series of picturesquely impressive panels in the upstairs corridor leading off from the head of the staircase he had painted in 1935. Here he arranged a succession of scenes from the pre-Hispanic life of Mexico. On the rectangular wall panels of this corridor, Rivera shows a more attractive and luminous color than ever before, with masses of figures projected in a somewhat simpler style than that of the earlier stairway murals (fig. 108). Color, it would seem, is the chief feature of these works, apart from a rather agreeable though quite conventional spatial quality arising from a geometric perspectivizing, with mountains in the background closing the space. Here, also, Rivera continues the practice of the neutral gray predella scenes, as in the Institute of Cardiology, which date back with variations to his early murals in the Ministry of Education.

Coloristically these murals emphasize (in addition to the brown of the Indians' bodies) a golden yellow as well as bright reds, blues, and light greens; the red is somewhat too insistent, however, and tends to throw the panels off key. The new color emphasis is unfortunately carried to discordant lengths in the scenes on the left side of the corridor, and a peculiar, unbalanced contrast exists between their intensity and the gray grisaille areas below.

On the other hand, the painter has done a tremendous amount of historical research for these as for many other works, e.g. Detroit, New Workers School, et cetera. This has enabled him to render a meticulously factual (except perhaps for the so-called portrait of Cortez) account of the precolonial history of his country, with scenes portraying in great detail the manners and customs of those days (fig. 108). Nevertheless it is a question to what extent these works may be considered aesthetically successful and to what extent they are glorified illustrations.

The work on the left wall, which occupied Rivera until 1950, has been continued since 1951 on the wall opposite the staircase with another group of panels; in these he has introduced a new feature that gives color to the previously gray predella panels, so that their earlier disturbing contrast with the strong upper colors is no longer present. These lower areas now have a bland blue-green-gray quality that is in far better harmony with the upper sections.

One of the important Rivera works of the 'forties is the series of mural scenes for the dining room of the Hotel Del Prado in Mexico City, entitled *Dream on a Sunday Afternoon in the Central Alameda* (1947–8). Here again he presents a history of Mexico from Cortez to the present day, sufficiently decorative and charming to please almost anyone. But as is often the case with Rivera murals, there was a catch in it. He included in the Reform-period panel a phrase from one of the precursors of that era, Ignacio Ramírez, saying, 'God does not exist.' There was enough reaction against this gesture to force the management to cover the murals, an action we may regret on the ground that they offer a new and unusually poetic quality in Rivera's art.[1]

Here he is not decorating merely for the sake of decorating but is rather creating a series of moods evoked out of the dream state that is his thesis. The people sleeping on benches, the better-dressed folk strolling in the Alameda—including the young Rivera in knickerbockers walking hand

---

[1] In 1956 the mural again was uncovered, when the painter removed the offending words. See *New York Times*, 15 April 1956.

in hand with a lady *calavera* and Posada—those awake and those asleep in the Reform period, and many other areas bespeak a half-Surrealist, half-personal poetry not often seen in this artist's work.

In the summer of 1949 the National Institute of Fine Arts paid him the tribute of a national exhibition in the Palacio de Bellas Artes, which continued into 1950; in 1951 they published a luxurious monograph on his life's work. The exhibition revealed the great skill of Rivera's Cubist pictures before his return to Mexico, the fine quality of his early murals, the charm of the easel pictures of the 'thirties, and the rather unfortunate

108

RIVERA. *The Temple of the War and Rain Gods*, detail from *Life in Pre-Hispanic Mexico*. FRESCO. NATIONAL PALACE, MEXICO CITY.

character of the many commercialized portraits of the 'forties. These last-mentioned works, which negate Rivera's undeniable talents as a colorist and draftsman, would seem to be indications of his loss of roots in the Mexican movement itself. They also show the ease with which such talents can be turned to the uses of profitable and academic portraiture. Certainly the murals of this period, with the exception of the Cardiology and sections of the Hotel del Prado dining room, offer evidence of serious retrogression in vigor and significance.

This fact is underlined by the well-publicized murals in the distribution chamber of the Lerma Waterworks just outside Mexico City, which were finished in 1951. The approach to this building is past a huge stone-mosaic sculptured figure of Tlaloc, the rain god, placed flat in the middle of a pool. The paintings inside the building are within the open rectangular distribution chamber, into which one looks from above. The four walls and floor of this well were done, contrary to advice of the Taller de Ensaye of the Polytechnic Institute, in a polyesterine paint that soon wore off the floor and disappeared into the pipes carrying the water to the city; only the wall paintings remain. Technicians at the Institute (whom Rivera had consigned to the devil) had prophesied that 'Mexico City will soon be drinking Diego's mural.'

Amoebae and other water organisms were originally painted on the floor. On the side walls are two very large caricature-like figures of 'man' and 'woman' arising from primeval forms of life. In the corners of these walls the painter has laid out a series of small compositions showing various kinds of activities that benefit from the bringing of water: gardening, swimming, and so on. (One of the swimmers is his daughter Ruth, a well-known architect). Over the opening to the tunnel is a pair of hands, used many times before (e.g. Detroit), and when the water pours over them they form what is perhaps the most satisfactory part of the entire mural. The space opposite, showing workers, managers, and engineers in a straight line, engaged in planning this waterworks, is appreciably dull in effect.

Although the chamber contains a number of good individual details and groups, the total result, particularly the lack of color harmony, is rather disappointing. The fact that paintings are done on the floor of a water chamber has very little meaning if within a few months those paintings are gone because of technical inefficiency.

The next of Diego's murals, *The Nightmare of War and the Dream of Peace*, was finished early in 1952 and was intended to be part of the large-scale government exhibition of Mexican art (precolonial, colonial, and modern) arranged for the Paris Museum of Modern Art and the Stockholm Museum. When the National Institute of Fine Arts authorities saw what he had painted, they felt it impossible for them to send such an obvious anti-United States, anti-French, and anti-British statement to Europe without compromising the Mexican government. The left immediately raised the cry of 'United States imperialism'—an increasing tendency since the end of World War II—claiming that the 'North Americans' were interfering once more in Mexican affairs, or at least influencing their conduct.

This transportable mural, painted in polyesterine on canvas and fifty square meters in area, contrasts the 'bellicosity' of the capitalist nations with the 'peacefulness' of the Communist nations. In the background, Western soldiers arranged in a Goya-like file are shooting a group of crucified Orientals. An overalled worker in the foreground, at the foot of one of these crosses, points left to a benevolent Stalin and Mao effering the dove of peace to a trio of caricatured figures representing Marianne, John Bull, and Uncle Sam. From the extreme right, where the background delineates the exploitation of the Orient, the conditions of the ideal society unfold in a series of well-clothed and well-fed workers, intellectuals, and soldiers; one group features Sra. Rivera imparting knowledge. Rivera in his old age has turned once more to the political beliefs and practices of his youth; but however the painting may serve the aims of anti-United States propaganda, it does little to enhance its author's artistic reputation.

On 22 November 1952 Rivera formally applied for readmission to the Mexican Communist Party, admitting his past 'sins' and condemning his own *Man at the Crossroads* mural (which included the portrait of Trotsky) as corresponding to 'the weakest period in the plastic quality of my painting.'[2] Yet such are the paradoxes of Mexican politics that in 1952–3 Rivera carried out an enormous decorative commission for the University City, another for Hospital No. 1 of the Social Security Administration, as well as a large outdoor mosaic mural on the Teatro de los Insurgentes.

This last work was attacked by the Archbishop of Mexico as contrary to the 'sentiments of all true Catholics,' because in its initial stages it showed the comedian Cantinflas in his customary ragged costume on which was sketched the Virgin of Guadalupe (who, according to legend, caused her image to appear on the cloak of the peasant Juan Diego in the sixteenth century). In a generous gesture to the harassed theater management, the artist finally omitted the figure of the Virgin from this panoramic history of the Mexican stage—another in the long series of typical Rivera incidents.

The year 1954 was marked by the death of his wife, the talented Frida Kahlo, and by his readmission to the Communist party. In 1955 he married again and went to the Soviet Union to be treated for a serious illness, leaving his home, his works, and his collection of precolonial art objects as a gift to the Mexican people. In 1956, however, he returned to Mexico.

---

[2] Reported in the *New York Times* of 23 November 1952, p. 30.

109

ZALCE. *Zapata*, section. FRESCO.
COLL. THE ARTIST.

Mexican Painting Today

Aside from the careers of the three leading muralists during the period since 1940 there has been a development of the Mexican school as a whole. Basically this development presents a double form in which a new generation of Mexicanist mural (and easel) painters evolves side by side with a newer group of nonpolitical and even formalist artists. The work of the latter, however, though theoretical in conception, never divorces itself from its environment.

Of the first group, one of the most interesting is Alfredo Zalce (b. 1908), already mentioned in connection with his membership in the Taller de Gráfica Popular and his 1945 *Estampas de Yucatán*. During this period he continued his mural paintings with a fresco in Secondary School No. 2 in Mexico City, 1942; another, in the Museum of Morelia, begun in 1945, is in the general tradition of Mexicanist works examined earlier. Since that time, the monumentalism observed in his Yucatán lithographs of 1945 has ripened into pictorial form. The light-toned and magnificently painted *Head of a Woman* (1948), which is done in the new vinylite medium, has the quality of pastel-tinted sculpture. Along the same formal lines and quite different in character and impact from his Morelia mural is the movable fresco section, *Zapata* (1952, fig. 109), a dark, brooding, and poetic work of such strength as to place Zalce in a category apart, at least in so far as this development indicates. These works are unquestionably part of the Mexicanist tradition of the past thirty years, but it is interesting to find that personal and individual variations are still possible.

Other noteworthy contributions to this type of mural painting are the already mentioned O'Higgins-Méndez works in a Maternity Hospital of the Social Security Administration in 1946, the O'Higgins mural in the Seattle Longshoremen's Union in 1945, the 1947 Méndez enlarged black-and-whites for the UNESCO meeting in Mexico City, and Arenal's portable mural for a rural school in Arcelia, state of Guerrero.

As we saw earlier, these men represent the second generation of muralists and generally balance the qualities of Rivera and Orozco in their work. A third generation of younger mural painters includes a group of Riveristas: e.g. Rina Lazo, Arturo García Bustos, Diego Rosales, and Marco Antonio Borreguí; a small group of Siqueiros followers: e.g. Francisco Pego and Federico Silva; and a larger number of Orozco disciples: e.g. Armando López Carmona, Guillermo Monroy, and Ramón Sánchez García. Finally there are those who represent a fusion of all three influences: e.g. Luis Robledo, Jorge Best, Fermín Chávez, and Arturo Estrada.

The work of the Rivera followers may be exemplified by the project of Rina Lazo, Arturo García Bustos, and Antonio Carrasco for the Community Co-operative Society of Atencingo, Puebla, in 1950, seven panels representing *The Struggle of the Farmers against Feudalism*. The Orozco group may be typified by the 1950 Guillermo Monroy pyroxilin mural in the Belisario Domínguez School of Tuxtla Gutiérrez, Chiapas. Mixed influences may be seen in the murals by Arturo Estrada in the vestibule of the Narciso Mendoza Cinema in Cuautla, Morelia, a vinylite-on-gesso job fifty-three meters square, showing *A Gesture of Independence* (1952).

In the main, these followers of the three leaders are by no means comparable in quality to their sources; they manifest a weakness for declamation that can never be accepted as a substitute for pictorial ability. This is perhaps truest of the imitators of Siqueiros, whose style may lend itself to superficial imitation in terms of perspective devices, and so on, but in the last analysis depends on the drive and emotive power of the man himself.

Among the new muralists of the 'forties, Jorge González Camarena (b. 1908) is perhaps the most noteworthy. From the very beginning of his career, this painter has been interested in the fusion of formal expression and poetic feeling, the two elements varying in respective importance depending on the particular stage of his evolution. Although his apprenticeship started under academic teachers who represented the very beginnings of modern Mexican art, the decisive influence was that of Rivera, when the latter, during the brief period of his directorship of the Academy, tried to break the old traditions of that institution.

In 1930 Dr. Atl gave González Camarena a studio, where he worked at commercial art to make a living and contributed drawings and articles to the press at the same time. This studio became a gathering place for so many young intellectuals that González Camarena, finding himself unable to work, left Mexico City. For three years he lived in an old ruined monastery at Huexotzingo in the state of Puebla, learning to know the Indians and their humble lives and studying precolonial art.

During this period he evolved a strange geometrical technique whereby the canvas space was divided into four squares, and then subdivided further into eighths, sixteenths, et cetera. Most of the early works, though mannered, show a striving for emotional feeling. Some, such as the *Peaks and Gorges*, are successful and represent the best of this period of self-evaluation. By the late 'thirties he had emerged from this geometrical style into a rather precise formal type of painting; a subdued but vibrating color quality allows the increasingly powerful forms their full scope of expression. The legends and beliefs he had encountered in Huexotzingo, the restoration of colonial murals that he had done in the monastery itself, were now a permanent part of his artistic equipment.

His first mural commission in 1939 began a series that includes a hotel, an office building, a church, two banks, and a brewery—a somewhat different type of outlet from the usual government-sponsored murals of the Mexican movement up to that point. It was the remarkable development of business in this period that made most of these projects possible, since few painters outside of the leading three had been considered for government commissions. Later González Camarena did such works as the tiny mural of 1948 for the Cuicuilco Museum, out past the new University City, and in 1950 the entrance hall of the Social Security Building on the Paseo de la Reforma—his most significant work to date.

His 1939 mural for the Hotel Fundición in Zimapán on the Pan-American Highway was followed by the 1941 panels in the lobby of the Guardiola Building in Mexico City, his first really important project. Here two rectangular panels show powerful male and female forms symbolizing the processes of life. In one, *Man* is seen as a dynamic form flying through space, muscles tense, in the act of transmitting his force through nerves, the flow of his blood, and so on. *Woman*, on the other hand (fig. 110), is the passive element, seen asleep and receptive, her right hand

110

GONZÁLEZ CAMARENA. *Woman*. OLEOCERA.
GUARDIOLA BUILDING, MEXICO CITY.

GONZÁLEZ CAMARENA. *Germination*.
OLEOCERA. BANCO DEL AHORRO,
MEXICO CITY.

holding an egg as symbol of her fertility, the lower background filled with placenta, blood, and undulating veins, with the entire arrangement before a cold moon, the woman symbol.

Both panels are dark in color and conservatively drawn, yet dramatically effective; they represent an adaptation of Michelangelesque form ideas brought up to date with the themes of modern science. These works may suggest anatomical illustration, yet because of their contrasting subdued and dynamic moods, their poetic feeling, they have a superior personal quality as well.

In 1945 González Camarena did a magnificent *Christ on the Cross* for the La Purísima Church of Monterrey (about 8 by 13 feet), combining his earlier formalism of composition with a wonderfully expressive mood. When this painting was first exhibited, women in the audience burst into tears.

244

The 1946 project at the Banco del Ahorro on the busy Calle Venustiano Carranza in Mexico City consists of a small movable panel about seven feet square called *Germination* (fig. 111). Here in the upper portion against a dark lavender background, a horizontal lavender-green arm stretches across the top, squeezing through its fingers large, glycerine-like drops into the mélange of light-green and gray forms below, and causing them to germinate. One of these is a greenish organism bursting out of a gray shell, while a desiccated skeleton lies head down among huge vegetable forms. From this series of imaginative shapes there emerges a feeling of the irresistible growth of organic life from the chaos of nature.

The following year (1947) González Camarena executed three portable square panels for the Banco Mercantil de México: *Industry, Banking,* and *Commerce.* These begin with a representation of Industry being born, a brown foetus fed by reddish blood vessels and enclosed in a gray womb surrounded by pinkish matter, which in turn is enveloped by a cogwheel

12

GONZÁLEZ CAMARENA. *Banking.*
OLEOCERA. BANCO MERCANTIL
DE MÉXICO, MEXICO CITY.

whose color changes from pink to gray in the change-over from organic to metallic material. Outside elements here show industrial pipe forms and machine parts in bluish gray. The whole is intended to represent the function of Industry in taking primary materials and converting them to useful products within its womb.

Banking, a somewhat generalized glorification of this activity (fig. 112), is perhaps the most attractive of the three panels. It consists of a faceless monumental figure in gray and brown emerging from brownish-gray and greenish rock forms, which presumably refer to the rocklike stability of banking's foundations; this is seen against an attractive blue-gray background. The third scene portrays the *Black Market Strangled by Free Commerce*, a reference to that widespread evil of the postwar period in Mexico. Black Market is a monster with red tongue and dark gray body surrounded by beckoning brown hands. Especially effective are the dynamically placed brown-gray hands at the bottom. General background effects here are bluish pink.

González Camarena's mural decoration in the offices of the Modelo Brewery was done in 1948, and is about 35 square meters in area. Within the limitations of such an assignment, the painter did well by the beer industry (fig. 113). Unfortunately, it is rather difficult to look at this mural without seeing the malt and hops under the arm of the powerful central male figure and the Rivera-esque figures at the extreme right who bring these products in. Yet the two center figures, the male and female symbols of creativity, give off a vital force far more exciting than the necessarily commercial purpose of the mural. Between their outstretched and Masaccio-like hands, placed one above the other, there flows a creative light. These forms emerge from an amorphous and interestingly textured mass that is capped by a mask made up of interlaced serpents, representing Tlaloc, the god of rain and lightning, a deity useful in furnishing the water and electric power for making the beverage.

The bodies of the two central figures are especially noteworthy for the vibrating effect of the colors used, as is the case also with the earlier murals. This is due in great part to the medium the painter utilizes, an *oleocera*, or combination of linseed-oil paste and wax, with which the colors are mixed. They are then applied with the aid of metal spatulas, serrated bars, and trowels, all of which give the peculiar vibratory quality he is after.

On the outskirts of the capital, in the little Museum of Cuicuilco, named after the ancient pyramid nearby, whose artifacts are shown there, González Camarena in 1948 did the small portable panel, *Eruption of Xitle*. This fiery scene shows the eruption of the neighboring volcano of Xitle, which some two thousand years ago covered what is claimed to be the oldest man-made structure in the Western Hemisphere, the Pyramid of Cuicuilco. Here the painter goes into an entirely different style. A speckled lavender pyramid and a gold-colored volcano are seen against

113
GONZÁLEZ CAMARENA. *Life and Industry*. OLEOCERA.
CERVECERÍA MODELO, MEXICO CITY.

114

GONZÁLEZ CAMARENA. *Mexico*. VINYLITE.
INSTITUTO MEXICANO DEL SEGURO SOCIAL, MEXICO CITY.

a deep rose background, the gold-pink lava flowing at the right with a purple cloud of smoke over it. It is a new conception and handling of color, worked out without the portrayal of human figures, but as interesting as anything done up to this time.

The most exciting of González Camarena's mural works so far is the long rectangle of 50 square meters, 1950, for the entrance lobby in the main building of the Social Security Administration of Mexico on the Paseo de la Reforma (fig. 114). Using vinylite for the first time in an important project, the painter has given an extraordinarily imaginative portrayal. A stone Mexican eagle covers almost the entire surface of the panel, its right half taking shape beneath the many scaffolds and the workmen on them. This is the Mexico of the future, brought into being through the untiring efforts of its people, whose progress up the stone

PHOTO GÓMEZ

face of this gigantic symbol is marked by ladders, catwalks, scaffolds, planks, and other building aids. At the very top, right, is the bluish head of the serpent symbol held in the gray-lavender beak of the eagle. In the right-hand corner, the wing emerges in strong lavender, with the tan claws visible in the right center foreground, holding the body of the serpent.

In the upper left center, the second wing, in lavender-white, takes shape out of a mass of gray rock suffused with an orange glow of fire that emanates from two gigantic horizontal grayish forms covering the lower left portion of the mural. These are a skeleton symbol of the Conquest, dressed in armor, and an Aztec-warrior skeleton in elaborate headdress, lying side by side. The general background of this impressive panel is violet for the left-hand side and light blue for the right.

What distinguishes this unusual interpretation of the growth of Mexico is its personal poetic approach. The new *patria* destroys the earlier

249

symbols with rocks tumbling down on the corpses at the left, as the wing of the eagle plows through the rocky mass above, causing an earthquake to bury the ancient ones in falling stone and molten lava. The abandoned scaffolding near the claws symbolizes the earlier phases of the rebuilding of Mexico, just as the two halves of the plumb line weight in the extreme lower right show the process of building in general.

González Camarena's feeling for textural qualities, seen in the earlier vibratory handling of his *oleocera* medium and its peculiarly stippled character, emerges here with particular force in the all-over pattern of rocky surfaces. These show the same meticulous clarity as the other forms in the painting, and indeed in his art generally—a clarity and a dream-like quality found both in the murals and in the numerous easel paintings. His easel work may be represented by the wonderfully mysterious *Convento de Huexotzingo* (1949, fig. 115), a picture of the secluded spot in which the painter spent decisive years during his early life, preparing himself for his participation in the contemporary movement.

115

GONZÁLEZ CAMARENA. *Convento de Huexotzingo.* OIL. COLL. THE ARTIST.

The bulk of González Camarena's work, it should be mentioned, has been done for commercial buildings and may perhaps mark one phase of the change of patronage in modern Mexico, i.e. from a purely governmental to an increasingly private character. Similar projects include the bank frescoes of Roberto Montenegro on the Avenida Venustiano Carranza, the factory mural (1952) of Fanny Rabel, various cinema murals, and others that characterize this side of the new patronage offered the Mexican muralist in recent years.

Here and there trade unions have offered their walls for mural decoration, e.g. the 1939 Electrical Workers done by the Siqueiros team and the Cinematographers Union by Antonio Ruíz. In the same limited way, there is slowly growing a tendency toward murals for private residences, exemplified in the effective job done by José García Narezo (b. 1922) for Sr. Mario López Lena in the latter's house on the Calle de Caracas in Mexico City. The striking modern building was designed in 1951 by Lorenzo Carrasco and Guillermo Rossell. Progressive architects are certainly aware of the possibility of integrating mural and sculptural decoration with contemporary architecture, but the reluctance of clients to go along with the idea or to spend the extra money makes its wide acceptance a rather remote prospect.

In both his mural and easel paintings the Spanish-born Narezo represents the still strong current of semi-academic nationalist or Mexicanist painting. His 1950 *The Shadowy Conch Shell* (collection of the artist) illustrates the poetic imagination of this young painter and the way in which he brings people and landscape together. Parallel in general significance, though stronger in expression, is the work of Juan Soriano (b. 1920), a self-taught painter of great decorative and formal strength, represented by his *Jarocha*, or Vera Cruz Woman, of 1944 (Museo Nacional de Artes Plásticas).

Fernando Castro Pacheco (b. 1928) has produced rich, Impressionist-derived, flowing color and sweepingly dramatic figures based on everyday themes, as in the striking *Hennequén* (fig. 116) of recent date. Here the peasant's body is pierced through in symbolic fashion by the sharp leaves of the hennequén.

José Chávez Morado (b. 1909), somewhat older than many of these young painters, represents again the continuity of what one may call, for lack of a better expression, the more established side of Mexicanism. His easel paintings may be exemplified by the *Dancers* (1951), whose verve and humorous quality, seen even more vividly in his earlier macabre work, are characteristic of one phase of Chávez Morado's expression. The other aspect, more distinctly didactic and political, emerges in the murals, especially in those for the new University City (1952, see fig. 123) and in the recent mosaics done on the Ministry of Communications and Public Works in collaboration with Juan O'Gorman and their respective 'teams.' Chávez Morado has been director of the Plastic Integration

Workshop of the Instituto Nacional de Bellas Artes, working on means of bringing together painting, sculpture, and architecture.

Rául Anguiano (b. 1915), like Chávez Morado a member of the L.E.A.R. and the Taller de Gráfica Popular, has achieved a great deal of deserved reputation in recent years as one of the group of artists and writers working at the Maya site of Bonampak. From there he has brought back a number of striking pen-and-ink sketches, such as the *Kayóm* (fig. 117, 1949), all reflecting the life of the descendants of the Maya Indians. Together with the work of his colleagues on the project, Anguiano's contribution represents a new high point in the Mexicanist movement. Without the slightest trace of the pretty or the folkloristic,

116
CASTRO PACHECO. *Hennequén*
OIL. COLL. THE ARTIST.

117

ANGUIANO. *Kayóm*. INK DRAWING.
MEXICO CITY, COLL. THE ARTIST.

these men have returned to the Indian a significance and a dignity that are justly his.

José L. Gutiérrez (b. 1902) has already been discussed in connection with his significant experiments in the various synthetic-paint media used increasingly by modern Mexican and United States painters, especially ethyl silicate, vinylite, and pyroxilin. In addition to this laboratory research conducted over a period of almost twenty years, Gutiérrez has been painting since about 1940, first in an illustrative Mexicanist style comparable to that of the original Revolutionary painters, and more recently in a bright-colored, sharply contoured, and illusionistic per-spectivized technique that reflects his use of the newer materials and his growth as a painter. The *Scorched Earth*, from his 1952 show at the government's Salón de la Plástica Mexicana, is a high-keyed pyroxilin painting on a curved masonite surface; it not only illustrates the textural possibilities of the medium but shows at the same time the painter's interest in polyangular effects and their space-creating qualities.

On one level, a greater concern with technical and formal problems manifests itself in the use of synthetics and 'public art' illusionistic devices, as in the Siqueiros group, which includes Gutiérrez, or in the new technique of González Camarena. It may emerge on an entirely different plane in those men interested primarily in 'pure painting.' The latter group, increasingly important in the last generation, represents an intensification and extension of the non-Revolutionary art of the late 'twenties and early 'thirties, the art that was sparked by Tamayo and the members of Los Contemporaneos. The current crop of formalist painters is not merely a continuation of the earlier group but also an improvement on it, to the extent that the younger men are far more conscious of the real meaning of color in easel painting, a serious deficiency in much of the older art, both Revolutionary and formal (except for Tamayo).

Among the outstanding members of this new group are Ricardo Martínez de Hoyos (b. 1918) and Guillermo Meza (b. 1917). Martínez de Hoyos offers an unusually sensitive color feeling, dealing in subdued grayish-brownish effects and geometric, formal-patterned arrangements both for his landscapes and for his figure pieces. There is a clear difference in the styles of his landscapes and his more anecdotal and mystical figure paintings. Paintings such as the *Santa Rosa in Ochre* (1949) present a distinctly nonillustrative and formalized approach to the problem of nature, which in this case is reduced to a series of curved lines to give direction and spatial quality. The entire picture is in ochre, except for the green lines of grass and the blue-gray background. A slightly later work, *La Tarde* of 1952 (fig. 118), shows against a striking vermilion background in the upper half of the picture a steel-gray maguey and house in simple but powerful geometrical arrangement, with two small figures standing by.

The figure paintings of Martínez de Hoyos have a different kind of feeling, moving over into a mystical area that may be compared with the expression of the older Rodríguez Lozano (whose colors, though, are far more violent and harsh, however deliberate their intent). In such pictures as *The Road*, with its typical blue-gray background, Martínez de Hoyos brings into play more vivid and colorful effects to augment the symbolic intent of the work; the men are in brown, the woman in various hues. All the figures have their backs to the onlookers as they move off into eternity, not sorrowfully but with full human dignity, and not particularly Mexicanist either. It is in pictures of this general literary quality that Martínez de Hoyos breaks with the nationalist tradition of Mexican painting. Even more significant is his consciousness of the importance of color as a vital vehicle for the painter's craft, a device that must increasingly take its place by the side of the draftsmanship that has long dominated Mexican painting.

Guillermo Meza is another poetic painter and landcape artist who until recently was known almost exclusively for his remarkable draftsmanship. Within the past few years, this talented draftsman has developed a soft palette of yellowish-green tones for his figures, with contrastingly streaked tones for background effects in the same general key. The lower portion of his compositions is often a yellowish red. The final result in

118

MARTÍNEZ DE HOYOS. *Afternoon (La Tarde)*. OIL.
HOUSTON, TEXAS, COLL. MR. & MRS. ROBERT D. STRAUSS.

most cases is a harmonious and skillful blend of colors. Figure pieces especially, such as the *Ceiva* (1949) or the *Leopard and Figures* (1950, gouache, fig. 119), have a poetic quality that is strong and clear without the usual sentimentalizing. While both of these pictures and many more like them are based on the life of Mexico and its people, there is not the slightest hint of the purely illustrative or nationalistic in the traditional sense. The *Ceiva*, apart from the wonderful flow of tree roots and their relation to the undulating lines of a young girl's body, presents a study of mood as well as a composition making full use of form and color relationships. In the *Leopard and Figures* the major note is the magnificent swing of the leopard's body in its S curve across the picture surface; its form and color dominate the entire work and put the human elements in shadow.

These sensitive and poetic newer painter-colorists represent an important and a more recent development in modern Mexican painting. The older men who were responsible for inaugurating the easel movement have also continued to paint during this period, as indicated earlier. The works of artists such as Rufino Tamayo, Carlos Orozco Romero, Carlos Mérida, Manuel Rodríguez Lozano, Agustín Lazo, Gabriel Fernández

Ledesma, Federico Cantú, Juan O'Gorman, Jesús Guerrero Galván, Frida Kahlo, and Julio Castellanos represent the backlog of older easel painting for its own sake. It may or may not be specifically nationalist in quality; its chief concern is with painting as such, an end not always achieved, primarily because of the lack of color skill in many cases.

Among these older painters Miguel Covarrubias is a somewhat special case. Beginning as a very effective caricaturist during the early 1920's, he turned to painting and lithography for a brief period and from those to anthropology and archaeology. His well-known book, *Island of Bali* (1937), was the fruit of these newer interests, and he has since continued to paint and to illustrate books of this nature. His most recent paintings

119

MEZA. *Leopard and Figures*. GOUACHE. LAFAYETTE, IND., COLL. DR. EDWARD AKELEY.

include the charmingly colored panel decorations in the Museum of Popular Arts and the Hotel del Prado in Mexico City and in the Museum of Natural History in New York. These works illustrate not only the decorative nature of his painting but his great knowledge of the many peoples in whom he has interested himself.

The development of easel painting in Mexico has been slow. The overwhelming effect of the mural and graphic movements, the nonexistence of a middle-class patron group until recently, are only part of the story. Even more consequential is the lack of familiarity with contemporary (and older) painting of other countries. Notwithstanding the advent of a new middle class and the increase of art galleries to cater to its aesthetic needs, patronage is still primarily restricted to nationalistic painting rather than to the so-called 'art for art's sake' painters. The latter, in addition to these problems, also suffer from the fact that their contact with modern painting has been mainly through the medium of magazine illustrations of works of art instead of original works. For these various reasons, most of these painters have not yet produced an art comparable in quality to that of either the muralists or the graphic artists.

Although dissatisfied with both the political and aesthetic character of muralism, many of the formalistic painters, because of their lack of contact with original works of art (there is still no museum in Mexico comparable to the Museum of Modern Art, the Metropolitan, Louvre, National Gallery, et cetera), have not been able to reach the same high level of performance. For a long time, therefore, most Mexican easel painting has been a weak echo of the murals and graphics or, in terms of intellectual dissatisfaction, a local brand of Surrealism or Magic Realism.

With the significant and notable exceptions of Rufino Tamayo and Carlos Mérida, modern abstract expression has left Mexican painting almost completely untouched. The expository character and strength of the Revolutionary tradition, the violent nationalism of the Revolution and post-Revolution periods, and the continued attacks of left-wing Mexican artists against foreign art have kept both European and United States art at a distance. Tamayo's career shows the lack of receptivity to 'modernism' in Mexico. Only in the United States and in Europe has he been able to achieve the recognition he merits. Even today, finally considered as one of the 'big four' because of this foreign acclaim, and patronized by various collectors, Tamayo remains an atypical phenomenon in Mexico, like the abstract point of view itself.

Tamayo's moving to New York in 1938 was an acknowledgment of this situation. At the same time, however, he found it necessary to spend at least a part of each year in Mexico, not merely from ordinary sentimental motives but because his artistic roots, his sense of color and other elements in his work, were there rather than in New York. Three important artistic events mark his sojourn in the United States: first, the effect of Picasso's art (cf. the 1939 Museum of Modern Art exhibition) from around 1939–40 on; then, the 1943 commission for a mural at Smith College—his first abstract mural—and finally the turn since 1946–7 toward a more violent form of expression.

The effect of Picasso may be identified in such pictures as the Museum of Modern Art's *Animals* of 1941 or the well-known *Singing Bird* of 1943 (fig. 120), both of which move in a new and heroic direction. Various parts of the body are carefully isolated from each other and deliberately placed in their respective positions, while compositional effects are extremely calculated. Yet however universal these symbols of Tamayo's may

120

TAMAYO. *Singing Bird*. OIL. VENICE, COLLECTION OF THE ITALIAN GOVERNMENT.

PHOTO COURTESY INSTITUTO NACIONAL DE BELLAS ARTES

258

now become as a result of this outside influence, the essential qualities, especially the color harmonies, are still very much those of Tamayo himself. Moreover, this color quality and the forms themselves are still close to the Mexican environment from which they are drawn. Thus, in the *Trembling Woman* of 1944 (fig. 121, Carrillo Gil collection) and in many others of this decade, he bases his forms on a papier-mâché type of figure very common in Mexico, especially the Judas figures used at Easter, with their imaginatively shaped and colored bodies. The same would seem to be true of many of his animal paintings of this period, which, while taking on the dynamism of Picasso's compositions, still derive in form from the fanciful and semi-grotesque molded paper dogs, wolves, and so on, that are part of Mexico's folk art.

The well-known *Trembling Woman* is characteristic of the most recent

121

TAMAYO. *Trembling Woman.*
OIL. MEXICO CITY,
COLL. DR. A. CARRILLO GIL.

PHOTO COURTESY INSTITUTO NACIONAL DE BELLAS ARTES

development in Tamayo's painting. Strongly foreshortened figures move in and out of a deeply perspectivized space, the emphasis being on movement as such instead of on the formal relation of the earlier paintings. Tamayo has been affected in a number of pictures by the fanciful imagination and humor of Paul Klee (as in the 1939 *The Doctor* of the Carrillo Gil collection); he injects into these deeply indented spaces a kind of macabre fantasy that is also in line with the Mexican tradition. At the same time, we cannot overlook the continuous and palpable effect of Picasso in these works—the leaping figures, the upturned heads of men and animals, the enlarged hands, the oblique references to *Guernica* elements in the older master's work—but always with Tamayo's own lambent color effects.

Between the first and second styles of this period comes the mural done in 1943 in the Hillyer Art Library of Smith College. Called *Nature and the Artist*, this 'un-Revolutionary' mural shows first *Nature* herself with four breasts signifying abundance; she is lying back in a position of surrender. At the left is *Water*, a blue female nude with water shooting from her hands. Above her is *Fire*, a red male figure; while behind Nature a coffee-colored figure, *Earth*, holds Nature in her arms. At the right-hand side of the mural, a blue male form represents *Air*. These five symbols are tied together by a rainbow arching across the top of the composition and representing *Color*, the basic element in all painting. To the right of these allegorical figures is a clothed man before his easel. Near him a lyre and compass instruct the painter to look at Nature through poetry and knowledge.

At the extreme right, the allegory ends with *The Observer and the Work of Art*, where a figure is completely absorbed in a piece of sculpture carved without any consideration of the Nature from which it was derived. The work of art must stand by itself and not require narration, naturalism of effect, or similar values. In Tamayo's own words: 'To emphasize the idea that when judging a work of art one must take it as a new creation, independent of the source from which it sprang, the Observer stands with his back to the group that symbolizes Nature.'[1]

This mural, with its somewhat literal symbolism, is a very tightly knit and strikingly colored composition. Its diagonals are carefully related, and effective tonalities range from red-ochre to darker ochres and finally to the coffee brown of earth, plus the striking blue of Air, the yellows, the greens, and the others. In comparison with his unfinished mural in the National School of Music and the abortive 1930 project in the National Museum of Archaeology, the Smith College work represents a tremendous forward step, pointing the way to Tamayo's achievement in the realm of abstract mural painting.

Whether or not the abstract element represented by Tamayo and

---

[1] Robert Goldwater, *Tamayo*, Quadrangle Press, N.Y., 1947, quoted on p. 35.

PHOTO JOSÉ VERDE, COURTESY SRA. INÉS AMOR

122

TAMAYO. *Birth of Nationality*. OIL.
PALACIO DE BELLAS ARTES, MEXICO CITY.

Mérida will become more influential in Mexican art remains to be seen.
Tamayo's 1952–3 mural paintings in the Palacio de Bellas Artes, in the
same building with murals by the other important masters, mark a new
phase of the development. The *Birth of Nationality* (fig. 122) is the first
of two panels on the second floor of the Palacio. Expository in theme, it
represents an adaptation of the sketch for the abandoned 1930 mural
project, and at the same time is entirely typical of Tamayo's most recent
color and dynamic development. It illustrates what can be accomplished
in combining narrative (even Revolutionary) content with significant
form and color.

The horseman of the Conquest moves sharply right, against one of
Tamayo's typical rich lemon-yellow backgrounds. The dark-brown body
and head of the horse (the head moving diagonally upward in a manner

reminiscent of Picasso) are surmounted by a grayish man-head, but the underside and the rear of the horse are done in a characteristic warm rose color. The horseman brings with him the culture symbols of the white man, such as the impressive detached column at the left, and leaps over the ruins of Indian civilization, symbolized by a tan-colored dead Indian at the lower right. From the head of this figure a child is seen to emerge, half-Indian, half-European. At the upper right two rose-colored suns meet to symbolize the conjunction of the Old World and the New. These elements, together with the dynamically moving horse and rider, exist between the lemon-yellow upper background and the glowing lavender and blue lower portion of the mural.

The second panel, on the opposite side of the great hall, was finished in 1953 and is known as *Mexico Today*. It consists of a fairly literal, although still typical of Tamayo, modernist presentation of a number of symbols expressing what has become an increasingly popular theme for Mexican muralists.

These works have met little favor from the Revolutionary artists because of their nonrepresentational qualities and even more because of the 'decadent' implications of all such painting. Actually, both murals, particularly the first one, are a significant step in the evolution of modern Mexican art. Within the compass of the contemporary world idiom, they retain not only the narrative content of Mexican history but also the flavor and color of that country.

The little dancing abstracts of Mérida, done in silicon on square concrete plaques on the façade of the Benito Juárez Housing Project, and his staircase mural in the same building (1949) represent another attempt to fit modern design to the needs of Mexican mural decoration. Although not at all so specific in theme as Tamayo's subjects, these forms have an Indian quality of their own which, from the point of view of pure design, relates admirably to the broken forms of the building's window arrangements.

Other artists in Mexico are becoming aware of the need, if not for abstract art itself, at least for a higher form of pictorial organization and color harmonics to replace the rather naïve realism characteristic of many of their colleagues, the weak echoes of Rivera and Orozco. The arrival in Mexico of *émigré* artists from Europe has also contributed a leavening element, to the degree that they represent a type of thinking which, though not as strong as the original Picasso-Braque-Léger-Matisse sources, gives the nationalist artist something new to consider.

The left wing in Mexico, still a powerful factor in the country's art, however non-left the government, feels there are other solutions to the problem of contemporary Mexican painting. That there is a problem is attested by Siqueiros's criticism of the Taller, which, he claimed, had not found its roots in the Mexican people but was depending on 'snob' trade, particularly that of foreigners. The Taller, in turn, accused him of not living up to the ideological premises of his own art. Generally, Siqueiros feels that the future of Mexican art lies in the outdoor mural, presented to as large an audience as possible and in as permanent a medium as can be achieved. For this end a dynamic social realism seems to him the most suitable form of expression, and we can agree that for Siqueiros it is the best and most successful vehicle. On the other hand, it may not be the best for those unable to reach his emotive heights and socially critical level. Unless there are a good many painters prepared to follow Siqueiros —and there is little indication so far of a school—the answer would seem to lie elsewhere.

The 1952–5 work on the University City by Siqueiros, Rivera, O'Gorman, and Chávez Morado may be taken to represent for the most part the 'popular art' conception of Siqueiros.[2] One of the most elaborate and expensive academic projects in the world, the University City is an impressive sight, with scores of fine functional buildings and the visible results of the work of artists engaged to decorate many of the façades.

Rivera's colored stone inlay design on the outside of the 110,000-seat stadium is an allegory on Learning. One panel shows the Engineer, Worker, and Architect offering the University City to the Mexican people, whose sacrifices have made possible the great achievements of today. The other panel shows the teaching staff of the University welcoming the students to the stadium for development of their strength and health through sports. These and similar themes are carried out in varying heights of relief, high in the center and diminishing at the sides.

O'Gorman, working on the outside of the Library (which he helped to design), has contributed two decorative schemes: a stylized flat relief of Aztec hieroglyphics of Water, Earth, Fire, and Sun, worked out on a wall in front of the enormous base on which the building is set; and four tremendous stone mosaics on the main structure. The latter symbolize the pre-Hispanic world, the colonial epoch, and the contemporaneous culture resulting from the mixture of those two strains. They are spread out in profuse historical and anthropological detail that attests to the thorough preparation (six years) and great grasp of the material by the architect-painter.

Chávez Morado, working on the Science Building, has completed several traditional Mexicanist murals in one part of this structure and a more striking Italian mosaic on an exterior panel below the main part of the building (fig. 123). Here he has brought together a series of conventional allegorical figures that represent the different phases of the world's culture, in a composition entitled *Return of Quetzalcoatl*. Seated on the serpent raft of this ancient god, the figures are carried to the right and into modern times, as it were. They include from left to right: Egypt (gold color), Middle Ages (green), Quetzalcoatl himself (red), Assyria (brown),

[2] See *Time*, 23 Feb. 1953, for illustrations of University City murals.

Greco-Roman civilization (brown figures with white robes), Orient (light green), and Moslem (purple). Against a background showing the Pyramid of the Sun, they symbolize the permanence of culture. At the left are the broken dark-blue weapons of war and at the right is the golden fire of inspiration and hope. The mosaic is placed above a flat pool so that the composition looks as though it were floating on the water.

Siqueiros's main contribution to the University City centers about the Administration Building (Rectoría), where four distinct areas had been allocated for his paintings. These consist of a cubical mass, or *vierendel*, that projects from the east side at a height of about twenty meters from the ground, three sides of which allow for two hundred and fifty meters of painting; two horizontal walls (south and north) comprising three hundred and twenty and one hundred and thirty meters of space respectively; and a huge vertical west wall six hundred meters in area (this last never carried out).

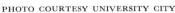

123
CHÁVEZ MORADO. *Return of Quetzalcoatl.*
MOSAIC. SCIENCE BUILDING,
UNIVERSITY CITY, MEXICO.

In addition to the effect given by synthetic paints and industrial chemical oxidizing agents, the finish of these murals is a combination of ceramics, mosaic, and various metallic adjuncts. The artist speaks of this as 'sculptural painting,' meaning not the usual idea of pictorial sculpture or colored bas-reliefs but the use of different superposed planes that may project in some instances as much as 60 centimeters. These (plus whatever actual sculptural forms may be added) have as their primary purpose an optical pictorial and textural effect. Since the project was so immense, Siqueiros was obliged to parcel out the work to two separate teams (the same is true of the Rivera, O'Gorman, and Chávez Morado undertakings), each with its own artist-leader.

The general theme of these murals is *The University at the Service of the Nation*. On the north wall, the first that one sees upon coming down the highway from Mexico City, is the narrow panel showing a huge symbolic hand in the act of creating a pictorial image, signifying *The Man Who Molds the Nation Reclaims the National and Finally the Universal Culture*. For

124

SIQUEIROS. *The Sage, Sociologist and Artist . . .*
ETHYL SILICATE. ADMINISTRATION BUILDING, SOUTH SIDE, UNFINISHED STATE, UNIVERSITY CITY, MEXICO.

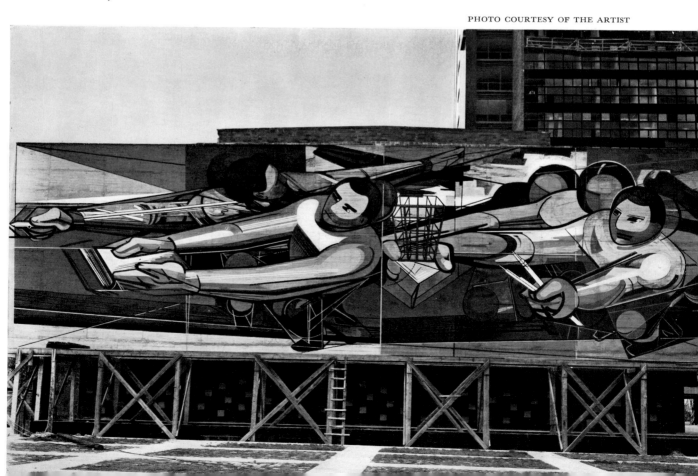

the projecting *vierendel*, the painter has envisaged the eagle and the condor, symbolizing the union between Mexico, Central, and South America. The second horizontal wall (on the south), visible from the out-of-town approach to the University City, shows how *The Sage, the Sociologist, and the Artist Bring to the Nation the Fruit of Their Studies for Their Scientific, Technical, Agricultural, Industrial, and Cultural Application* (fig. 124), resulting in a rather literal sequence of outstretched arms. The last wall, a vast vertical space fronting on the highway and the first to be seen on entering the University grounds, would have represented the spark and light of culture.

The difficulties of the entire University City mural project, it would seem, arose not only from the size and outdoor nature of the assignments (less a problem to Siqueiros than to the others) but also from the fact that the various artists did not express themselves as freely here as one would have expected from their previous work. The paradox of working for a government with whom the artist has political differences apparently inhibits comfortable expression. This would be true even if no holds were barred. Indeed they all, curiously, settled on literary and 'harmless' themes for their respective works.[3] Unfortunately, the strength of any of these men has been in a critical attitude, however expressed: Rivera's eloquent references to the past, Chávez Morado's macabre humor, O'Gorman's mood-filled and incisive attacks on fascism, Siqueiros's whirlwind fury against any invader and any transgressor.

In the last year of the Alemán administration (1952) and during the early years of the presidency of Adolfo Ruiz Cortines, when these works were being carried out, there were still enough issues about which an artist could be Revolutionary, apart from attacks on 'imperialism' and exhortations for 'peace.' The government Party of Revolutionary Institutions (P.R.I.), Mexico's official and now institutionalized Revolutionary party, had built such wonders as the University City and other projects of equal grandiosity, but many things still remained to be done for the people. Of these there is very little said in the present murals, which are in turn decorative, pompous, intellectualized, or just declamatory. The lions had been tamed—given such an occasion as the new University, there was perhaps little choice, but the removal of their teeth did not leave these men at their best.

This cannot be taken to mean, however, that the Revolutionary tradition is dead in Mexican art; it does indicate that the great strength of its masters so far has been in the expression of profound social convictions rather than in the realm of officially correct allegories. At the same time, it brings forward the point thatt his art has in recent years

---

[3] Siqueiros later added to his symbolic hand image the four crucial dates in Mexican history—1520, 1810, 1857, and 1910—and ended this list with a '19—' in pointedly red paint. This defiant gesture, however, does not affect the basic character of the work.

tended to fall into the trap of pictorial and political clichés. The future health of Revolutionary art, it appears, will depend on the addition of design and color elements that can come only from enlarged acquaintance with the art of other countries and other times. It is little use to point with great pride, as one leading Mexican painter has done,[4] to the glorious tradition of social painting represented by Goya if contemporaries do not learn from him or others like him, past and present, in terms of technique.

There are still unnumbered ways in which the ideals of the Mexican Revolution, the ideals of a better life for the majority, can be expressed by artists. These need not be in any of the already established and canonized forms, however good those have been. Nor need they necessarily be carried out with the aid of the modern tradition, although this is not so farfetched. Whichever path is followed, instead of bringing culture down to the level of the people it is much more important to raise people to the level of culture. In the final analysis, this will not be accomplished with the kind of purely illustrative expression that has been increasingly purveyed by so many Mexicans. A country capable of producing the monumental abstract art of precolonial times, the decorative folk art, and the powerful Revolutionary painting of our own times can surely appreciate a new development, organically constructed in the tradition of either the old or the modern masters, or both.

Toward this end a way must be found to bring the younger artists of Mexico into contact with various artistic traditions. Reading about them in books and magazines is far from satisfactory. Originals must be provided by one means or another; a museum of art that goes beyond the purely local product would be a valuable addition to the cultural potential. Today in Mexico this need looms larger than ever. Most artists recognize that something must be done. With the death of Orozco and the increasing age of Rivera, a great period is drawing to a close. Siqueiros now stands as the leading Revolutionary painter, working in a highly personalized, even romantic vein difficult to emulate; Tamayo remains the leader of the abstract group. These men represent in their respective ways the best that Mexico has to offer. What they have to say can be preserved and in the future developed by the younger men if they have the initiative and are given the tools and leadership that is necessary.

With Mexico's further emergence from the phase of agrarian revolt into one of industrial evolution, new needs will be encountered, new problems will arise to be solved. One can believe and hope that the leading role of the artist in this society, a role established from the beginning, will continue into the new epoch, and that Mexican painting will carry on its activity as tribune of the people and conscience of their Revolution.

---

[4] Jesús Guerrero Galván, 'El nuevo movimiento en la pintura Mexicana,' *El Popular*, Mexico, 3 August 1952.

Bibliography

Abreu Gómez, Emilio, 'Jesús Guerrero Galván,' *Hijo Pródigo*, Mexico, año 2, vol. 6, no. 20, Nov. 1944.

Acosta, Julio, 'Nuevos pintores mexicanos,' *Hijo Pródigo*, Mexico, año 3, vol. 10, no. 31, Oct. 1945.

ALFARO SIQUEIROS

Alfaro Siqueiros, D., 'Carta a Orozco,' *Hoy*, Mexico, no. 398, 7 Oct. 1944.

Alfaro Siqueiros, D., *Como se pinta una mural*, Ediciones Mexicanas, Mexico, 1951.

Alfaro Siqueiros, D., 'El joven doctor Atl,' *Hoy*, Mexico, 24 Sept. 1944, no. 396.

Alfaro Siqueiros, D., *El Muralismo de México*, Ediciones Mexicanas, Mexico, 1950.

Alfaro Siqueiros, D., 'En la Guerra, Arte de Guerra! Manifiesto,' *Forma*, Santiago, Chile, I, nos. 8 & 9, Jan.–Feb., 1943.

Alfaro Siqueiros, D., 'Hacia una nueva plástica integral,' *Espacios*, Mexico, Sept. 1948, no. 1.

Alfaro Siqueiros, D., 'La crítica del arte como pretexto literario,' *México en el arte*, no. 4, Oct. 1948.

Alfaro Siqueiros, D., 'La obra de Diego Rivera,' *Hoy*, Mexico, no. 387, 22 julio 1944.

Alfaro Siqueiros, D., 'La pintura mexicana moderna,' *Hoy*, Mexico, no. 385, 8 julio 1944.

Alfaro Siqueiros, D. & Kirstein, L., 'La reciente obra mural de Siqueiros en el conjunto del muralismo Mexicano,' *Hoy*, Mexico, 26 junio 1943.

Alfaro Siqueiros, D., 'Manifiesto de los pintores de América,' *Vida americana*, Madrid, no. 1, 1921.

Alfaro Siqueiros, D., 'Mi pintura en Chillán,' *Hoy*, Mexico, no. 276, junio 1942.

Alfaro Siqueiros, D., *No hay mas ruta que la nuestra*, Secretaría de Educación Pública, Mexico, 1945.

Alfaro Siqueiros, D., *Siqueiros: Por la vía de una pintura neorealista o realista social moderna en México*, Instituto Nacional de Bellas Artes, Mexico, 1951.

Alfaro Siqueiros, D., 'Un ensayo de pintura colectiva,' *Romance*, Mexico, vol. 1, no. 4, 15 Mar. 1940.

Alfaro Siqueiros, D., 'Un hecho artístico embrionariamente transcendental en Chile,' *Hoy*, Mexico, 20 Feb. 1943.

'California group studies fresco technique with Siqueiros,' *Art Digest*, New York, vol. 6, no. 19, 1 Aug. 1932.

David Alfaro Siqueiros: Trece grabados en madera. Text, W. Spratling, Taxco, 1931.

Mural del Hospital de la Raza-Siqueiros (8 pls.) Mexico, Ediciones de Arte Público, n.d.

'White walls and a fresco in California,' *Arts & Decoration*, New York, vol. 41, no. 2, June 1934. (Murphey house, Siqueiros).

Altolaguirre, Manuel, 'La pintura quemante,' Hoy, Mexico, 20 Nov. 1943.

Amabilis, J. Manuel, 'La obra de Diego Rivera,' *El arquitecto*, Mexico, ser. 2, no. 5, Sept. 1925. (Chapingo).

American Artists Congress. Two papers presented.... 15 February 1936 by Orozco and Siqueiros; and the catalogue of the exhibitions of the Mexican delegates... at the A.C.A. Gallery...., A.C.A. Gallery, N.Y., 1936.

'An international portfolio, Mexico; modern Mexican murals carry on an old tradition', *Arts & Decoration*, New York, vol. 41, no. 3, July 1934.

Abraham Ángel. Talleres gráficos de la nación, Mexico, 1924.

Anguiano, Raúl, 'La plástica en Bonampak,' *Espacios*, Mexico, no. 4, Jan. 1950.

Anguiano, Raúl, 'Las artes plásticas y el cine,' *Espacios*, Mexico, no. 1, Sept. 1940.

Anguiano, Raúl, *Popular Proverbs*. 6 lithographs with introduction by Justino Fernández. La Estampa Mexicana, Mexico, 1943.

Arenal, Angélica (intr.), *Siqueiros, 70 Obras Recientes*, Instituto Nacional de Bellas Artes, Mexico, 1947.

'Art of the Americas,' *Art News Annual, XVIII*. The Art Foundation, New York, 1946.

Artaud, Antonin, 'Le Mexique et l'esprit primitif: Maria Izquierdo,' *L'amour de l'art*, Paris, vol. 18, Oct. 1937.

Atl, Dr. (Gerardo Murillo), *Diez Dibujos del Dr. Atl*, Ediciones Arte Mexicano, Mexico, 1939.

Atl, Dr. (Gerardo Murillo), *Valles y Montañas de México: 80 Dibujos del Dr. Atl*. Catalogue Departamento de Artes Plásticas, Mexico, 1948.

Azuela, Mariano, *The Under Dogs*, trans. by E. Munguia, Jr., pref. by Carleton Beals, illustrated by J. C. Orozco, Brentano's, N. Y., 1929.

Balmori, Santos, 'La pintura de Carlos Mérida,' *Espacios*, Mexico, no. 2, Winter 1948–9.

Barreda, Octavio G., 'Carlos Orozco Romero,' *Hijo Pródigo*, Mexico, año 3, vol. 11, no. 34, Jan. 1945.

Barreda, Octavio G., 'Juan Soriano,' *Hijo Pródigo*, Mexico, año 3, vol. 8, no. 25, abril 1945.

Barreda, Octavio G., 'Rufino Tamayo en 1944,' *Hijo Pródigo*, Mexico, vol. 5, no. 18, Sept. 1944.

Benson, E. M., 'Orozco in New England; murals at Dartmouth College,' *American Magazine of Art*, Washington, D. C., vol. 26, no. 10, Oct. 1933.

Berdecio, Roberto, 'Sobre la crisis en la pintura social,' *Espacios*, Mexico, no. 1, Sept. 1948.

Bergamín, José, 'La Piedad, un fresco de Rodríguez Lozano en la penitenciaría del D. F.,' *Ars*, Mexico, vol. 1, no. 3, marzo 1942.

Bergamín, José, 'Pintura de la justicia,' *Hoy*, Mexico, no. 254, 27 Dec. 1941.

Boston, Institute of Modern Art. *Modern Mexican Painters*, selected with an intr. by MacKinley Helm, Boston, 1941.

Brenner, Anita, 'A Mexican renascence,' *Arts*, New York, vol. 8, no. 3, Sept. 1925.

Brenner, Anita, 'An artist from the Maya country; Carlos Mérida,' *International Studio*, New York, vol. 83, Apr. 1926.

Brenner, Anita, *Idols Behind Altars*, Payson & Clarke, Ltd., N. Y., 1929.

Brenner, Anita, 'The Mexican Renaissance: its rise and eclipse,' *Harper's Magazine*, New York, vol. 182, no. 2, Jan. 1941. (also in *Mexican Life*, Mexico, March 1941).

Brenner, Anita, 'Une renaissance mexicaine,' *Renaissance de l'art*, Paris, vol. 11, no. 2, fév. 1928.

Brenner, A. & Leighton, George R., *The Wind that Swept Mexico*. With 184 historical photographs by G. R. Leighton, Harper's, N. Y., 1943.

Breton, André, 'Frida Kahlo,' *Hijo Pródigo*, Mexico, año 4, vol. 12, no. 38, May 1946.

Cantú, Federico, *Letanía Lauretana* (19 engravings). Privately printed, Monterrey, 1946.

Cardoza y Aragón, Luis, 'Jesús Guerrero Galván,' *Mexican Art & Life*, Mexico, no. 3, July 1938.

Cardoza y Aragón, Luis, 'José Clemente Orozco, pintor mexicano,' *Revista nacional de cultura*, no. 22, Sept. 1940; no. 23, Oct. 1940.

Cardoza y Aragón, Luis, *La nube y el reloj*, Ediciones de la universidad nacional autónoma, Mexico, 1940.

Cardoza y Aragón, Luis, 'La obra de Orozco en la iglesia del Hospital de Jesús,' *Cuadernos americanos*, año 3, vol. 15, no. 3, mayo-junio 1944.

Cardoza y Aragón, Luis, 'New murals by José Clemente Orozco,' *Mexican Life*, Mexico, December 1937.

Cardoza y Aragón, Luis, 'Nuevas notas sobre Alfaro Siqueiros,' *México en el arte*, Mexico, no. 4, Oct. 1948.

Cardoza y Aragón, Luis, 'Rufino Tamayo. Un nuevo ciclo de la pintura de México,' *Cuadernos Americanos*, Mexico, año 7, vol. 40, no. 4, July–Aug. 1948.

Castro Leal, Antonio, 'José Clemente Orozco en la Exposición Nacional de sus Obras,' *México en el Arte*, Mexico, no. 6, December 1948.

Catlin, Stanton L., *Art moderne mexicain*, Braun et Cie., Paris, 1951.

Cervantes, Enrique A., *Pintura de Juan O'Gorman en la Biblioteca 'Gertrudis Bocanegra' de Patzcuaro, Michoacán*, Mexico, 1945.

Charlot, Jean, *Art-Making from Mexico to China*, Sheed and Ward, N. Y., 1950.

Charlot, Jean, *Art from the Mayans to Disney*, Sheed and Ward, N. Y. and London, 1939.

Charlot, Jean, 'José Clemente Orozco, su obra monumental,' *Forma*, Mexico, vol. 2, no. 6, June 1928. (trans. in *Art from the Mayans to Disney*)

Charlot, Jean, 'Orozco's Stylistic Evolution,' *College Art Journal*, IX, 2, Winter 1949–50.

Charlot, Jean, 'Renaissance Revisited,' *Magazine of Art*, vol. 39, no. 2, Feb. 1946.

Charlot, Jean, 'José Clemente Orozco,' *Magazine of Art*, vol. 40, no. 7, Nov. 1947.

Charlot, Jean, 'Rufino Tamayo,' *Magazine of Art*, vol. 38, no. 4, April 1945. (Smith College).

Charlot Murals in Georgia. Intr. by Lamar Dodd, photographs by Eugene Payor and comments by Jean Charlot. University of Georgia, Athens, 1945.

Chávez, Ignacio, *Diego Rivera, sus frescos en el Instituto Nacional de Cardiología*, El Colegio Nacional, Mexico, 1946.

Claudel, Paul, 'Jean Charlot,' *Mexican Life*, July 1931.

Colección Anahuac. *Arte Mexicano*, Editorial de Arte, Mexico, 1948, vol. 3, Orozco; vol. 8, Rivera; vol. 14, Siqueiros; vol. 17, Anguiano.

Contemporary Art of Latin America. Series 2, Pan-American Union, Washington, D. C., 1945.

Cortes Juárez, Erasto, *El Grabado Contemporáneo, 1922–1950*. Ediciones Mexicanas, Mexico, 1951.

Cossío del Pomar, Felipe, 'La pintura social en México,' *Cursos y Conferencias*, Buenos Aires, año 7, no. 5–6, Aug.–Sept. 1938.

Crespo de la Serna, Jorge, 'Les circonstances et l'évolution des arts plastiques au Mexique, 1900–1950,' *México en el Arte*, édition speciale en français, Mexico, 1952.

Danes, Gibson, 'Juan O'Gorman,' *Southwest Review*, vol. 28, no. 1, Autumn 1942.

Darío, Jaime, 'En torno a mi pintura,' *Espacios*, Mexico, Sept. 1948, no. 1.

de la Encina, Juan, 'La pintura Mexicana moderna,' *Revista Nacional de Cultura*, no. 16, febo. marzo 1940; no. 19, junio 1940.

Díaz y de Ovando, Clementina, *El Colegio Máximo de San Pedro y San Pablo*, Instituto de Investigaciones Estéticas, Mexico, 1951.

Dickerson, Albert I., *The Orozco Frescoes at Dartmouth*, Dartmouth College, Hanover, N. H., 1934. Foreword by Orozco.

Downing, Todd, *The Mexican Earth*, Doubleday, Doran & Co., N. Y., 1940.

Duran, Daniel, *Carnaval de Huejotzingo*. Drawings by Desiderio Xochitiotzin. Privately printed, Puebla, 1949.

Edelman, Lilly, *Mexican Painters and their influence in the United States*, Service Bureau for Intercultural Education, N. Y., 1938.

Edwards, Emily, *Modern Mexican Frescoes, a guide and map*, Central News Agency, Mexico, 1934.

Edwards, Emily, *The frescoes by Diego Rivera in Cuernavaca*. Cultura, Mexico, 1932.

Egleson, James D., 'José Clemente Orozco,' *Parnassus*, New York, vol. 12, no. 7, Nov. 1940.

Engravings of the Mexican Revolution. Folio of 85 engravings by members of the Taller de Gráfica Popular, La Estampa Mexicana, Mexico, 1947.

Evans, Ernestine, *The frescoes of Diego Rivera*, Harcourt, Brace, N. Y., 1929.

Farías, Ixca. *Biografía de pintores jaliscienses, 1882–1940*. Ricardo Delgado, Guadalajara, 1940.

Fernández, Justino, 'Anguiano pintor realista,' *Hoy*, Mexico, 11 Sept. 1943.

Fernández, Justino, 'Arte moderno y contemporáneo,' in *México y la cultura*, Secretaría de Educación Pública, Mexico, 1946.

Fernández, Justino, *Arte moderno y contemporáneo de México*, Universidad Nacional de México, Mexico, 1952.

Fernández, Justino, 'Cecil Crawford O'Gorman,' *Anales del instituto de investigaciones estéticas*, vol. 3, no. 11, Mexico, 1944.

Fernández, Justino, 'Contemporary painting and sculpture in Mexico,' (in Born, Esther, *The new architecture in Mexico*, N. Y., 1937).

Fernández, Justino, 'De una charla con J. C. Orozco,' *Anales del instituto de investigaciones estéticas*, vol. 2, no. 5, Mexico, 1940.

Fernández, Justino, *Diego Rivera: 10 reproduciones en color*. E. Fischgrund, Mexico, 1946.

Fernández, Justino, *El arte moderno en México*, Ediciones Porrúa, Mexico, 1937.

Fernández, Justino, 'El pintor de nuestro tiempo,' *Anales del instituto de investigaciones estéticas*, no. 16, 1948.

Fernández, Justino, *J. C. Orozco, forma e idea*, Librería de Porrúa hermanos, Mexico, 1942.

Fernández, Justino, *José Clemente Orozco: ten reproductions of his mural paintings*, E. Fischgrund, Mexico, 1944.

Fernández, Justino, 'La obra de Montenegro,' *Hoy*, Mexico, 27 Nov. 1943.

Fernández, Justino, 'La poesia salvaje de Maria Izquierdo,' *Hoy*, Mexico, 25 Sept. 1943.

Fernández, Justino, 'Los frescos de Orozco en el templo de Jesús Nazareno,' *Hijo Pródigo*, Mexico, año 1, vol. 3, no. 12, marzo 1944.

Fernández, Justino, 'Los teules de Orozco,' *Universidad de Mexico*, no. 13, Oct. 1947.

Fernández, Justino, 'Meza, pintor de lo imposible,' *Hoy*, Mexico, 7 agosto 1943.

Fernández, Justino, 'Obras recientes de Orozco,' *México en el Arte*, no. 6, Dec. 1948. (Escuela para Maestros and National Mus. of History).

Fernández, Justino, 'Orozco, genio de América,' *Cuadernos Americanos*, Nov.–Dec. 1949. (reprinted in *College Art Journal*, IX, 2, Winter, 1949–50).

Fernández, Justino, *Orozco, Rivera y Siqueiros*, E. Fischgrund, Mexico, 1948.

Fernández, Justino, *Prometeo, ensayo sobre pintura contemporánea*, Porrúa, Mexico, 1945.

Fernández, Justino, 'Raúl Anguiano,' *Hijo Pródigo*, año 3, vol. 8, no. 27, junio 1945.

Fernández, Justino, *Rufino Tamayo*, Imprenta Universitaría, Mexico, 1948.

Fernández, Justino, 'Significación de Orozco,' *Cuadernos Americanos*, año 5, vol. 30, no. 6, Nov.–Dec. 1948.

Fernández, Justino, 'Textos de Orozco,' *Instituto de investigaciones estéticas*, Mexico, Imprenta Universitaría, 1955.

Fernández, Justino, 'Un regalo a los Estados Unidos,' *Hoy*, 9 Oct. 1943.

Frescos en Autlán' (José A. Monroy) *Hoy*, no. 433, 9 June 1945.

Gallardo, Cira Cesár, *El Maestro Rural*. Illustrated by G. Fernández Ledesma, Secretaría de Educación Pública, Mexico, 1943.

Gamboa, Fernando, 'Calaveras,' *México en el Arte*, Nov. 1948, no. 5.

García Maroto, G., 'La obra de Diego Rivera,' *Contemporaneos*, Mexico, June 1928. II, 1.

Garner, Bess Adams, *Mexico: notes in the margin*. Houghton, Mifflin, Boston, 1937. (Rodríguez Market murals).

Goldwater, Robert J., *Rufino Tamayo*, Quadrangle Press, N. Y., 1947.

Gómez Mayorga, Mauricio, *Jorge González Camarena*, Pintores de México, 2, Ediciones Mexicanas, Mexico, 1951.

'González Camarena en la Cervecería Modelo,' *Espacios*, no. 4, Dec. 1949–Jan. 1950.

Goodrich, Lloyd, 'The murals of the New School,' *Arts*, N. Y., vol. 17, no. 6, Mar. 1931.

Gray, Cleve, 'Orozco's Recent Frescoes,' *Art in America*, vol. 36, no. 3, July 1948. (Hospital de Jesús)

Gual, Enrique, *Rufino Tamayo*, privately printed, Mexico, 1950.

Guides to Mexican frescoes, Frances Toor Studios, Mexico, 1937, nos. 1–10.

Guerrero Galván, J., 'El nuevo movimiento en la pintura Mexicana,' El Popular, Mexico, 3 August 1952.

'Guillermo Meza', *Espacios*, no. 23–24, Jan.-Apr., 1955.

Gutiérrez, 'José L. Gutiérrez,' *Mexican Life*, Feb. 1947.

Haight, Anna Lyon, *Portrait of Latin America as seen by her print makers*, Hastings House, N. Y., 1946.

Helm, MacKinley, *Man of Fire: José Clemente Orozco*, Harcourt, Brace, 1953.

Helm, MacKinley, *Modern Mexican Painters*, Harper's, N. Y., 1941.

Henestrosa, Andres, 'El corrido Mexicano, su caracter popular y su función pública,' *Espacios*, August 1950, nos. 5 & 6.

Huerta, Efrain, 'David Alfaro Siqueiros: ducos,' Universidad, Mexico, vol. 3, no. 18, July 1937.

Kirstein, Lincoln, 'Siqueiros in Chillán,' *Magazine of Art*, vol. 36, Dec. 1943.

Kirstein, Lincoln, 'Siqueiros: Painter and Revolutionary,' *Magazine of Art*, vol. 37, January 1944.

'La pintura mural en México,' *Artes de México*, nos. 5 & 6, Dec. 1954.

Lira, Miguel N., 'Julio Castellanos,' *Universidad*, Mexico, vol. 3, no. 14, March 1937 (Coyoacán mural).

Méndez, Leopoldo, *En nombre de Cristo*: *7 litografías*. Departamento de Bellas Artes, Mexico, 1939.

Méndez, Leopoldo, *Folio of 25 engravings*, La Estampa Mexicana, Mexico, 1943.

Méndez, Leopoldo, *Río Escondido*: *diez grabados*, La Estampa Mexicana, Mexico, 1948.

Mérida, Carlos, *Estampas del Popol-Vuh*, Graphic Arts Publications, Mexico, 1943.

Mérida, Carlos, *Carnavales de México*: *diez litografías originales en color*, Mexico, 1940 (published in U.S. by F.A.R. Galleries, N.Y., 1941.)

Mérida, Carlos. *Images de Guatemala*, Quatre chemins, Paris, 1928(?).

Mérida, Carlos, 'Mexico's younger generation,' *Magazine of Art*, vol. 31, no. 6, June 1938.

Mérida, Carlos, *Modern Mexican Artists*, Frances Toor Studios, Mexico, 1937.

Mérida, Carlos, *Orozco's frescoes in Guadalajara*. Photos by Juan Arauz Lomeli. Ed. by Frances Toor, Mexico, 1940.

Mexican People. 12 original signed lithographs by artists of the Taller de Gráfica Popular. Associated American Artists, N. Y., 1947.

México a Chile. Empresa Editora Zig-Zag, S.A., Santiago, 1942 (Chillán murals).

Mexico City; National Institute of Fine Arts. *Exposición Nacional Diego Rivera*: *50 Años de su Labor Artística*. Catalogue with commentaries by Carlos Chávez and Fernando Gamboa, Mexico, 1951.

Mexico City: Secretaría de Educación Pública. *Escuelas Primarias*, *1932*, Mexico, 1933.

Mexico City: Secretaría de Educación Pública. *Las Escuelas de Pintura al aire Libre*, with Preface by Alfredo Ramos Martínez, Editorial "Cultura," Mexico, 1926.

México en el Arte, 'La Obra total de Goitia en la Galería Cervantes,' *México en el Arte*, no. 6, Dec. 1948.

México en el Arte, Édition Speciale en français, Mexico, 1952.

'Mexico: World's Fanciest Campus,' *Time*, LXI, no. 8, 23 Feb. 1953.

Millán, Verna Carleton, 'Guerrero Stages a Comeback,' *Inter-America*, vol. 3, no. 9, Sept. 1944.

Millán, Verna Carleton, *Mexico Reborn*, Houghton Mifflin Co., Boston, 1939.

Molina Enríquez, Renato, 'La pintura mural: Fermín Revueltas, *Forma*, Mexico, vol. 1, no. 3, n. m. 1927.

Montaño, Jorge, 'Rufino Tamayo: Leader of a new Mexican school of painting,' *Mexican Life*, Nov. 1929.

Montenegro, 'El pintor Roberto Montenegro,' *Forma*, Mexico, vol. 2, no. 7, 1928.

Montenegro, 'Frescos de Roberto Montenegro,' *Contemporaneos*, Mexico, vol. 2, no. 38–39, July-Aug. 1931.

Myers, Bernard, 'The Modern Mexican Movement,' *American Artist*, vol. 16, no. 6, June 1952.

Neruda, Pablo, 'Los frescos de Xavier Guerrero en Chillán,' *Ars*, Mexico, vol. I, no. 5, mayo 1943.

New York, Riverside Museum. *Latin American exhibition of fine arts*: *Brazil, Ecuador, Mexico, Venezuela, 1940*, New York, 1940.

New York, The Museum of Modern Art. *Diego Rivera*, New York, 1931.

New York, The Museum of Modern Art. *Frescoes of Diego Rivera*, Plandome Press, New York, 1933.

New York, The Museum of Modern Art. *The Latin American Collection of the Museum of Modern Art*, Edited by Lincoln Kirstein, New York, 1943.

New York, The Museum of Modern Art. *Twenty Centuries of Mexican Art*. In collaboration with the Mexican government, New York, 1940.

Obregón Santacilia, Carlos, 'Jorge González Camarena,' *Ars*, Mexico, vol. 1, no. 4, abril 1942.

OROZCO

Autobiografía de J. C. Orozco, Ediciones Occidente, Mexico, 1945.

'Clemente Orozco,' *Arte en México*, special number, 15 Nov. 1939.

Homenaje de El Colegio Nacional al Pintor José Clemente Orozco. Ediciones de El Colegio Nacional, Mexico, 1949.

José Clemente Orozco, Exposición Nacional. Notas acerca de la técnica de la pintura mural en los ultimos 25 años, por Orozco. Secretaría de Educación Pública, Mexico, 1947.

José Clemente Orozco; *pinturas en la Universidad de Guadalajara, Jalisco*, Mundial, Mexico, 1937.

José Clemente Orozco, Sexta Exposición de Obras Recientes: *Estudios y Bocetos para los Murales 1947–1948*. El Colegio Nacional, Mexico, 1948.

Los Frescos de Orozco en Dartmouth, N. H., Secretaría de Educación Pública, Mexico, 1944.

Obras de J. C. Orozco en la Colección Carrillo Gil. Text by Justino Fernández, priv. printed, Mexico, 1949.

Obras de, etc. . . . (part II) complemento y notas del Dr. Alvar Carrillo Gil, Mexico, 1953.

'Orozco en Jiquilpan,' *Hoy*, vol. 16, no. 206, Feb. 1941.

'Orozco's frescoes in Guadalajara,' Frances Toor Studios, Mexico, 1940. Biog. by Toor, critique by Mérida.

Orozco 'Explains,' Bulletin of the Museum of Modern Art, N. Y., vol. VII, no. 4, 1940.

'Orozco's Justice Frescoes in Mexico City,' *Magazine of Art*, vol. 34, Oct. 1941.

Orozco, J. C., 'Si pintas ¿Para que hablas?' *Cultura México*, Mexico, año 2, no. 2, julio—dicbre. 1943.

Sánchez Gutiérrez, Edmundo, *José Clemente Orozco*, Fischgrund, Mexico, 1941. (Jiquilpan murals)

Veinte Dibujos de J. C. Orozco en la Exposición de Agosto de 1945 en el Colegio Nacional, México, 1945.

Pach, Walter, 'Impresiones sobre el arte actual de México,' *México Moderno*, Oct. 1922.

Pach, Walter, 'L'art au Mexique,' *L'amour de l'art*, Paris, vol. 8, Mar. 1927.

Parker, Howard, 'Las nuevas acuarelas de Carlos Mérida: Mérida's new watercolors,' *Mexican Folkways*, Mexico, vol. 7, no. 3, July-Sept. 1932.

Parkes, Henry Bamford, *A History of Mexico*, 2d ed. revd. Houghton Mifflin, Boston, 1950.

People's museum association, Detroit. *The Diego Rivera frescoes*, Detroit, 1933.

Pérez Martínez, Hector, 'Carlos Orozco Romero,' *Mexican Folkways*, vol. 7, no. 4, Oct.-Dec. 1932.

Philadelphia Museum of Art. *Mexican Art Today*. Intr. by Henry Clifford, Essay by L. Cardoza y Aragón, Philadelphia, 1943.

Plenn, Abel, 'Fermín Revueltas,' *Mexican Life*, Mexico, March 1934.

Plenn, Abel, 'The woodcuts of Leopoldo Méndez,' *Mexican Life*, Mexico, Sept. 1933.

Posada. *José Guadalupe Posada, 1851–1913*. Folio of 25 original prints. La Estampa Mexicana, Mexico, 1942.

Posada. *100 original woodcuts by Posada*. Foreword by Jean Charlot. Taylor Museum, Colorado Springs, 1947.

Posada. *Posada, Printmaker to the Mexican People*. Catalogue with text by Fernando Gamboa. Art Institute of Chicago, 1944.

Prieto, Julio, 'El grabado contemporáneo en México,' *Boletín Seminario Cultura Mexicana*, no. 3, agosto 1944.

Prieto, Julio, 'Esquema del desarrollo del grabado contemporáneo en México,' *Letras de México*, año 7, vol. 1, no. 15, 9 Sept. 1943.

Ramos, Samuel, 'L'esthetique de Diego Rivera,' *México en el Arte*, Mexico, 1952.

Ramos Martínez, María Sodi de, *Alfredo Ramos Martínez*, The Martínez Foundation, Los Angeles, 1948.

Reed, Alma, *José Clemente Orozco*, Delphic Studios, New York, 1932.

Reed, Alma, *Orozco*, Fondo de Cultura Económica, Mexico, 1955. Eng. ed., Oxford Univ. Press, N. Y., 1956.

Reed, Alma, 'Orozco and Mexican Painting,' *Mexican Life*, Mexico, March 1932.

Rivas, Guillermo, 'A new mural by Juan O'Gorman,' *Mexican Life*, May 1942.

Rivas, Guillermo, 'David Alfaro Siqueiros,' *Mexican Life*, Dec. 1935.

Rivas, Guillermo, 'Dr. Atl: a most unusual personality,' *Mexican Life*, Dec. 1933.

Rivas, Guillermo, 'Federico Cantú,' *Mexican Life*, Sept. 1937.
Rivas, Guillermo, 'Jorge González Camarena,' *Mexican Life*, Feb. 1940.
Rivas, Guillermo, 'Jorge González Camarena,' *Mexican Life*, Dec. 1941.
Rivas, Guillermo, 'Julio Castellanos,' *Mexican Life*, Sept. 1936.
Rivas, Guillermo, 'Manuel Rodríguez Lozano,' *Mexican Life*, Nov. 1949.
Rivas, Guillermo, 'More walls to paint,' *Mexican Life*, Dec. 1930.
Rivas, Guillermo, 'Paul O'Higgins,' *Mexican Life*, Feb. 1937.

RIVERA

'Diego Rivera paints a novel theme for San Francisco art school,' *Art Digest*, New York, vol. 5, no. 20, 1 Sept. 1931.
'Dynamic Detroit,' *Creative Art*, New York, vol. 12, no. 4, Apr. 1933.
Rivera, Diego, 'Frida Kahlo y el arte mexicano,' *Boletín Seminario Cultura Mexicana*, tomo I, no. 2, Oct. 1943.
Rivera, Diego, 'Los judas,' *Espacios*, Mexico, no. 3, Spring 1949.
Rivera, Diego, *Raices políticas y motivos personales de la controversia Siqueiros-Rivera*, Imprenta Mundial, Mexico, 1935.
Rivera, Diego. Acuarelas, 1935–1945. Colección Frida Kahlo. The Studio Publications, New York, 1948.
Rivera, Diego, 'The revolution in painting,' *Creative Art*, New York, vol. 4, no. 1, Jan. 1929.
Rivera, Diego & Wolfe, Bertram, *Portrait of America*, Covici Friede, N. Y., 1934.
Rivera, Diego & Wolfe, Bertram, *Portrait of Mexico*, Covici Friede, N. Y., 1937.
'Rivera Murals: New Workers School,' *Architectural Forum*, N. Y., vol. 60, no. 1, Jan. 1934.
'The new Rivera murals in San Francisco,' *Studio*, London, vol. 103, no. 469, Apr. 1932.

Rodríguez Lozano, Manuel. *Rodríguez Lozano*, Universidad Nacional, Mexico, 1942.
Rogo, Elsa, 'David Alfaro Siqueiros,' *Parnassus*, New York, vol. 6, no. 4, Apr. 1934.
Roh, Franz, *Realismo Mágico: post expressionismo*, Revista de Occidente, Madrid, 1927.
Salazar, Rosendo, *México en pensamiento y en acción*, Avante, Mexico, 1926.
San Francisco, Golden Gate international exposition, 1939–1940, Department of Fine Arts. Mexico (*Contemporary art: official catalogue*.) San Francisco, 1940.
San Francisco Museum of Art, *Diego Rivera: drawings and watercolors*, San Francisco, 1940.
Schmeckebier, Laurence E., *Modern Mexican Art*, University of Minnesota Press, Minneapolis, 1939.
Schmeckebier, Laurence E., 'Orozco's graphic art,' *Print collector's quarterly*, New York, vol. 21, no. 2, Apr. 1934.
Schmeckebier, Laurence, 'The Frescoes of Orozco,' *Mexican Life*, March 1933.
SIQUEIROS, see ALFARO SIQUEIROS
Smith, Robert & Wilder, Elizabeth, *A Guide to the Art of Latin America*, Hispanic Foundation. The Library of Congress, Washington, D. C., 1948.
Strode, Hudson, *Timeless Mexico*, Harcourt Brace and Co., N.Y., 1944.
Tablada, José Juan, 'José Clemente Orozco, the Mexican Goya,' *International Studio*, N. Y., vol. 78, no. 322, March 1924.
Tablada, José Juan, 'Mexican Painting of Today,' *International Studio*, N. Y., vol. 76, no. 308, Jan. 1923.
Tablada, José Juan, 'The arts in modern Mexico,' *Parnassus*, N. Y., vol. 1, no. III, March 1929.
Tablada, José Juan, 'Un pintor de la mujer: José Clemente Orozco,' *El Mundo Ilustrado*, 9 Nov. 1913.
Taller de Gráfica Popular. *Album TGP Mexico*. Prologue by Leopoldo Méndez, introd. by Hannes Meyer, La Estampa Mexicana, Mexico, 1949.
Taller de Gráfica Popular, *El Libro Negro del Terror Nazi en Europa*, El Libro Libre, Mexico, 1943.
Taller de Gráfica Popular. *Engravings of the Mexican Revolution*, La Estampa Mexicana, Mexico, 1947.
Tamayo, Rufino. 'Unas palabras de Rufino Tamayo, *Espacios*, no. 3, Spring 1949.
Tamayo, 20 años de su labor pictórica, Exposición del Instituto Nacional de Artes Plásticas, Mexico, 1948.

Tannenbaum, Frank, *The Struggle for Peace and Bread*, A. A. Knopf, N. Y., 1950.

Tannenbaum, Frank, *Peace by Revolution*, Columbia University Press, N. Y., 1933.

Toor, Frances, *Treasury of Mexican Folkways*. Illustrated by Carlos Mérida. Crown Publishers, New York, 1947.

Torriente, Loló de la, 'Conversaciones con D. A. Siqueiros sobre la pintura mural mexicana,' *Cuadernos Americanos*, año 6, vol. 36, Nov.-Dec. 1947.

Toscana, Salvador, *Federico Cantú, obra realizada de 1922–1948*, Ediciones Asbaje, Mexico, 1948.

Valles y montañas de Mexico. 80 dibujos del Dr. Atl, obras de 1904–1948. Exposición del Museo Nacional de Artes Plásticas, Mar.-Apr. 1948. Secretaría de Educación Pública, Mexico, 1948.

Velásquez Chávez, A., *Contemporary Mexican Artists*, Covici Friede, New York, 1937.

Velásquez Chávez, A., 'David Alfaro Siqueiros, la tercera época,' *Ars*, Mexico, vol. 1, no. 4, 1942.

Velásquez Chávez, A., 'El sentido cultural de la obra de Diego Rivera,' *Universidad*, Mexico, Oct. 1937.

Villaurrutia, Xavier, 'Historia de Diego Rivera,' *Forma*, Mexico, vol. 1, no. 5, 1927.

Villaurrutia, Xavier, 'Maria Izquierdo,' *Mexican Folkways*, vol. 7, no. 3, July-Sept. 1932.

Villaurrutia, Xavier, 'Rufino Tamayo,' *México en el Arte*, Aug. 1948.

Villaurrutia, Xavier, *La pintura mexicana moderna*, González Porto, Barcelona, 1936.

Westheim, Paul, 'David Alfaro Siqueiros, análisis de la forma,' *Espacios*, no. 4, Jan. 1950.

Wolfe, Bertram D., *Diego Rivera*, Pan-American Union, Washington, D. C., 1947.

Wolfe, Bertram D., *Diego Rivera, his life and times*, A. A. Knopf, N. Y., 1939.

Woodman, Santiago, 'The murals of Juan O'Gorman,' *Mexican Life*, Feb. 1941.

Zalce, Alfredo, *Estampas de Yucatán*, La Estampa Mexicana, Mexico, 1946. Preface by Jean Charlot.

Zigrosser, Carl, 'Mexican Graphic Art,' *Print collector's quarterly*, London, vol. 23, no. 1, Jan. 1936.

Index

279

282

DATE DUE

MAR 31			
MAY 20			
NOV 2 8			
MAR 2 8 2000			
GAYLORD			PRINTED IN U.S.A.